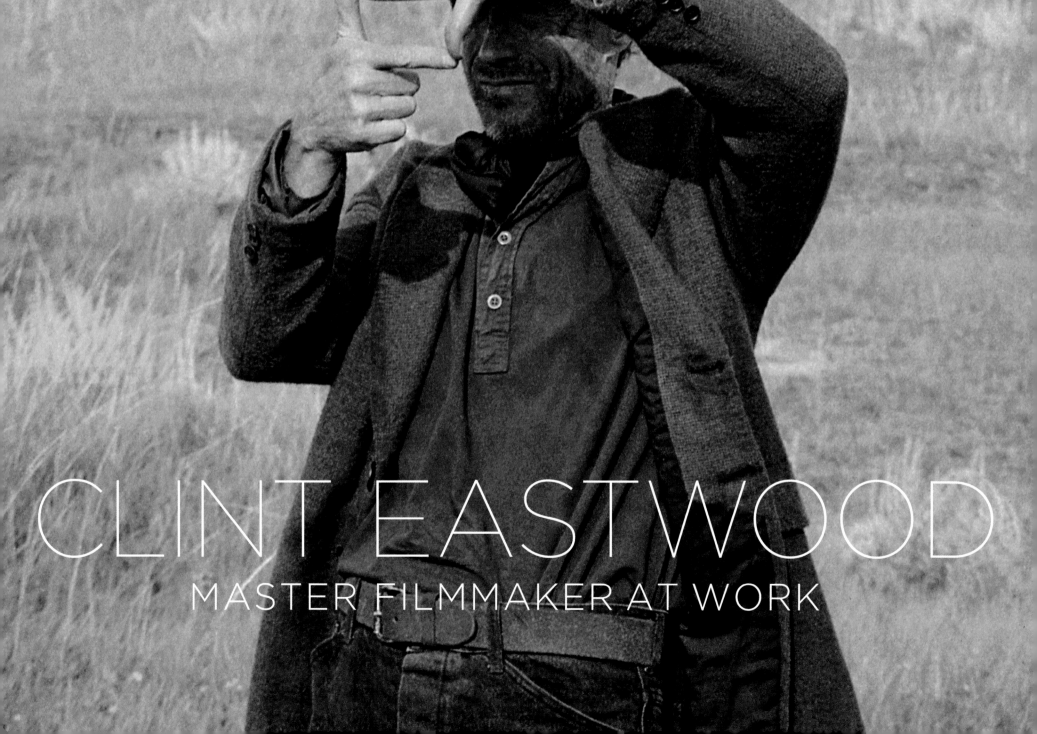

CLINT EASTWOOD
MASTER FILMMAKER AT WORK

FILMMAKER LEGACY

CLINT EASTWOOD

MASTER FILMMAKER AT WORK

MICHAEL GOLDMAN

Foreword STEVEN SPIELBERG *Preface* MORGAN FREEMAN

ABRAMS, NEW YORK

CLINT EASTWOOD
MASTER FILMMAKER AT WORK

MICHAEL GOLDMAN

Foreword STEVEN SPIELBERG *Preface* MORGAN FREEMAN

Packaged by LISA FITZPATRICK

Design MARK MURPHY

A SWAN STUDIO Production

ABRAMS
THE ART OF BOOKS SINCE 1949

115 West 18th Street
New York, NY 10011
abramsbooks.com

"IT'S REALLY NOT AN AUTEUR THING, IT'S AN ENSEMBLE."

CLINT EASTWOOD

A SWAN STUDIO production
Thanks to TECHNICOLOR for their support

CONTENTS

"CLINT IS NOT ONLY THE MOST EMOTIONALLY INVESTED FILMMAKER WE HAVE TODAY,
BUT ALSO THE MOST ECLECTIC IN HIS OPENNESS IN CONSIDERING ALL GENRES."

STEVEN SPIELBERG

FOREWORD

STEVEN SPIELBERG

LIKE MOST OF MY GENERATION, I WAS INTRODUCED TO CLINT EASTWOOD THROUGH THE ADVENTURES OF HIS CHARACTER, ROWDY YATES, ON *RAWHIDE*, A SHOW I WAS QUITE DEVOTED TO BACK THEN. MUCH LATER, I MET CLINT AT UNIVERSAL STUDIOS, WHILE WE WERE BOTH BUSY, IN OUR OWN WAYS, EARNING OUR DIRECTOR'S STRIPES.

I think the reason we hit it off is that we were both techies. We couldn't stop talking about cameras, lenses, film stock, and the stories we were hoping to tell someday. It was all shoptalk, about our similar legacy at Universal Studios and our love for our craft—never tiring of talking shop to this day—and we are still good friends nearly forty years later.

The first job Clint did for me as a director was an episode of *Amazing Stories* that I had written called "Vanessa in the Garden." We got to work together again when my company, Amblin, produced *The Bridges of Madison County* for Clint in 1995. I later brought *Flags of Our Fathers* to Clint, and Clint brought me *Letters from Iwo Jima*. And after that, Kathy Kennedy and I brought *Hereafter* to Clint in 2010. She produced and I executive produced in partnership with Clint's Malpaso team.

These opportunities allowed me to observe Clint at work. Among the earliest and clearest impressions is that Clint can break your heart and mend it, all in the space of a two-hour film, and he accomplishes this without a whiff of sentimentality.

I came to understand that Clint's directorial style is brilliantly unique and unadorned. He's a cinematic filmmaker, of course, but to me, he's also a stage-oriented director. The staging of many of his scenes relies less on where the camera specifically is, and a lot more on how he moves his characters around the frame. In that sense, he is one of the greatest blocking directors ever, like Michael Curtiz and Howard Hawks. The way he gets his actors to tell their stories, their body language, is something serious film students and filmmakers greatly admire.

I've also grown aware that Clint demands from his audience a laconic sort of patience . . . like the man himself. If it's a Clint Eastwood movie, you are not usually going to get out-of-the-gate action from the first frame, and this is because Clint has an innate respect for the intelligence of film audiences and includes them as his collaborators. He's going to involve us in his storytelling one heartbeat at a time. Thus, in my opinion, by the end of any Clint Eastwood–directed project, viewers feel like they have gone on a personal journey that often reflects who they are. That's how Clint shows his respect for audiences—they are constantly in his thoughts, a part of his journey as he's spinning his yarns or recreating his truths.

That is why this is an important book, even if you are not as consumed with the nuances of filmmaking as Clint and I are. Clint is unique among American filmmakers, and he crafts his films around basic emotional themes that anyone is likely to take to heart. How he does it is inexorably tied to who he is. So achieving a greater understanding of Clint's "who," "how," and "why" through the eyes of those who have worked with and know him best is a rare and precious opportunity afforded by this book.

(Opposite) Adam Beach in *Flags of Our Fathers*. (Above) A portrait of Clint Eastwood at night during filming (*Letters from Iwo Jima*).

For me, personally, I'm lucky to call him a close friend, who happens to work in the same business as I do. But as a filmgoer, I am, like you, also fortunate—we all get to be inspired by his work.

Clint even composes his own music, and at the very least, is deeply involved in creating his themes, as this book will explain. Thus, Clint not only expresses his point of view through the story he is telling and how he directs it. He is also making the effort and taking the time to sit down at a keyboard and tell us how he feels musically. That is unique in our entire field, and probably in the entire Directors Guild of America.

It's my view that Clint is not only the most emotionally invested filmmaker we have today, but also the most eclectic in his openness to considering all genres. He may have played the same Western antiheroes again and again, but as a director, you can never accuse Clint of repeating himself. This is quite obvious in a film like *Bird*, but even the movies he directs and produces that are not outwardly what you would call personal movies—they are nonetheless deeply personal to him. This may rub up against the iconic representation of Clint as the brooding, disconnected Man with No Name—the character that first brought him to cinematic immortality. But it is precisely the best available pathway for understanding Clint Eastwood, the man.

—November 2011

(Opposite) Clint Eastwood directing a scene from *Flags of Our Fathers*. (Top R) Eastwood with producer and friend Steven Spielberg when *Flags of Our Fathers* debuted, in 2006. (Center R) Spielberg and Eastwood talk shop on the Warner Bros. lot in 1985 when Eastwood was directing an episode of Spielberg's *Amazing Stories*. (Bottom R) An image from *Flags of Our Fathers*—a project that Spielberg brought to, and produced with, Eastwood. (Page 18) Cast and crew chairs neatly arranged during the filming of *Million Dollar Baby*. In fact, Eastwood and crew are rarely found in their seats when working. (Page 19) Eastwood examines his script, pondering the next shot in Nelson Mandela's office (*Invictus*).

"CLINT WANTED ME TO BE IN HIS NEW WESTERN. I HAD ALWAYS WANTED TO DO A WESTERN,
AND HAD ALWAYS CONSIDERED *THE OUTLAW JOSEY WALES* TO BE ONE OF THE GREATEST WESTERNS
EVER MADE. SUDDENLY, HERE WAS A CHANCE TO RIDE WITH CLINT EASTWOOD."

MORGAN FREEMAN

PREFACE
DEFINING CHEMISTRY

MORGAN FREEMAN

AS SOMETIMES HAPPENS ON RESTLESS NIGHTS, I WAS FLIPPING THE CHANNELS AROUND THREE O'CLOCK IN THE MORNING RECENTLY WHEN, SUDDENLY, *PLAY MISTY FOR ME* POPPED UP ON MY TELEVISION SCREEN—THE FIRST FILM DIRECTED BY CLINT EASTWOOD, IN 1971.

Clint's transition into being a director on that film happened just a few years after many of us first started taking notice of him, when he returned from Italy in the mid-1960s, having established himself as the biggest badass around with the spaghetti Westerns he starred in for Sergio Leone—*A Fistful of Dollars*, *For a Few Dollars More*, and *The Good, the Bad and the Ugly*.

Clint made *Misty* long before I ever worked with him, or even met him for that matter. But that movie still brings back fond memories for me, because it caused me to examine him in a new way—he was a filmmaker now. I felt that *Misty* gave us a whole other look at Clint Eastwood from the badass we had become accustomed to. He was making statements cinematically, from his first film as a director onward. Even movies like *The Gauntlet* (1977), which was basically wall-to-wall violence, or a psychological thriller like *Tightrope* (1984) started giving us characters with strange, but human, vulnerabilities. Since then, he's been building such vulnerabilities and flaws into virtually all of his stories and characters—even the legendary Dirty Harry.

I admire that sort of thing, and so I started paying even closer attention to Clint's films as the years went by. But I never dared hope I could ever work with him. However, by the early 1990s, I heard about a screenplay called *The William Munny Killings*. I was working with Kevin Costner on *Robin Hood: Prince of Thieves* (1991), and he told me about it, saying he thought there was probably a part in it for me, but that Clint Eastwood had the script and Costner didn't know what he was planning to do with it.

About a year later, I was in Zimbabwe, shooting a picture called *The Power of One*, when, out of the blue, I got a call from my agent, saying Clint wanted me to be in his new Western. I had always wanted to do a Western, and had always considered *The Outlaw Josey Wales* to be one of the greatest Westerns ever made. Suddenly, here was a chance to ride with Clint Eastwood; there was no arm-twisting involved. I said yes immediately, and so, that first day I walked onto the *Unforgiven* set in 1992, I finally met the man I had been following all those years.

We became friends instantly, but from a professional point of view, as an actor, I could not have asked for more. He didn't try to tell me how to play my character; he didn't try to intellectualize everything. He did tell me what he thought about things, and he had everything organized perfectly. But he didn't tinker with the script and he didn't tinker with the actors. I gave the part of Ned Logan what I thought it deserved, and that was just fine with Clint.

(Opposite) During production, camera operator Stephen Campanelli (L), wearing a Steadicam rig, Morgan Freeman in costume, and Clint Eastwood discuss an imminent shot. (Above) Clint Eastwood and Morgan Freeman, working together on the second of their three projects (*Million Dollar Baby*).

We did it all again, of course, on *Million Dollar Baby* (2004) and *Invictus* (2009). On all three projects, he worked fast, which I love; left me alone to do my job, which I really love; and basically was as close to perfect as any director I've ever worked with.

I was blessed to get a couple of award nominations and an Academy Award (for the role of Eddie "Scrap-Iron" Dupris in *Million Dollar Baby*), and lots of other accolades, and I was pleased with the work. But the real reward was to work, learn from, and enjoy my time with Clint Eastwood.

The central reason why that means a lot to me is that Clint's way of working, and the way he relates to his cast and his crew, tells you directly that he believes in you. That is very empowering for an actor or anyone else on set. He's professional, he's relaxed, and he's a real leader.

So for these reasons, and because I'm extremely prejudiced in favor of telling the world about this great artist and person, I hope you will find this look inside his filmmaking world valuable. If nothing else, you might learn something about how to treat colleagues, how to be professional, how to respect people, how to avoid micromanaging people, and perhaps most valuable if you ever find yourself trying to make a movie, you will learn how to be quiet, calm, and in control of yourself. What Clint Eastwood learned long ago, and can teach the rest of us, is that people get off being left alone to do their jobs. All he asks is that you come ready, just like him.

Will I work with Clint again in another movie? I sure hope so—all he has to do is give me a call. I even offered to play the young boy in *Hereafter*, but he told me I wasn't right for the part, if you can believe that. But whether or not we do more movies together, we're friends, and that's more important. We have something together that works. Sinatra had a song called "How Little We Know" with a line that says, "Who cares to define what chemistry this is?"

That's my relationship with Clint Eastwood. It's hard to define. It just is, and I'm luckier for it.

—November 2011

(Opposite) Morgan Freeman in his Academy Award–winning role as Eddie "Scrap-Iron" Dupris, friend of Clint Eastwood's character, Frankie Dunn.

(Top R) Clint Eastwood playing Dunn, a hardened boxing trainer/manager, and (Bottom R) with Hilary Swank during shooting (*Million Dollar Baby*). Swank says Eastwood influenced her deeply, to the point that she considers him almost a surrogate father.

(Page 24) *J. Edgar*'s ornate production design is evident in this overhead shot of the Stork Club set. (Page 25) Costume design and props, including vintage microphones, are on display in a scene featuring the young Hoover (Leonardo DiCaprio) testifying before Congress in *J. Edgar*.

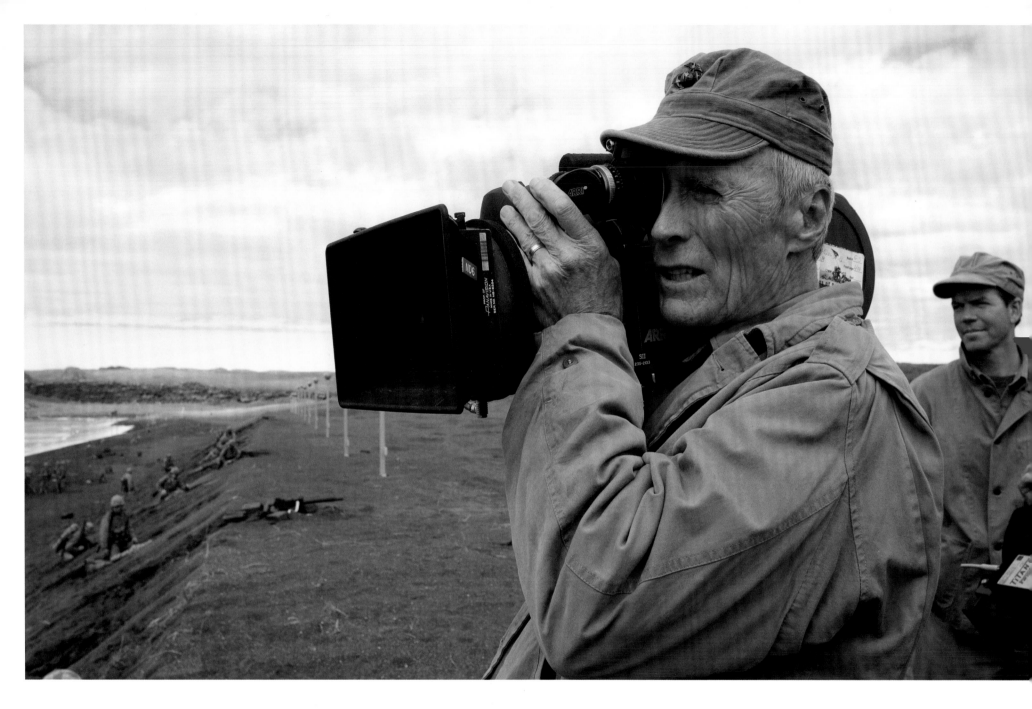

"HE'S A TREE PERSON, NOT A FOREST PERSON—
HE FIGURES OUT WHAT HE WANTS TO DO ON HIS OWN, FIGURES OUT HOW TO DO IT AND
THEN DOES IT BRILLIANTLY."

BOB DALY, FORMER WARNER BROS. CEO, 2011

INTRODUCTION
GOOD, CREATIVE, AND PRUDENT FILMMAKING

WHEN THE LATE STEVE ROSS, THE FORMER CEO OF WARNER COMMUNICATIONS, RECEIVED A TWO-PAGE MEMO FROM CLINT EASTWOOD ON JANUARY 31, 1984, HE PROBABLY DIDN'T REALIZE IT ANY MORE THAN EASTWOOD DID, BUT THE DOCUMENT CAME AS CLOSE AS ANY DOCUMENT EVER WOULD TO OFFICIALLY CODIFYING EASTWOOD'S FILMMAKING PARTNERSHIP WITH WARNER BROS.

The memo was essentially a polite thank-you to Warner Bros. for its support of his film *Sudden Impact*, but along the way, it declared succinctly Eastwood's satisfaction that the studio had become the home he had always needed in order to pursue what he called in the memo "good, creative, and prudent filmmaking."

"I consider myself part of the team, and not a stranger working at a different studio each time we make a film," Eastwood wrote. "Over the years, we have been making our deals with Warner Brothers from picture to picture, which is again an expression of a very unusual relationship in that contracts are not necessary between us for our past, present, and future activities and that our handshake has held well over the years."

Later, he added that he hoped his good relationship with the studio and his high-performing track record would "stay that way for a long time to come," which, of course, remarkably, they have—thirty-five years and counting since he first moved to the studio.

What came to be known as the Handshake Memo was written eight years after Eastwood moved his company, Malpaso Productions, into the modest stucco bungalow on the Warner lot where it remains to this day. He did so at the invitation of Ross and his colleague Frank Wells, the studio's president who had previously been his lawyer and, along with Ross, was a dear friend. Eastwood moved there ostensibly to make *The Outlaw Josey Wales*, and simply never left. With *Josey Wales*, he brought to his new home the filmmaking momentum he had begun at Universal Studios four pictures back. In the ensuing years, Eastwood made his cozy bungalow the place from which he evolved into one of the world's most gifted and revered filmmakers, shifting how the industry and his fans perceived him from being an iconic film actor into something much greater.

AS SIGNIFICANT AS EASTWOOD'S IMPACT HAS BEEN ON THE MOVIE BUSINESS OVERALL, IT'S CLEARLY BEEN EVEN MORE SIGNIFICANT ON THE MANY INDIVIDUALS WHO HAVE COLLABORATED CLOSELY WITH HIM OVER THE YEARS.

(Opposite) Clint Eastwood gazes through the viewfinder of a handheld camera to consider composition of a shot of the Marine landing at Iwo Jima on a beach in Iceland (*Flags of Our Fathers*). Producer Rob Lorenz stands behind. (Above) Decades earlier, Eastwood contemplates a different shot during production for *Sudden Impact* (1983).

THE INFLUENCE

In the decades since launching his directing career with *Play Misty for Me* in 1971, Eastwood the filmmaker has of course enjoyed incredible box office success and years of critical acclaim, and has had a major and visible impact on the bottom line at Warner Bros., on the filmmaking industry, and on popular culture. The numbers and accolades are both well known and staggering—through 2011, Eastwood had three Best Director Academy Award nominations, with two Oscars in that category; two nominations for acting in a leading role; the Irving G. Thalberg Memorial Award; two Best Picture Oscars and two more nominations; five actors directed by Eastwood with acting Oscars, five more actors nominated for Oscars; and multiple nominations and wins for technical/craftsmanship Oscars—ranging from sound to music to editing, cinematography, art direction, and visual effects. And that doesn't even begin to count multiple Palme d'Or nominations at the Cannes Film Festival, dozens of other film festival nominations and awards, critics' awards, and trade guild and industry association awards.

Virtually none of Eastwood's films have lost money, some became monster performers for Warner Bros. and its partners, and all have been made economically, on time, and below, at, or very close to their projected cost. Eastwood's films and career have been the subjects of numerous books, critical analyses, and other media coverage, and have been taught in universities and at film schools. His memorabilia is on display at the Warner Bros. museum, in the Academy of Motion Picture Arts and Sciences archive, and at the Wesleyan University film archive, among other places.

These and other facts and statistics on Eastwood's global achievements and honors made him a venerated filmmaker inside Hollywood long before the critics got around to warming up to his work on a consistent basis. From the point of view of those within the industry, Eastwood's approach is the gold-standard way to make motion pictures.

"Clint is essentially the icon for efficient movie production, and I think everyone across Hollywood, not just Warner Bros. people, will tell you that," says Barry Meyer, Warner Bros. chairman and CEO. "As far as what he's done for this studio—if there were a Warner Bros. Hall of Fame, Clint would be the first person in, and he'd be elected unanimously. For a studio executive, he's a dream come true—a trustworthy guy and a creative guy with great instincts, who is responsible with money and involved in all aspects of his projects. He's soup to nuts—a true producer/director, and then he does his own music. You just don't find that elsewhere. Over the years, he became a great, iconic filmmaker, and we learned to completely trust him. The entire relationship is built on trust."

And as his colleagues point out, Eastwood is not merely a filmmaker. Part of their admiration comes from seeing the level of savvy he exhibits as a producer on his films and in the marketing process to promote them. Joe Hyams, the longtime Warner Bros. marketing executive, now retired, who was assigned to Eastwood's projects, worked alongside Clint for decades, designing campaigns, creating trailers, navigating the media and reviewers, and attending industry events with him.

Eastwood, Hyams insists today, "knows his material better than anyone." He calls his old friend "a fantastic movie producer, and even better with marketing. I'd fight with him on a few things over the years, and he'd let me win occasionally, but usually he was right. He has tremendous instincts. I can recall Warner Bros. would sometimes have a couple different ads, and they would send them over to us and ask us to test them out. He'd take me into the alley at the studio, and when a couple workmen would come along, he'd call them over and ask them which poster they liked better. That was the market research. They were common guys, and he felt he was a common guy like them."

As significant as Eastwood's impact has been on the movie business overall, it's clearly been even more significant on the many individuals who have collaborated closely with him over the years. Like Hyams, when interviewed, they uniformly imply, directly or indirectly, that his ability to form, maintain, and manage meaningful and respectful relationships with the people he works with at all levels—from studio chief to common crew—is central to what has made him such a successful and creative filmmaker.

(Above) Clint Eastwood directed himself initially in 1971's *Play Misty for Me*. (Opposite) Eastwood prepares a shot—he collaborated closely with mentor Don Siegel behind the camera long before *Misty* launched his directorial career.

This collegial tone was entrenched during the Ross era, according to former Warner Bros. co-CEO Terry Semel, and it was a tone that fit perfectly with Eastwood's nature. Semel and others say Ross created a personal relationship–based working atmosphere that made the Warner Bros. empire and perks available and fun for all to enjoy, as long as they worked hard to make great and profitable motion pictures. It was all built on the foundation of a gregarious style of collaboration that Semel suggests Ross, whom he fondly calls "the father of us all," believed in and actively promulgated. Semel recalls "people at other studios, particularly [former Universal Studio chief] Lew Wasserman, derided us for flying people around on jets and helicopters and things. But that was the way Steve Ross lived his life. He set the atmosphere for those in the Warner family, and Clint became a leader [within this environment]."

And in terms of resources, Eastwood was a conscientious leader, as he remains to this day. He was never one to let an asset go to waste—the Warner Bros. jet, when in Eastwood's custody, for instance, was frequently incorporated into the work as much as it was used for play. In fact, Eastwood's former producer David Valdes insists that Clint frequently found ways to use the Warner jet as, essentially, a cargo plane, to transport people and material to and from movie locations.

"On *Pale Rider* [1985], Clint chose the two main Idaho locations himself [a remote area for the mining operation, and the Sawtooth National Recreation Area for the Western town site]. During that production, I don't believe there was one crew member who flew to Ketchum [Idaho] via commercial airliner," Valdes recalls. "We had to bring all of our construction crew from Los Angeles—painters, plasterers, you name it—because there were just a handful of union-based crew in Sun Valley. So we flew them all in on the Warner jet. Clint always felt that if you have a private jet available, it should not be reserved solely for VIPs. On many movies, Clint would allow me to pack that Warner Bros. Gulfstream with as many people and as much equipment as possible. We got an entire construction crew to Idaho without paying for one commercial ticket, plus most of the shooting crew. It was Clint's solution for making things easier and better for us, and at the same time, rewarding crew members that would never have the chance to fly privately.

"I would fly up to Idaho with nine carpenters on a Monday morning, and they would be building the town by that afternoon. I would do my work, and then take the empty jet back to Burbank that evening. I'd work in L.A. the remainder of the week, and then, the next Monday, I'd do the same thing all over again. For all of us, it was nothing short of fantastic. My kids were little, and on a show like *Pale Rider*, or most Clint movies for that matter, I didn't have to be away from home for long periods of time. On a movie these days, I'm gone seven or eight months. With Clint, you were usually gone two to three months at the most. That was part of the family environment that people talk about on a Clint Eastwood movie. But it was always designed to ensure we got the work done as efficiently and inexpensively as possible."

In other words, the adventure of working for Eastwood is typically mixed with the labor, with the results readily apparent, then and now.

After the Ross era ended, Semel and Bob Daly took over stewardship of the studio, and the handshake endured. Upon their departures, succeeding administrations at Warner Bros. have also maintained the relationship virtually unchanged. Today, both Daly and Semel suggest that a line of management continuity at Warner certainly played a major role in this, but at the end of the day, the uniqueness of Eastwood as a filmmaker, and as a man, has been the determining factor in this ongoing partnership.

"From Ted Ashley to Frank Wells [under Ross] to John Calley and Terry and me, and Alan Horn and Barry Meyer and [current president] Jeff Robinov, there has been very little turnover at Warner Bros. in the sense that almost everyone had already been working there, and the head of production always came from inside the company," explains Daly. "So it was particularly stable studio management, and almost everyone had a relationship with Clint. We all knew enough to let Clint do his own thing. He's a tree person, not a forest person—he figures out what he wants to do on his own, figures out how to do it and then does it brilliantly."

(Opposite, L–R) Camera operator Jack Green and first camera assistant Baird Steptoe listen to director Clint Eastwood, dressed in character, plan a shot in the mountains of Idaho during the making of *Pale Rider*. (Above) Reproduction of the famous Handshake Memo Eastwood sent to Warner Bros. in 1984. (Right) Eastwood with former Warner Bros. chairman Robert Daly on the set of *Space Cowboys*.

(Above) Director Clint Eastwood and star Ken Watanabe consult during filming, while in adjacent photo, also from *Letters from Iwo Jima*, Eastwood, Rob Lorenz, and Tom Stern (L–R) plan a shot. (Opposite) On location in the Sawtooth National Recreation Area of Idaho during the grueling *Pale Rider* shoot (1984).

PERSONAL TOUCH

What Daly is driving at is the notion that, as remarkable as Eastwood's professional success as a filmmaker has been, it can't be disconnected from the direct personal influence he exerts on those he collaborates with. His effect on them is palpable when speaking with longtime collaborators. Valdes, for instance, talks glowingly of his Malpaso time, even years after leaving the company to pursue other opportunities.

"Professionally, it not only made me a better producer, but it also made me a better person," Valdes says. "Today, in work and in my personal life, I just know that anything conceived can be achieved. When people say, 'You can't do that,' I now take that as a challenge, and know that we can do it if it's important enough. I simply tell them, I worked with a guy who always did it. If they ask who, I simply say 'Clint,' and suddenly, that iconic, monosyllabic name gets the impossible accomplished. It was a great part of my life working with him—something I'll always treasure."

Rob Lorenz has been Eastwood's producing partner for almost a decade, since Valdes left, and has settled into the office next to Clint's at the bungalow. For him, the topic of Eastwood's personal impact on his life is so poignant that he has trouble fully explaining it.

"I don't even know where to begin," Lorenz says. "I've learned so much from him—his management style, his directing style. I've learned so much, not just about the process and about this business, but about how to work with people, treat people, and about life—taking care of my body, my health. There are all sorts of things, but it is really hard to talk about, to be honest."

Professionally, this influence results in what many people refer to as the stress-free Eastwood set—a phenomenon that permeates every creative, physical, and logistical aspect of the work. Mable McCrary, who has served as Eastwood's script supervisor since *Space Cowboys*, in 2000, feels strongly about this point, suggesting that Eastwood's calm sets are a direct result of his nature, and his insistence on treating everyone the same.

"There is a great deal of respect," McCrary says. "We have worked together a long time. We know each other's work and have [high regard for each other]. So there are no egos—if Clint shows no ego, then none of us have any reason to. That makes it a comfortable place to work—you show up and work with friends. Our cooperation fosters an attitude of comfort for the actors. They know they will feel comfortable and relaxed when they come to the set. Everyone knows what to expect. That all comes from the top."

Those who provide the money and tools for Eastwood to ply his trade feel precisely the same way. They repeatedly emphasize that, while the studio's arrangement with Eastwood certainly makes economic sense, it goes far beyond financial considerations. Current and former studio executives who have known Eastwood for decades insist that his personality traits and skill set make him perhaps one of the most distinctive filmmakers they have ever worked with.

"The relationship with Clint satisfies the criteria to make good business sense, obviously," says former Warner Bros. president and CEO Alan Horn. "But it goes way deeper than that. He's low key. He's solid, dependable, extremely talented, a nice guy. He can act, direct, write songs. That makes for a great studio partner and for great movies. I'm lucky to have him for a friend."

Terry Semel feels Eastwood deeply impacted his life on a personal level, and enjoys reminiscing about their adventures together even more than the filmmaking successes.

"He's really the most remarkable man," Semel says. "We got to spend tons of time together over the years. He would come and spend time with my family in our house in Saint-Tropez in the summers, and that might sound glamorous, but he would just show up and ask if he could stay with us. He'd travel with one little bag. He'd always pull up to the plane in his little pickup truck with that one bag, even if he were going away for a couple weeks. He has a style that is hard to resist.

"It was on one of those trips to France that he started getting interested in helicopters, where he got the bug. He decided to get his license so he could fly them. One day, I remember talking to him about how he would fly us out, in the event of a big earthquake in Los Angeles. We lived near each other, and we talked about a system for landing his helicopter in my backyard if there was ever an urgency, and we planned our own little escape route."

(Above) Clint Eastwood with *Mystic River* actors Kevin Bacon and Laurence Fishburne. (Below R) Eastwood's longtime Warner Bros. publicist, Joe Hyams, shows the director a test publicity one-sheet for *Bronco Billy* on the set of that film. Eastwood has always been intimately involved in the marketing of his movies.

But what is really unusual is the fact that Eastwood's current and former cast and crew, ranging from major movie stars to high-ranking department heads to those in more modest roles, speak in oddly similar tones about him. Many at all levels of the crew hierarchy enjoy relationships with Eastwood that aren't dissimilar to those described by studio executives.

"My kids grew up in the same era as Clint's kids," relates Alan Murray, who, along with Bub Asman, has been Eastwood's co-supervising sound editor for decades. "It's nice to see my oldest son [Blu Murray, now an assistant editor at Malpaso] join the family and work on films with Clint, [and his children] Kyle and Alison. I remember when [Blu] was five years old, and his favorite movie was *Bronco Billy*. I told Clint about it, and he agreed they should meet on the sound stage later that week. It was pure magic that day when my son entered the room, and there standing in front of him was the real Bronco Billy. Clint immediately went into character and called out, 'Well howdy, little pardner, come on over and say hello.' The next thing I know, my son is sitting on Clint's lap, talking about cowboys and Indians as only a five-year-old can."

"I was invited to help the production set up a wireless video monitoring system when they were shooting *Mystic River* in Boston, and I was only supposed to set it up, show them how to run it, and fly home," recalls Liz Radley, Eastwood's video and computer graphics supervisor. "Rob Lorenz called me and said Clint wanted me to stay for the run of the movie, despite the cost of having me on-site across the country when it wasn't really necessary. I took that as a huge gesture of loyalty, and because he made that gesture, I've made sure to make myself available for every one of his movies since then. Clint is all about loyalty, and when you show it, he reciprocates."

Indeed, the word "loyalty" comes up repeatedly when talking to those who have been with Eastwood for any significant amount of time.

Howard Bernstein, for instance, has worked with Eastwood since 1967, and, in partnership with Roy Kaufman, has been his business manager since 1969. Bernstein and Kaufman, however, were raw, inexperienced newbies in the gritty world of Hollywood business management when Eastwood placed that faith in them. They were two years into gigs working for the accounting firm owned by the late Irving Leonard, a close friend of Eastwood's, who had been managing Clint's affairs since he started acting in the 1950s. When Leonard tragically died of a heart attack at the age of fifty-three, instead of shifting to another established firm, Eastwood simply asked Bernstein and Kaufman to stay on.

Bernstein believes Eastwood did so simply because "he is intensely loyal, and when he saw we had the intention to take care of Irving's widow, I think he appreciated that. There were people telling him to move on with Irving gone, but that is not Clint. We were pretty young, but he didn't care. He just stuck with us."

A much younger, more recent collaborator—actress Hilary Swank—has felt precisely the same way since earning an Academy Award in 2005 for her starring role, under Eastwood's direction, in *Million Dollar Baby*. Among the themes in that film was the evolution of a father-daughter relationship between her character and Eastwood's gruff boxing trainer, Frankie Dunn. Swank remains so devoted to Eastwood that she insists her life has clearly imitated the art of the film relationship.

"That movie relationship definitely paralleled our relationship in real life," she declares. "I've become very close with Clint and with his wife, who is one of my best friends. We've skied together, and he loves animals, as I do. He has the biggest heart. I say that if he ever wants me to help with something, he only has to call. And I don't mean just for acting. If he wants me to come to his set and work craft services, he only has to call, and I mean that."

(Above) Clint Eastwood, his ubiquitous monitor in hand, gives instructions to Leonardo DiCaprio during filming of *J. Edgar*. DiCaprio says Eastwood helps actors achieve "ultimate confidence" when working for him. (Below R) DiCaprio in character as J. Edgar Hoover.

Swank is hardly the only A-list actor to feel that way. Virtually every actor contacted for this project expressed similar devotion. As recently as mid-2011, Leonardo DiCaprio certainly did, shortly after finishing his star turn in the title role for the psychological character study, *J. Edgar*. Soon after shooting concluded, DiCaprio was clearly enamored with his first experience working for the filmmaker, and declared him to be "almost a father figure—a guy who gives you nearly absolute artistic freedom."

Actor/filmmaker Forest Whitaker also speaks of Eastwood as a mentor/father figure, and not only because Eastwood gave him an opportunity for his first lead role in a feature film, with *Bird* (1988), at a time in his life when Whitaker was doubtful that he had what it took to be a professional movie actor.

"I was running from the demons of mediocrity within myself at the time," Whitaker says today. "I had never had a lead [movie] role. Clint gave me the opportunity, and then he taught me to go out and dance on a ledge, to face my fear. He had that belief in me, and it's a lesson I've used on all projects ever since."

In fact, Whitaker speaks appreciatively of Eastwood showing up to a screening of the first feature film he ever directed—an HBO drama called *Strapped* (1993)—and then spending time in the parking lot offering input. "I was blown away by his generosity. [As recently as 2010,] I sent him a script I'm developing on Louis Armstrong, and he invited me over to his office and gave me his thoughts and advice about directing myself, since I have never directed a film I acted in before. Just to see Clint do things like that, and do them so well, makes you feel anything is possible. I'm much more confident today as an actor, a filmmaker, and a person because of Clint Eastwood."

Such anecdotes and rhetoric abound in the Eastwood universe. That personal touch, the empowerment and loyalty that Eastwood offers everyone he collaborates with and expects in return, combined with his obvious artistic talent and experience, have allowed him to officially direct thirty-two feature films as of this writing, and to be deeply involved in virtually all aspects of production and postproduction on several others that technically bear the names of other people under the credit "director." (Eastwood directed, for example, most of 1984's *Tightrope*, but screenwriter Richard Tuggle started the project, and his deal officially gave him the credit.) The quality and nature of many of these films, the lengthy track record, critical acclaim, awards, and box office stability over decades have all combined to place Eastwood at or near the head of the line of America's living film directors.

Critics can debate his exact place in that line. But there is no question those interested in films, filmmaking, or the nature of teamwork or leadership can benefit from understanding Eastwood's methods and mind-set. His tendency to be soft-spoken about his working method, and to underplay the nature of the strategic thinking and the impact on him of decades of experience in front of and behind the camera, belies the reality that there are very particular reasons why Eastwood prefers few takes, uses a single camera, gravitates toward low lighting, and avoids interfering with the writing process and actor preparation for the most part, among many other things. But there are reasons—often unique or unexpected ones—and a thinking process and a working method that are truly of Eastwood's own making behind all of it. This volume's intent is to open a door, aim a lens into his filmmaking world, and reveal those lessons for all to see.

"IT'S THE PAINTING OF IT ALL THAT INTERESTS ME . . .
WHY DOES AN ARTIST MAKE A CERTAIN STROKE? JUST BECAUSE IT SEEMED LIKE
THE RIGHT THING TO DO AT THE TIME."

CLINT EASTWOOD, 2011

PROLOGUE
THE GROOVE

CLINT EASTWOOD DEFENDS GETTING HIS HAIR CUT WHILE ON THE JOB, IN QUINTESSENTIALLY SIMPLE TERMS. "WHEN YOU FIND A GOOD BARBER, YOU TAKE HIM WHEN HE'S AVAILABLE," EAST-WOOD CHUCKLES, RISING OUT OF HIS DIRECTOR'S CHAIR, AWAY FROM A PAIR OF SNIPPING SCISSORS.

He scurries over to briefly whisper something into the ear of his star, Matt Damon. It's an early January afternoon in 2010, in Emeryville, California, on the set of his thirty-first directorial effort—a love story tinged with supernatural elements, called *Hereafter*.

The movie is hardly stereotypical Eastwood fare—not that he's ever had a stock genre or style in his films since he first officially took the helm more than forty years ago. But with *Hereafter*, he is constructing a leisurely paced, offbeat trio of loosely linked stories about connecting to loved ones alive and dead. On this particular day, Eastwood is guiding Damon and actress Bryce Dallas Howard through their characters' awkward attempts to launch romantic interplay during a mundane cooking class—a sequence shot inside Paulding & Company, a small, real-life cooking school facility in Emeryville.

Aside from the on-set haircut and some tasty gourmet food, ranging from the ubiquitous poached salmon that Eastwood routinely picks at while filming to a spicy jambalaya that Damon raves about all afternoon, the shoot is typically efficient, economical, and wholly lacking in chaos. In fact, all of the elements of *Hereafter's* cooking school scenes are captured on celluloid by cinematographer Tom Stern's team in just a matter of hours, as Eastwood gently, but strategically, manipulates the day's energy.

At the heart of Eastwood's agenda this day is his commitment to covering the subtle interaction between Damon's character and Howard's as thoroughly as possible, from many different directions and perspectives. Even while shooting it, Eastwood is thinking about how he might edit the scene, and is covering the action with the goal of giving co-editors Joel Cox and Gary Roach multiple options down the road. The strategic volume and nature of the coverage of the scene are typical. Although Eastwood never storyboards, rarely even blocks out such scenes, and does, as the legends say, shoot few takes with only one lens at any given time, he does use lots of lenses to capture pieces of such scenes repeatedly from different directions and angles—almost always with a single camera. On the surface, this meticulous coverage might appear to contrast with the stereotype of Eastwood as the fastest shooter in Hollywood, but that stereotype revolves around the number of takes, not the depth of coverage. The truth is, he's both fast and thorough.

When asked about this dichotomy, Eastwood first offers his stock answer—"I like to keep the BS to a minimum." However, in truth, he and his team have a well-honed, methodical process for how the director wants his camera to capture elements for virtually all dramatic, character-driven, non-action-related moments in his films.

(Page 36) Eastwood works on location in Boston during the filming of *Mystic River*. (Page 37) The ornately designed and detailed interior of the Green Emerald Bar built for that film. (Opposite) Clint Eastwood and actor Christopher Carley prepare a scene while shooting *Gran Torino*—a movie filmed entirely on location in Michigan. (Below) Matt Damon as George Lonegan with actress Bryce Dallas Howard during the *Hereafter* cooking class scene.

He will, as he did in the cooking school scene for *Hereafter*, start wide with what is sometimes called the master shot, or in the words of first assistant cameraman (in charge of lenses) Bill Coe, "what we call the big stinking wide shot. It's basically the wide shot over the shoulders, and moving in closer to the close-ups. We try to give Clint these shots with a minimal amount of technical infringement, so he can concentrate on the essence of the scene, the acting."

Eastwood will push in using almost every lens available until he feels he has achieved comprehensive coverage of the encounter. Then his team will switch the camera to the other side and repeat the exercise.

(Top L) Clint Eastwood and Don Siegel on the set of *Dirty Harry*. (Top R) Matt Damon and Eastwood share a light moment during the London location shoot for *Hereafter*. (Bottom) Vincent Bonasso, playing a tailor, fits Eastwood's character for a suit as the camera team films them on a Detroit-area stage for the climaxing moments in *Gran Torino*. (Opposite, L–R) Cinematographer Tom Stern, actor John Carroll Lynch, and Clint Eastwood are seen reflected in the mirror of the barbershop used in *Gran Torino*.

Tom Stern, Eastwood's cinematographer for eight years at this point, after doing a twenty-year tour of duty as his chief lighting technician (gaffer), chuckles when asked if his boss and friend would ever consider shooting a scene like this with multiple cameras, to acquire different perspectives simultaneously. That's because Eastwood almost never uses multiple cameras for any reason, "unless we're blowing stuff up," Stern suggests. And Eastwood's reason for that, according to Stern, is that multiple cameras aren't the best way to lure the best emotions from multiple actors in a dialogue scene. Instead, Eastwood believes emotional performances unfold best in front of a single, cozy camera.

"Getting more coverage gives editors the opportunity to shorten or jazz up a scene a bit, which is important in this case because there is a tremendous amount of narrative exposition there—the scene involves pages of dialogue," Stern explains. "Clint knows that good actors normally play to the camera, no matter how many of them you have. If Matt Damon is in a wide shot, he's playing it one way, and differently for his close-up—an actor of that caliber knows how to use the camera accordingly. So if you use multiple cameras in that situation, the actor can't play it just for the wide shot or the tight shot, and therefore, they can't be as good as they can be. So instead, Clint will take his time, and move a single camera around when necessary. That's a different thing than just doing take after take, as many filmmakers do."

Eastwood's camera team can readily explain the technical and creative reasons for this style. But for Clint, it's mostly instinctual, born from a lifetime in and around filmmaking, studying and participating in the art. Thus, when pressed, he resists overarticulating a process that has become completely organic and seamless to him over the years.

The director says simply, "There's no rule on it—it's just the way that works for me. I tell people, 'Do whatever suits you at the time.' It's the painting of it all that interests me. It's a lot like painting. Why does an artist make a certain stroke? Just because it seemed like the right thing to do at the time."

And so, on this day, the crew constantly shuttles around the kitchen location, in order to strategically create conditions that allow Eastwood to capture a variety of quiet, intimate moments between Damon and Howard, in as many ways as the environment will permit. He does so even though he hasn't mapped out any of it, nor held extensive meetings over it, nor even discussed most of the technical details with his team before he started shooting it.

A key portion of the scene calls for Howard to wear a mask for a blind taste test, with Damon slowly spooning a variety of mystery ingredients into her mouth. Eastwood, standing beside the actors, stares at his handheld wireless monitor to ponder composition and framing, and each time gently pushes for the encounter to be more intimate as they film it from different angles.

"Sweep his hair, fix her mask, get closer, push the spoon in deeper," he urges in a whisper. At one point, reversing the angle, Eastwood asks Stern to switch to a tighter lens. Later, Eastwood lopes over to Damon and whispers something in his ear. The actor replies with a belly laugh, and instantly snuggles closer to Howard.

Damon, working for the second time with Eastwood, on the heels of 2009's *Invictus*, was making no secret of plans to direct films himself—in fact, he would announce his directorial debut in late 2011. And so, when Eastwood speaks—even jokes—he's listening intently.

"He was cracking a joke, but within his joke, he was trying to get me to slow down a hair there," Damon says, polishing off yet another cup of jambalaya. "With his monitor, Clint is checking the frame line, standing real close to the camera. He's watching us act with his naked eye, but he's also watching the frame line so he can visualize how the shot [will appear on film]. When he stopped me, I assume he saw something there—something about the intimacy of the thing. The sequence could be cut a number of different ways, from straightforward to lyrical with music over it, to close shots of the spoons going back and forth, in and out of our mouths. I think Clint saw something he liked and felt if we could do it slower and more sensually, it would be great.

"Everything he says—they are always helpful notes, and even his jokes can be strategic. You have to understand, on a movie set, things can get out of control, people's nerves can come into play—it's a fragile working environment and ever changing. His jokes, little comments, and relaxed attitude are designed to counter that—to keep things really calm so everyone can do their best work. Plus, of course, a director's personality comes out when they direct, and most sets are a reflection of those personalities. Clint's a relaxed man, so the set is relaxed."

Eastwood's personality does, indeed, dominate the environment as the afternoon winds down, but in an understated way. Paradoxically, he is able to exert control by loosening the reins. He simply empowers each veteran collaborator to do the things that experience has taught him will come about if he provides his team the right information and environment, while he focuses most of his attention on his actors' needs. Much of his influence on his crew, in fact, has been exerted long before they ever arrive on set—everything from locations to colors to costumes to lighting are carefully preplanned by Eastwood's colleagues and then implemented without fanfare, with slight adjustments applied whenever Eastwood, or anyone else with a good idea, speaks up. This group has been together for so long, and so successfully, that many of the chosen elements designed or executed by others on the team pass Eastwood's muster with hardly any comment. And yet, at some point, like pieces in a particularly organic puzzle, those separate choices and tasks inevitably meld together, as Eastwood's overall vision is eventually exposed on film.

The work is finished by dusk. Eastwood piles into a Ford Ranger 4x4 and prepares to drive himself home to Carmel, a couple of hours away from the Emeryville location. "See you later," he says through a rolled-down window, to no one in particular, and with a wave, he's down the driveway and gone.

(Opposite) Clint Eastwood instructs extras playing audience members at Bronco Billy's Wild West Show (*Bronco Billy*). Eastwood puts great thought into casting and utilizing extras in his pictures. (Above) Clint Eastwood and late actor Stefan Schnabel chat during a break in shooting *Firefox* in 1981.

ONE YEAR LATER...

In early March 2011, the Malpaso team reconstitutes itself in another cramped location—the venerable Smoke House restaurant in Burbank, California, directly across the street from Eastwood's office on the Warner Bros. lot. This time, they are briskly filming scenes for Eastwood's follow-up to *Hereafter*—*J. Edgar*, a 2011 release about legendary FBI boss J. Edgar Hoover. Eastwood fondly recalls dining at the Smoke House in the 1950s, while a contract player for Universal Studios. He says that when the production went shopping for a single location to stand in for two different restaurants in two different periods of Hoover's life, he recalled the place across the street.

"We looked at a lot of restaurants," he explains, while his team prepares the restaurant's interior so he can film his star, Leonardo DiCaprio, as a young Hoover, about to meet his future companion and colleague, Clyde Tolson (played by Armie Hammer) for the first time. "We wanted a booth-type restaurant with old, dark wood—a smoky kind of place like they had in those years. Sometimes, you don't see what is in front of you, but eventually, I remembered this place."

During the course of this day, Eastwood's team will transform the Smoke House first into the Mayflower Hotel's restaurant in 1927, where Hoover and Tolson first meet, and later, into Harvey's Restaurant in 1933, where the two men will reconvene to discuss Hoover's secret file on Eleanor Roosevelt. Despite the need to transform actors, light, makeup, costumes, table settings, food (technically, it's "stunt food" and will later be donated to an animal shelter), walls, and backdrops,

(Above) Armie Hammer (L) and Leonardo DiCaprio in a restaurant scene for *J. Edgar*, filmed at the Smoke House restaurant in Burbank, CA. The location was then promptly re-dressed and re-used that same day for a scene in an entirely different restaurant. (Opposite) The Stork Club scene from the same film—vintage clothes, props, hair, music, and lighting scheme all contributed to the illusion.

as well as deal with a few minor problems along the way, Eastwood's team is calm and matter-of-fact as they get organized.

For the Harvey's Restaurant sequence, Charlie Saldana, Eastwood's longtime key grip, hammers a wood panel between the ceiling and the top of the same booth where the earlier scene was shot, in order to create a false wall and, thus, a completely different background. Longtime camera operator Stephen Campanelli stretches his legs before slipping into the Steadicam rig (a motion-stabilizing camera mount worn by camera operators to give them freedom of movement to follow action). He's getting ready to film the Hoover and Tolson characters walking through the busy, smoke-filled restaurant, weaving their way between tables and diners.

For the entrance, Campanelli, guided by dolly grip Greg Brooks, to prevent him from tripping, expertly maneuvers backward, navigating the maze of the restaurant ahead of the actors until they take their seats. For a Steadicam shot of this type, Eastwood is not able to hover close to the camera as he normally does, since it moves so erratically, so he picks a corner spot to stand near the booth and watches his actors approach. In so doing, he inadvertently interferes with a homemade remedy his crew has concocted to solve a minor problem. Gaffer Ross Dunkerley has noticed a small shadow cast by Campanelli and his camera rig on the floor. To eliminate it, Dunkerley asks Saldana to hold and rotate a small screen as the actors and cameraman pass by, to briefly block light, and therefore the shadow, in that one spot. Eastwood, however, chooses exactly that spot to stand in, and concentrating so intently, he never hears Dunkerley's whisper, asking him to move, thus preventing Saldana from turning the screen sufficiently.

"He may have not heard me, but more likely, he was ignoring me because he was concentrating on the performances," Dunkerley sighs immediately afterward. Then he politely requests a rare retake of the shot, after explaining the situation to Eastwood, who ends up doing two more takes of the walk through the restaurant, after a brief microphone malfunction.

A short time later, DiCaprio requests another timeout to fix a problem with a contact lens, but promises Eastwood he'll be "speedy" in resolving the problem. The director laughs at this, knowing DiCaprio is referring to Hoover's private nickname, bestowed upon him in the movie by his mother (Judi Dench).

"Hurry up and wait. That's the movie business," the director mutters to himself.

At 7:30 P.M., an even more unusual event occurs—Eastwood recalls cast and crew after releasing them moments earlier. "Flag on the play" crackles over radios, ordering people back inside—one of the few times you will hear walkie-talkies on a Clint Eastwood set. A single shot was forgotten before the crew was released—a quick bit featuring Hoover and Tolson engaging in a champagne toast.

(Opposite) Like many before him, Leonardo DiCaprio took the lead role in *J. Edgar* specifically to work with Clint Eastwood. (Above) The famed Warner Bros. tower hovers over extras who are part of the horse-racing scenes in *J. Edgar*. Actors were filmed on makeshift bleachers in the studio parking lot and combined with real and digital elements to give the illusion of period racetracks.

As the crew files back inside the Smoke House, Eastwood and his team tease one another, calling the incident an "Abby Singer moment." Abby Singer was a production manager and assistant director in Hollywood years ago, who became famous for incorrectly telling cast and crew that the second-to-last shot of the day was the last—a shot that eventually came to be known as the "Abby Singer shot." Eastwood points out that you can never end on the Abby Singer shot. The faux pas is rectified in minutes.

Aside from a handful of prominent exceptions over the years, such moments are about as dramatic as it gets on Eastwood sets, and the director's bemused reaction is about as petulant as he is likely to get these days. Stories circulate, of course, of Eastwood losing his temper or raising his voice when his precious and economical production flow is somehow interrupted for trivial or avoidable reasons, but those who know him best and longest say those are ancient stories, if they happened at all. Indeed, after the Abby Singer moment, as the crew files out a second time, Eastwood goes out of his way to praise DiCaprio and Hammer on the smallest of things. "Nice job with the small talk" earlier in the day, he tells them, referring to improvised tableside chitchat.

Such seemingly innocuous praise brings a wide smile to DiCaprio's face. He calls Eastwood a director who "gives his actors ultimate confidence, and trusts everyone's instincts the way he trusts his own." And by "everyone," DiCaprio means not only actors—crew members at every level offer variations on the same theme.

The small speed bumps of the day are long forgotten. It was a day that reminded an interested observer—the film's screenwriter, Dustin Lance Black—"of jazz," and Black is not the first person who has worked with Eastwood to make that comparison.

"It's the same in the sense that you don't lock yourself in too much—you let yourself discover something new at the moment," says Black, who was on set

throughout the making of *J. Edgar*, but with almost no rewriting to do, he spent most of his free time watching filming and working on his next screenplay. "He may start the shot high and wide, but then he moves in and tries to discover things. He sees shots in his mind, and then he is fortunate to have this crew that knows him so well, and they go out and move real fast to put that exact shot together in a matter of minutes."

And so, once again, an Eastwood production day went so smoothly that, on the surface, the process could be easily mistaken for being less complex and creative than it really was. Perhaps, as Matt Damon suggests, "making movies is easy when you have put sixty years into it." But Rob Lorenz suggests that, at the end of the day, harmony on an Eastwood set largely flows out of a unique, "unusually balanced and controlled leadership style" on Eastwood's part.

If that's true, then, by definition, Eastwood must have someone to lead. Over the decades, his Malpaso team has developed such a finely tuned rapport with him that, at times, it can be hard to tell where Eastwood's direct input ends and his hands-off instincts take over, permitting his colleagues to put their fingerprints on his canvas, and subtly and seamlessly influence the greater whole, rewarding Eastwood for letting them do their thing.

In any case, once again, the day's work ends as casually as it began, and shortly after eight P.M., Eastwood's team slips off to catch shuttles back to the parking garage. Yet another successful chapter in the life of a Clint Eastwood production is in the books. Lorenz refers to such days as "hitting a groove," where two powerful paradigms converge. "You realize full confidence, and simultaneously work with a team that understands you real well," the producer explains. Clearly, even after more than forty years directing movies, Eastwood and his crew still have their groove on.

(Above) Exactingly designed props lend an air of realism to the Stork Club scene in *J. Edgar*. Prop master Mike Sexton spent months researching the smallest details and acquiring props like glasses, cups, lamps, and more for the period piece.

"THEY ARE REALLY PART OF HIM.

IT'S LIKE CLINT IS THE HEAD AND THE CREW ARE THE BODY."

ACTOR KEN WATANABE, 2011

CHAPTER ONE
THE WELL-OILED MACHINE

WHEN CLINT EASTWOOD ACCEPTED HIS INITIAL BEST DIRECTOR ACADEMY AWARD IN 1992 FOR *UNFORGIVEN*, THE FIRST PEOPLE HE THANKED WERE HARDLY HOUSEHOLD NAMES—HIS PRODUCER, DAVID VALDES, CINEMATOGRAPHER JACK GREEN, "AND ALL THE CAMERA CREW."

Thirteen years later, accepting the same award for his work on *Million Dollar Baby*, after paying tribute to his wife and his mother, Eastwood again placed his crew before anyone else, including, by name, camera operator Stephen Campanelli, first assistant cameraman Bill Coe, cinematographer Tom Stern, ASC, production designer Henry Bumstead, art director Jack Taylor, and set decorator Richard Goddard. Eastwood then went on to explain to the millions watching that his team shot *Million Dollar Baby* in just thirty-seven days.

"It takes a well-oiled machine to do that, and that well-oiled machine is the crew," he declared.

That single, succinct sentence boiled down what essentially lies at the core of Eastwood's filmmaking philosophy—pick the best crew, empower them, respect them, keep them together as long as possible, and trust them completely. This belief in "his team" has been unshakable in Eastwood's mind and method his entire career, which is why he has declared in numerous interviews, "I'm no auteur."

Eastwood is fond of telling people that the primary reason he's kept his core team together for so long is because "I don't have a lot of explaining to do with people I've worked with before. They know the routine—there isn't a lot of wasted motion. A lot of times, crew members ask a thousand questions, but I don't want to do a thousand and one if I can help it."

However, the true story runs deeper—it is, above all else, a story of the success of a decades-long collaboration between Eastwood and a small, devoted group of fellow artists and colleagues. Eastwood, in fact, deeply respects his team, and genuinely feels they are the best in the business. Although colleagues insist that Eastwood's demeanor is the reason his sets run so quiet and smooth, Eastwood reverses that notion by suggesting "they are the ones that make me look good."

"It's like a guy throwing a ball," he says. "It looks effortless for [professional quarterback] Tom Brady. But someone else has to put a lot of strain into it. A ball, a

golf swing, working on a movie—it appears effortless when done by someone who knows what they are doing, and it appears strenuous when you don't know what you are doing. My guys know what they are doing."

Thus Eastwood is creatively joined at the hip with his "guys," and works with them in a way largely devoid of ego, hierarchy, and much of the pretension one normally sees in Hollywood.

Actor Ken Watanabe, who worked intimately with the director on *Letters from Iwo Jima*, marvels at the tight interweaving of Eastwood with his crew. At Watanabe's request, Eastwood permitted him not only to star in the film, but also to supervise translation of the script from English to Japanese, and to work with

[Opposite] Some of Clint Eastwood's closest, longtime partners help him film explosions in the California desert. (L–R) Michael Owens, Eastwood, Tom Stern, Rob Lorenz, and Buddy Van Horn. [Above] Also during production of *Letters from Iwo Jima*, Stern (C) and Owens consult with Eastwood.

"CLINT DOESN'T ONLY CAST ACTORS—HE CASTS THE CREW, AS WELL," ROB LORENZ EXPLAINS. "AND IF THEY DO IT WELL, HE ASKS THEM TO KEEP COMING BACK. FOR THE MOST PART, THAT'S WHAT THEY DO."

costume designer Deborah Hopper and the prop team to select vintage World War II–era Japanese army uniforms and props. Thus, Watanabe interacted closely with virtually the entire Eastwood team.

The way Watanabe sees things, "Clint always trusts, more than anyone else—he trusts the whole crew. Everybody. They are really part of him. It is like Clint is the head and they are his body."

Central to this philosophy is the fact that Eastwood has kept core elements of his team together more consistently and longer than probably anyone in Hollywood history. There have been changes—key changes, in fact—but, relative to industry norms, these changes are few and far between. When they do happen, it's usually due to unavoidable conflicts, personal reasons, health reasons, retirement, or death. Some of those who have left or retired have periodically returned, or remain willing to, if and when Eastwood calls.

"Clint doesn't only cast actors—he casts the crew, as well," producer Rob Lorenz explains. "He intentionally seeks out people who know their jobs and have a lot of experience in their craft, and he then trusts them to do that job. He trusts they will be better prepared than he is when it comes to their particular area. And if they do it well, he asks them to keep coming back, and for the most part, that's what they do."

Certainly, this preference emanates out of Eastwood's personal values. But that isn't the only reason Eastwood strives to keep his team together. His colleagues believe it also boils down to the fact that his filmmaking method simply works best when it's being executed by those who have experienced it first-hand and repeatedly.

"I really think Clint makes movies in such a unique way that it's not always evident that someone who is not familiar with it can just step into it," says Tom Stern. "I think he is wise to recognize this, and that is probably one reason why he has maintained such continuity on the team."

WINDING THREADS

Few filmmakers have stayed loyal to a core team to the extent Eastwood has. His belief in the notion applies to virtually his entire filmmaking crew, as well as those who work with him in other capacities. His agent (Leonard Hirshan) has been with him for fifty years, his lawyer (Bruce Ramer) for more than forty years, his business managers (Howard Bernstein and Roy Kaufman) for more than forty years, and so on down the line. Bill Gold, who designed most of Eastwood's movie posters for forty years, insisted in 2011, at the age of ninety, that "Clint is my best friend in the world." Composer Lennie Niehaus, who first met Eastwood in the army at Fort Ord in Northern California in the 1950s, composed, conducted, orchestrated, arranged, and supervised music for Eastwood's films for more than twenty-seven years. Today, Niehaus declares, "I owe him a lot—he's the one who put my name on the map as a movie composer."

It's not surprising that a visually acute director like Eastwood has also been extremely close to his production designers over the years. He has worked with a few, including a lengthy stretch with legendary designer Edward Carfagno, for eight pictures in the 1980s. That work came after the late Henry Bumstead, another industry legend, had designed the Western town that plays a central role in *High Plains Drifter* in 1973. Eastwood was quite taken with the work, but Bumstead had commitments to honor with Alfred Hitchcock, George Roy Hill, and others, and so Eastwood waited until making another iconic Western, *Unforgiven* in 1992, to work with him again. Bumstead then worked on every Eastwood picture until his death in 2006, following his work co-designing *Letters from Iwo Jima* with another industry veteran, James Murakami, who has now taken his place.

(Above, L–R) Producer Brian Grazer (L) and Clint Eastwood's producing partner, Rob Lorenz, watch a shot unfold on the set of *J. Edgar* on a handheld monitor identical to the one Eastwood uses. Historical photo: Alfred Hitchcock (center), another of Henry Bumstead's regular collaborators, celebrates Bumstead's birthday on the set of *Vertigo* in 1958. Hoover's porch from *J. Edgar*. Producer Rob Lorenz and visual effects supervisor Michael Owens discuss an exterior shot with Clint Eastwood (*Letters from Iwo Jima*).

Charlie Saldana has worked as Eastwood's key grip (the crew member who logistically supports the camera and electrical departments) for more than thirty years, since being hired by former cinematographer Bruce Surtees on *Escape from Alcatraz* in 1979. Since then, Saldana has continued to fulfill that role on all but two of Eastwood's films.

Canadian camera operator Stephen Campanelli connected with Malpaso in the early 1990s. He was working on a movie in China with Surtees's successor, Jack Green, ASC, and recalls wanting desperately to please Green because he was linked to Eastwood.

"I worked really hard to impress Jack, and eventually, Jack told Clint I was a really good Steadicam operator with a good eye," Campanelli recalls. "Clint told him to try and get me for the next movie, but Jack pointed out I was Canadian and needed U.S. work papers. Clint asked him how good I really was, and Jack vouched for me, so Malpaso filed the paperwork, and I ended up in a cornfield in Iowa in 1994 working for my idol on *The Bridges of Madison County*."

Eastwood's early costume supervisor Glenn Wright brought current costume supervisor Deborah Hopper into the Malpaso fold to serve as women's costume supervisor on *Tightrope* in 1984. That led her to collaborate with Wright and others on Eastwood films for several years before earning her first costume design credit on *Space Cowboys* in 2000. She has been with Malpaso ever since. Likewise, the late Phyllis Huffman started as Eastwood's casting director on *Honkytonk Man* in 1982, and worked on most of his films until shortly before her death following *Letters from Iwo Jima* (2006).

Such threads wind on and on, binding the Malpaso team together in all sorts of ways, from first assistant cameraman Bill Coe to hair department head Carol O'Connell to script supervisor Mable McCrary to construction coordinator Mike Muscarella, prop master Mike Sexton, transportation coordinator Larry Stelling, first assistant director David Bernstein, and many more. Many of them were promoted from within or had worked with someone on the Eastwood crew when they earned their positions. Bernstein's, Muscarella's, and Sexton's fathers, in fact, all worked with Eastwood over the years.

As industry technology and techniques evolved, new crew members in new positions joined up. Visual effects supervisor Michael Owens, whose digital work is now essential to Eastwood films, has been with him since *Space Cowboys* in 2000, and video and computer graphics supervisor Liz Radley also joined on that show. Digital colorist Jill Bogdanowicz of Technicolor is brand new by comparison—she started color-correcting Eastwood's films with *Flags of Our Fathers* in 2006.

It's especially instructive to understand the genesis of Eastwood's relationships with certain key department heads who have been with him for a long time, in crucial jobs and as close confidants. For instance, Eastwood is so comfortable with Joel Cox, his editor of almost forty years, that he relies heavily on Cox's input when making most important creative or technical decisions. Cox and cinematographer Tom Stern are probably the most senior Eastwood department heads currently active at this point, but over the years, Bumstead and a couple of others also provided high-level input into Eastwood's decision-making process—a small, evolving group that Stern jokingly refers to as "the Star Chamber."

"Those of us with seniority—Clint will definitely give us a say in key decisions," Stern suggests.

Understanding the backgrounds and roles of current, longtime senior team members such as Cox, Stern, producer Rob Lorenz, supervising sound editors Alan Murray and Bub Asman, and stunt coordinator Buddy Van Horn, who has been with Eastwood since the beginning, is crucial to fully understanding how moviemaking works at Malpaso.

(Above) Cinematographer Tom Stern plans a shot on the rugby field (*Invictus*).

THE EDITOR

Joel Cox, ACE, now cuts Eastwood's films in partnership with his son-in-law, Gary Roach, but there was a time when he was the fresh face in the editing room. He had been working as a postproduction assistant at Warner Bros., learning editing, sound effects, music, looping, and much more, when Rudi Fehr, the studio's long-time head of production, arranged for him to interview with Eastwood's longtime editor, Ferris Webster, for an assistant position on *The Outlaw Josey Wales* in 1975.

As is often the case with Eastwood, it was the little things that made the director notice Cox, laying the building blocks for a decades-long friendship and collaboration. Cox, who won an Oscar for *Unforgiven* in 1992 and was nominated for an Oscar for *Million Dollar Baby* in 2005, has been involved in each of Eastwood's films in one way or another since *Josey Wales*.

But Cox didn't really interact with Eastwood until the editing team packed up its equipment and moved to finish *Josey Wales* near Eastwood's home in Carmel, California—a tradition that continues to this day.

"I drove up to Carmel Saturday morning, we met there and unloaded all the equipment into a little apartment Clint had for us," says Cox. "I went in Sunday and unpacked everything and set it all up. I wasn't asked to do it—I just did it. Clint came in and was clearly pleased. He knew we were in Carmel to work, not take a vacation, and was glad to see I knew it also."

While finalizing that film, Webster missed a few days due to a personal matter, and Cox worked directly with Eastwood to make final adjustments. The director then asked him to stay on as Webster's permanent assistant. From that early period as assistant onward, Cox routinely worked directly with Eastwood, with Webster's blessing, and eventually, according to Eastwood, it was Webster who urged him to make Cox co-editor. Cox worked in that capacity with Webster on several films between 1976 and 1982, and then took over when Webster retired, starting with *Sudden Impact* in 1983, and has been there ever since.

Cox emphasizes he had the technical skills for the job from the start, but learned from Eastwood to rely on first instincts. "He taught me never to second-guess myself. He told me that's how he directs, and it's how he wants me to edit. If you second-guess yourself, you start making changes you shouldn't make. Clint believes editing a movie is all about making the most out of emotional moments. He taught me that, and we've worked well together for thirty-six years. When a relationship clicks, it just clicks."

(Opposite) Cinematographer David Worth and Clint Eastwood lead the cast up a hill (*Bronco Billy*). (Pages 56–57) The Malpaso crew prepares to continue filming the climactic shoot-out in *Pale Rider*.

(Above L) Deborah Hopper, women's wardrobe supervisor on *Pale Rider* (and now Eastwood's longtime costume supervisor), wears one of her own costumes for a wordless cameo as "lady in the bank" in the film, alongside then gaffer Tom Stern, who tries to get a light reading before filming her. (Above R) Camera operator Jack Green offers suggestions for a shot to Clint Eastwood during the making of *Bronco Billy*. Eastwood calls the camera operator "my right arm" when he is shooting a movie.

THE PRODUCER

Rob Lorenz has been Eastwood's producing partner since *Blood Work* in 2002. He moved up to the job from the first assistant director position, which in turn he had earned after serving as second assistant director since *The Bridges of Madison County* (1995). He found himself suddenly thrust into the first AD position in a pinch during the *Absolute Power* (1997) location shoot.

"I was second assistant director on my first show for Clint, and we were about a week into production on *Absolute Power* in Maryland, trying to film an elaborate stunt where a car gets knocked off a cliff," Lorenz recalls. "We were trying to get out of there in one day, but things got a little disorganized and we had trouble placing the camera properly. Clint was watching a storm cloud come in while we were trying to get the camera right, so we rolled film. There was a special camera inside the car as [the car] went over, but in the chaos and confusion to get the shot quickly, the camera in the car rolled out, and we couldn't go forward with the stunt. Then the skies opened up on us. Clint called wrap, and at that point, I presumed I would probably be sent home.

"But that night, the first AD decided for his own reasons to quit the production, and so I got a call at one o'clock in the morning telling me I was now first AD. I had never firsted before and we were shooting a huge stunt on a Clint Eastwood movie. Had we been in Los Angeles, they probably would have brought in someone new, with more experience. But we were in Maryland and there was no one else available. So I ran the set the next day, and Clint was happy with how it turned out. We did two more days of stunt-related work, and they were offering to fly in someone new for Clint, but he just said, 'Rob is doing fine. Let him do it.'"

The movie wrapped ahead of schedule, and Lorenz thus became Eastwood's first AD. In ensuing years, Lorenz, eager to learn directing, managed sets in a way that was designed to make sure Eastwood could maintain his focus on the actors, and the relationship blossomed. As Eastwood had done with others before him, Lorenz was eventually promoted to producer from first AD, for a time doing both jobs, and remains Eastwood's producing partner to this day.

In late 2011, Lorenz announced he would direct his first film, with Eastwood starring, something Clint agreed to do, he says, because he liked the story about an aging baseball scout, but also "because it's Rob."

"He'll do a great job directing," Eastwood says. "He's also a terrific producer. You have to have somebody who is equally enthusiastic as you are, and understands you and has the passion to do it with you. He really enjoys the filmmaking process, and makes things easier for me. I keep him involved in everything—we're very compatible."

(Top L) Rob Lorenz (*Flags of Our Fathers*). (Top R) Jack Green and Clint Eastwood, dressed in character as Gunnery Sgt. Tom "Gunny" Highway (*Heartbreak Ridge*). (Bottom) Cinematographer Tom Stern and Eastwood discuss how to film the scene in *J. Edgar* in which the body of the Lindbergh baby is discovered by passersby.

THE CAMERA MEN

Eastwood calls Bruce Surtees the "predecessor to all my cinematographers—he was the guy that Jack Green, Tom Stern, and all of us learned our boldness from. Bruce was absolutely fearless with light levels and everything else."

As the first of just three regular cinematographers for Eastwood, Surtees was the connective tissue that links Eastwood, his directing mentor, Don Siegel, and the camera crew and visuals that have come out of the Eastwood camp since his filmmaking career began. (In fact, only four Eastwood-directed films have been shot by someone other than Surtees, Green, or Stern.) The son of cinematographer Robert Surtees, Bruce caught on as a camera operator for Siegel when Siegel was directing Eastwood in *Coogan's Bluff* (1968) and *Two Mules for Sister Sara* (1970).

When Siegel and Eastwood prepared to team up again in 1971 for the haunting psychological drama *The Beguiled*, the filmmakers were on a budget, according to Eastwood, and liked Surtees's style. Thus, they decided to move him up to cinematographer.

"When Don was directing, he and I tended to work closely together to make those decisions," Eastwood recalls. "It was fun on smaller films like *Coogan's Bluff*, and we weren't afraid to do crazy stuff, different stories, which *Beguiled* certainly was. We wanted a bold look at a reasonable price, so Bruce fit the bill."

Surtees went on to shoot Eastwood's directorial debut, *Play Misty for Me*, in 1971, and nine more films that Eastwood either acted in or directed between *Misty* and 1985's *Pale Rider*.

"Clint and Don totally gave me a break," Surtees said in an interview a few months before his death in February 2012. "It was an easy transition—we had already worked together, and Clint knew what he was doing by the time we started on *Misty*. Right from the start, he had such good instincts about casting and staging, where he wanted to place the camera and catch the action. He knew what he was doing to get the most impact."

Along the way, Surtees eventually took on Jack Green as his camera operator, at Eastwood's request, and also asked Tom Stern to be his gaffer for 1982's *Honkytonk Man*. Over time, he routinely encouraged both to get more directly involved with Eastwood. That set a template devoid of egos or hierarchy that lasts to this day, in which Eastwood consults routinely and intimately with not only his cinematographer, but directly with his operator and gaffer, as well.

When Surtees got sick while filming *Tightrope* (1984), Green filled in near the end of production. Surtees returned for *Pale Rider*, but after that production was over, he approached Eastwood and suggested he turn the cinematography job over to Green.

(Above) Eastwood and Lorenz confer for a moment during an interior day shoot for *Hereafter*. (Page 60) Cinematographer David Worth (L) and Clint Eastwood mull over a *Bronco Billy* urban sequence that takes place in a penthouse apartment. (Page 61, L–R) Worth, camera operator Jack Green, and assistant cameraman Leslie Otis set up a shot on a camera crane on a rainy Idaho day during the *Bronco Billy* shoot.

"I did want Jack to get his chance," said Surtees. "He did a good job when I was in the hospital, he had been working with Eastwood for a long time, and knew everything we were doing. So it was no problem for him to take over, and I went on to something else."

Green recalls Surtees's generosity with great emotion because their relationship started off rocky. Green had already been chosen by Eastwood to be his camera operator by the time Surtees returned to serve as cinematographer on *Firefox* (1982). Green had entered Eastwood's universe on his own, first doing aerial camera work separate from Surtees for *Play Misty for Me*, and then working as camera operator on *Every Which Way but Loose* (1978), *Bronco Billy* (1980), and *Any Which Way You Can* (1980)—three films shot by other cinematographers (the first by Rexford Metz and the next two by David Worth). They first worked together on *Firefox*, and Green says Surtees, quite understandably, was wary of working with a camera operator not of his own choosing.

"For Bruce and I, *Firefox* was like the first round of a professional fight, where a lot of jabs are thrown but you only hit air," says Green. "I was helpful to Clint because I had worked with him before, but I don't know how helpful I was to Bruce. So there was a little reaction there. By *Tightrope*, we had some time together under our belts, and then I finished it for him, so by the time *Pale Rider* came around, we had locked into a productive way of working together. He eventually asked me to work for him on *Beverly Hills Cop* [1984], and by then, we were close friends. He was the most interesting director of photography I have ever worked with. He worked as if the set was a canvas and he a painter with a large brush in his hand.

"But unbeknownst to me, after *Beverly Hills Cop*, we came full circle, because that is when Bruce went to Clint and suggested he move me up to DP. That was so generous of him—I'll never forget it."

Beginning with *Heartbreak Ridge* (1986), Green shot thirteen films Eastwood starred in and/or directed through 2000's *Space Cowboys*, earning an Academy Award nomination for his work on *Unforgiven* in 1992, among other accolades. After *Space Cowboys*, telling Eastwood he was looking to move into directing films (as of this writing, he has directed two features), Green gave way for Stern to take over the camera chair. Stern was an unusual selection in the sense that he had never operated a movie camera—his expertise was in lighting as a gaffer, and that is a rare path toward the job of cinematographer.

"Tom told me he was getting into the camera guild and asked me if I ever had an opening, would I consider using him as cinematographer, and I said sure I would," Eastwood recalls. "Bruce had brought him in, he had worked for me a lot, and was great with lighting, so I figured he knew what we were looking for."

"It's pretty unusual when you think about it, that Clint would promote me, or the fact that all his cinematographers have been promoted from within," says Stern. "It shows the level of continuity in the organization. That is connected to Clint's wonderful, but very unusual, management style."

Stern originally met Surtees on a TV commercial in the early 1980s. After that job wrapped, Surtees tried to get Stern onto *Firefox* as a gaffer, but the spot was already filled. However, the job became open heading into *Honkytonk Man*, and Surtees finally brought Stern on board.

Ironically, before Green departed and just before Stern was elevated to cinematographer for *Blood Work*, Stern was planning to retire because he was finding it grueling to live part of the year in the U.S. and part of the year in France, where his wife is from. He had already postponed retirement once to serve as gaffer for legendary

(Above L) Clint Eastwood spent hours inside the supersonic jet cockpit built on a stage to capture several scenes in *Firefox*. (Above R) During production of *Million Dollar Baby*, he kept up with any tweaks to the script with script supervisor Mable McCrary.

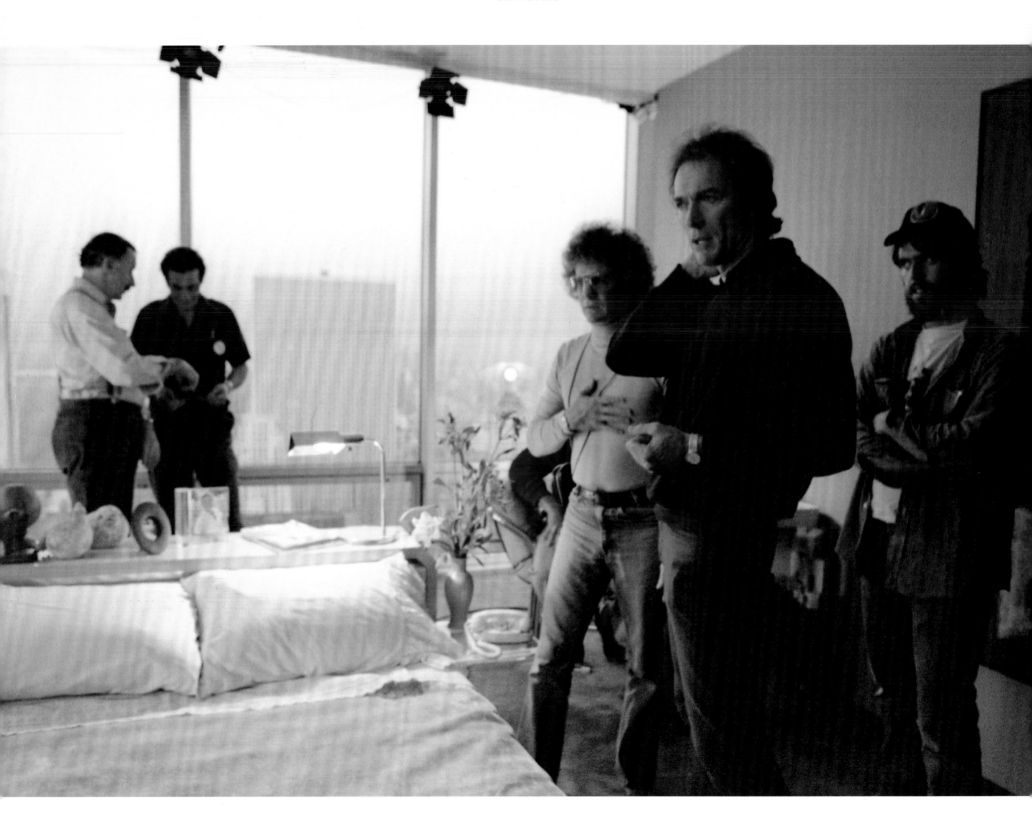

cinematographer Conrad Hall on Sam Mendes's *American Beauty* in 1999, which started a close association that ended when Hall passed away in 2003, following *Road to Perdition*. As Hall fell ill, Stern once again planned to call it quits. Unable to collaborate anymore with his mentor, he felt it would be hard to work as a gaffer for anyone else, "because Conrad was so amazing. I just didn't think I could enjoy working for another cinematographer anymore—that I couldn't be more creative than I was with him.

"And I certainly had never planned to be a cinematographer after thirty years as a gaffer," he adds.

"But then Clint called out of the blue and asked if I'd shoot *Blood Work*. I took a day to think it over, and came up with an analysis that the worst thing in the world is to be stuck in the past, and the only way to avoid that is to keep trying new things, even if there is a likelihood of failure. If I failed, I'd have to leave in shame, but then again, I was planning to leave anyway, so I figured I didn't have much to lose. I told Clint I'd do it, and I've been there ever since."

Since that time, Stern has earned an Academy Award nomination for *Changeling* (2008), and has become critically acclaimed for maintaining and experimenting with the preferred Eastwood/Surtees low-light aesthetic (see Chapter Five).

THE STUNTMAN

No crew member has worked with Eastwood longer than Buddy Van Horn. Despite technically retiring after 2008's *Gran Torino*, Van Horn returned to help coordinate a few sequences for *J. Edgar* in 2011 at Eastwood's urging. He now firmly insists he is, in fact, retired for good, "unless Clint calls me again."

In the 1960s, Van Horn worked with Eastwood on a few *Rawhide* episodes before their respective film careers began, but their relationship didn't really form until Don Siegel asked him to be Eastwood's stunt double on *Coogan's Bluff* in 1968. He worked on several other films directed by Siegel, and others that starred Eastwood, before finally signing on as Eastwood's regular stunt double and coordinator for *High Plains Drifter* in 1973. After that effort, the only Eastwood-directed pictures he missed over a thirty-five-year period were *The Outlaw Josey Wales* (1976), because of a scheduling conflict, and *White Hunter, Black Heart* (1990), because the African location shoot did not include stunts.

"I probably go back further than anyone with Clint in the sense that I also worked on many of those Universal (B movies) that Clint had one or two lines on as a day player when he was starting his career, and then on *Rawhide*," says Van Horn. "But we became close when I started working with him and Don Siegel. I knew right away working on *Coogan's Bluff* that he would become a director. He was always at the camera and watching Don and everything that was going on. He's a lot like Don—no nonsense guys who don't mess around."

Van Horn even directed three Eastwood films at his boss's request—*Any Which Way You Can* (1980), *The Dead Pool* (1988), and *Pink Cadillac* (1989), though he jokes that "*Pink Cadillac* isn't exactly my favorite."

He insists he never asked Eastwood to let him direct those pictures, but happily did so when his boss made the request. The impression Eastwood gives today is that Van Horn knew him and his style and team so well that it just made more sense to have Van Horn direct than recruit an outsider when Eastwood's scheduling issues made it difficult for him to take the helm himself.

"I just tried to do it the way Clint wanted me to do it," Van Horn says. "But I wasn't looking to direct. We just went fast, and if there was a problem, Clint and I would talk it over. I stopped doing it after that third picture when I had some health problems, but came back to do stunt work and second unit whenever Clint needed me."

(Above L) Clint Eastwood on the set of *Firefox*. (Left) Cinematographer Jack Green consults with Eastwood during filming (*The Bridges of Madison County*). (Opposite) Green, then camera operator, and Eastwood on a snowy bluff in Idaho as they shoot scenes for *Pale Rider*.

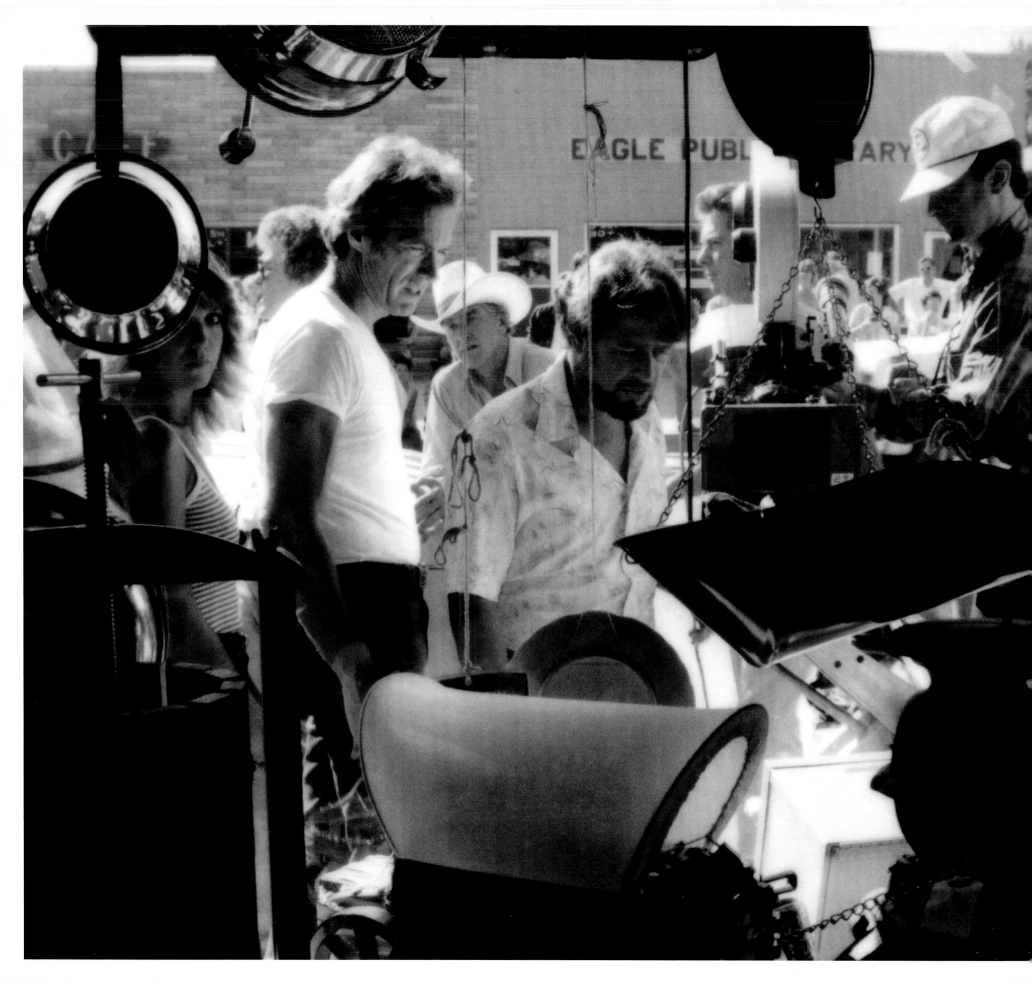

THE SOUND GUYS

Escape from Alcatraz was a watershed project for two more longtime team members—co-supervising sound editors Alan Murray and Bub Asman. In their case, however, they actively pursued spots on the crew.

"Back in those days, we were both working at Paramount on the feature film sound staff," says Murray. "Bub and I heard that Clint was bringing *Escape from Alcatraz* to Paramount for postproduction and sound mixing. Keep in mind, we graduated high school during the *Dirty Harry* years and Clint had just released *Josey Wales*. Clint was our hero. So when his cutting room moved back to the studio after shooting, Bub and I were on hand to introduce ourselves to Clint's film editor, Ferris Webster. Many lunches later, we had convinced Ferris of our ambition and he, in turn, introduced us to the film's director, Don Siegel. We auditioned for the job by doing a temp sound mix on the movie, so that Don could present it to the studio. But we didn't actually meet Clint until we were sitting in a screening room at Paramount playing back the movie with its temp mix. The lights went down, we heard someone settle in behind us, and we wondered who it was. We watched the movie, and when the lights went up, a familiar voice began to discuss the work. It was Clint, of course, and we were delighted that he had positive things to say about the sound job. He then asked us to stay on throughout the final mix."

[Opposite] Clint Eastwood consults with Jack Green (*Bronco Billy*). [Above L] Composer/music supervisor Lennie Niehaus listens to Damon Whitaker play the saxophone. Forest Whitaker's younger brother played the young Charlie Parker in *Bird*. [Above R] Also for *Bird*, Lennie Niehaus did a quick cameo as a hotel piano player.

On the next film, back at Warner Bros. for *Bronco Billy* (1980), Webster lured both men away from Paramount, and they have been working for Eastwood ever since. Asman took a hiatus in the late 1980s, but was back by 1989.

In those early years, Murray and Asman essentially were Eastwood's entire sound department in a uniquely lean operation.

"We pretty much did it all," says Asman. "For the first fifteen or so shows, we would walk Foley [physically creating and recording footsteps and other sound effects to match moving images], we would cut sound effects, dialogue, we did ADR [automated dialogue replacement], and much more. It wasn't until the shows got more complicated and expensive and the timelines got tougher that we started hiring a bigger sound crew."

Both men have been nominated for and won Academy Awards for their sound editing work for Eastwood. And yet, they talk about their good fortune in being members of the Eastwood team as if they still were those eager young men from three decades ago. Both say Eastwood's loyalty to them over the years has motivated them to the point where "we couldn't bear to miss a show," Asman insists.

"Every movie we do now is more than a movie—they are about Clint's legacy—especially the last ten years or so," adds Asman. "Most directors would be [taking it easy] at his age, but he keeps making bigger, better movies. If he needs us, we have to be there to help."

"CLINT HAS THE ABILITY TO HOLD ON
TO WHAT HE LIKES ABOUT SOMETHING, AND NEVER GET LOST."

DAVID WEBB PEOPLES
SCREENWRITER (UNFORGIVEN), *2011*

CHAPTER TWO
YOU LIKE IT OR YOU DON'T

PAUL HAGGIS WAS MINDING HIS OWN BUSINESS, BURIED DEEP INSIDE THE FRENZY OF DIRECTING AND PRODUCING THE FEATURE FILM HE HAD WRITTEN, *CRASH* (2004), WHEN CLINT EASTWOOD SUDDENLY INVADED HIS LIFE.

Haggis had been a well-respected TV writer/producer/director for years, but *Crash* was his first big studio feature film project, and he had his hands full with it at the time he received his first call from Eastwood. As fate would have it, two years later *Crash* would win the Best Picture Academy Award, but around the time Eastwood came calling, Haggis was still doing battle with *Crash*'s looming deadlines. He had previously written another screenplay—*Million Dollar Baby*—and had his agent send it to Eastwood on the odd chance that he might consider acting in it. Haggis had spent little time contemplating the potential consequences of such a request, and in fact, was far too busy with *Crash* to think much about *Million Dollar Baby* at all.

Certainly, during the rush to finish *Crash*, neither Haggis nor anyone else could have foreseen that Eastwood's arrival on the scene would cause *Million Dollar Baby* to suddenly speed through production and earn a Best Picture Academy Award a year ahead (2004) of when *Crash* would pull in the same honor, making Haggis the first person in history to write two consecutive Best Picture winners. In fact, although he liked what he had done with the *Million Dollar Baby* script (based on a short story by F. X. Toole, the pen name of real-life boxing trainer Jerry Boyd), he felt it was unorthodox and would be a tough sell to a studio. And besides, he had plenty of other things going on.

"But Clint got back to us real quick, said he loved the script and could he direct it?" Haggis recalls. "I said, 'Hold on, I'm directing it.' And then I thought about it for ten more seconds, and it dawned on me that if Clint Eastwood wanted to direct something I wrote, it would be incredibly special and I'd be honored. So, of course, I said yes."

Then Haggis went back to work on *Crash*. But a few weeks later, Eastwood called again and "he casually asked what I was doing," Haggis relates. "I was really busy with *Crash*, but it was Clint Eastwood, and if he might need me, I better be available, so I said I wasn't doing much."

[Page 66] The late, Academy Award–winning production designer Henry Bumstead's detailed production design for *Million Dollar Baby*'s fictional Hit Pit Gym. [Page 67] A de-saturated image of actor Kazunari Ninomiya in *Letters from Iwo Jima*. [Opposite] Costars Hilary Swank and Clint Eastwood film a scene on the Hit Pit Gym set [*Million Dollar Baby*]. [Above] Part of this film's extensive set dressing overseen by Bumstead.

Eastwood told Haggis he had a book he was thinking of adapting into a screenplay to direct—*Flags of Our Fathers*, about the historic battle for Iwo Jima. Eastwood said he would send Haggis the book if "his partner" agreed. That partner, of course, was Steven Spielberg, who owned rights to the book, brought it to Eastwood's attention, and who would eventually produce the film for him. While Eastwood ramped up *Million Dollar Baby*, Haggis finished *Crash*, and read the *Flags* book.

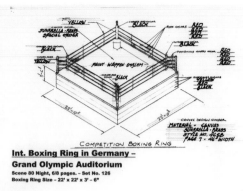

Int. Boxing Ring in Germany –
Grand Olympic Auditorium
Scene 80 Night, 6/8 pages. – Set No. 126
Boxing Ring Size – 22' x 22' x 3' – 6"

COMPETITION BOXING RING

(Above L) Morgan Freeman in his Academy Award–winning role as Eddie "Scrap-Iron" Dupris in *Million Dollar Baby*.
(Above R) A Malpaso design for one of the film's fictional boxing arenas, built at the Olympic Auditorium. (*Source: Jack Taylor*)

"I called Clint and said I loved the book, but had no idea how to make it into a movie, and he said, 'Let's go visit Steven and see what he says,'" Haggis recalls. "He picked me up in his truck and drove me to a meeting with Spielberg. I knew I would never get the job, but I figured, when else in my life will I ever get a meeting with Clint Eastwood and Steven Spielberg? I swear to God that the first half hour they just talked about meeting Fellini and Orson Welles—I was in heaven."

Enamored with the company he was keeping, Haggis agreed to take a whack at a screenplay based on *Flags of Our Fathers*. Throughout production of *Million Dollar Baby*, Haggis struggled with the assignment, but eventually got the story to where Eastwood and Spielberg wanted it, and the project suddenly sprung to life.

As is typical for Eastwood, he declared himself satisfied with Haggis's initial draft. Haggis offered a rewrite unasked, but to this day, the writer remains convinced that Eastwood didn't even read that draft.

"He shot the first draft anyway," he adds. "He also shot the original *Million Dollar Baby* script word for word."

BIRTHING *LETTERS FROM IWO JIMA*

Then, as *Flags of Our Fathers* went into production, Eastwood surprised Haggis again by sharing his idea to do a second movie about Iwo Jima, from the Japanese point of view. He again threw the task at Haggis, and once more, the writer couldn't turn Eastwood down, but he did want some help.

"I didn't understand why he asked me—it needed to be done from a Japanese perspective," Haggis says. "I told him I'd try to find someone like that. I couldn't find

a Japanese writer, but I found a Japanese-American writer, Iris Yamashita, who had an interesting idea for it."

Yamashita had exactly zero credits or industry experience, but she came to Haggis's attention after winning a screenwriting contest. She was so green that she initially presumed, when Haggis contacted her, that when he referred to "a companion film" to *Flags of Our Fathers*, he meant "some kind of extra or short film for the DVD. I didn't think he meant a theatrical film. When I realized what he was talking about, I was pinching myself."

"As soon as Paul called, I started doing tons of research on [the lead character] General Kuribayashi. I came up with this idea of telling the story not only from his point of view, but from the point of view of a Japanese private, a regular guy, who was stuck in the middle of this battle."

Haggis helped Yamashita flesh out the idea, and she quickly churned out a treatment.

"Paul told me she had a lot of ability, I met her, she seemed great, and we talked a bit about the story," Eastwood recalls. "That was about it, but then, a week later,

(Below) Early sketches of American troops in the invasion of Iwo Jima, from art director Jack Taylor—drawings for designing visual effects sequences for *Flags of Our Fathers*.

Paul calls and tells me she has a layout for the story. I had only given Iris the little book I had gotten from Japan, the book filled with letters written home by General Kuribayashi in the years before the war, so I was impressed. I read the treatment and it was terrific—that story was pretty much what the picture ended up being. I told him to have her write the script up and then we made the film. It was just luck of the draw that we came across Iris, and that she was so innovative."

(Above) Saigo (Kazunari Ninomiya) on the Japanese bunker set (*Letters from Iwo Jima*).

That story, of course, became *Letters from Iwo Jima*. Haggis and Yamashita developed it together, Yamashita wrote the screenplay, and their work was nominated for an Academy Award in 2006—two years after Haggis was nominated for an Academy Award for his adapted screenplay of *Million Dollar Baby* and one year after his success with *Crash*. Haggis and Yamashita both marvel that Eastwood didn't flinch at the notion that an inexperienced writer like her could pull it off.

"He's a guy who trusts the people he works with," Haggis explains. "He trusted me, and I trusted Iris. That was good enough for him. The same way that he loves the initial instincts of actors—he loves that in writers, as well."

Yamashita emphasizes that Eastwood's trust when it comes to the development and writing process is so all-encompassing that he almost never gives traditional notes. During the writing of *Letters from Iwo Jima*, she says Eastwood did discuss her research process and offered broad guidelines. But all the traditional input she got

during the writing process came from Haggis. And even at the script's most intense stages, the process was almost entirely removed from what Yamashita calls "the long development hell period" that typically surrounds movie scripts in the studio world.

"He doesn't want to control every aspect of the process as many directors do," she says. "He doesn't want you to go through that long development hell period where the director is micro-organizing or supervising every little aspect. In fact, on this script, Clint called me after I turned in the first draft, and said it was 'a real page turner.' I kept waiting for 'but' and 'my notes are,' but there weren't any. My agent was floored and didn't believe me that Clint had no notes."

That's not to say her script did not get input. In addition to Haggis, Ken Watanabe, the film's star, made suggestions, including two key ones that were incorporated. The first involved enhancing a flashback to when General Kuribayashi was an envoy in the United States before the war—a scene designed to illustrate his connection to the U.S. The second involved changing the way in which Kuribayashi commits suicide near the end of the film. Yamashita originally had him engaging in a traditional seppuku (ritual suicide) ceremony. But Watanabe pointed out that battle conditions would have prevented that. Other notes came from historical advisers on more mundane matters.

But Yamashita's point is that Eastwood gave her what she calls "the flexible option" to decide what to incorporate and how. "The finished movie is very close to what I originally wrote," she emphasizes.

"He doesn't give notes, but he does love research," Haggis adds. "In this case, he had read a great deal about [Iwo Jima], and that is the whole reason we had the book of letters [Kuribayashi] wrote—Clint found the book and became intrigued by it. He's voracious when it comes to reading, and he knows every detail. That's why his films are so rich by the time he starts shooting them—he knows so much about the subjects. During the writing process, he'll send me things—articles or pictures about the subject or to tell me about someone he met. So he did a lot of research and came up with ideas that ended up in those two films, but he doesn't overmanage that process."

Today, Yamashita looks back on the seamless ease of the collaboration as ironic. It was an incredible and important learning experience, obviously, and it made her a better writer, but it was also the kind of situation "that can spoil a writer."

"It taints your experience as a screenwriter, because it is probably the best experience you are ever going to have in this business," Yamashita explains. "Clint can develop movies this way—he's sort of straddling the best of the independent and the studio worlds. But he lets it all run so smoothly. With anyone else, you need to have a long and difficult development period."

71

STORY IS THE PROCESS

Scripts obviously flow into Malpaso from all directions, but there is no "development department" or development executive to manage them. There is only Eastwood and Rob Lorenz. If someone whom either of them respects suggests they read a script or book, they usually do so. If they both feel strongly about what they've read, and get positive reinforcement from informally surveying close confidantes—like Eastwood's longtime agent, Leonard Hirshan, and Eastwood's wife, Dina—then they begin a process of finding out if Malpaso can acquire or option the material.

Producer Kathleen Kennedy, who has firsthand experience bringing projects to Eastwood, suggests that, at this stage, he's strictly in disciplined-producer mode even as, creatively, he's hunting stories to bowl him over.

"Even as he is thinking about the characters, he is immediately taking into consideration what the size of the production might be," Kennedy adds. "He identifies very early on approximately how much he wants to spend. So he doesn't have a lot of patience for people who want to throw in the kitchen sink [financially]. It's therefore easy to produce with him, because his goals are so clear. He expects everyone around him to be austere in the sense of how they approach [producing] the movie."

Once Eastwood shows interest in acquiring a script, the next step in the process is for producer/production manager Tim Moore to work with Rob Lorenz and Malpaso controller Jason Gondek on a preliminary budget built around their understanding of Eastwood's spending discipline.

"We read the script, run the numbers, and then [Lorenz] usually makes a schedule for the shoot, since he was Clint's first assistant director for so many years and knows better than anyone how long it takes Clint to shoot a script," Moore explains. "We then discuss budget with Clint, and after he agrees to the number, we turn it in to the studio and promise we can make the movie for that number. As far as the business end goes, Clint knows exactly where he wants to spend and where he doesn't. He'll figure out ways to make [a project viable] by saving money in production design, shooting short days, and so on. There is no waste—budget never gets in the way of a movie he wants to do."

Thus, many Eastwood films move from acquisition to green light to production at light-speed. None of this is to say that final Eastwood movies are identical to their original scripts. It's just that the bulk of significant additions or subtractions, if any, come during the editing phase (see Chapter Eight). He normally shoots everything

(Opposite) Hilary Swank and Clint Eastwood discuss how she should hit the speed bag during filming of *Million Dollar Baby*.

as written, improvising subtle changes during production only if logistical circumstances or weather require it, or if someone presents a clearly better idea than what was originally planned.

In fact, Eastwood showed this flexibility his first time out as director, during the filming of *Play Misty for Me*. The film includes an extended sequence in which Eastwood's character, Dave Garver, and his love interest, played by Donna Mills, spend time at the Monterey Jazz Festival. The sequence was not in the script, but Eastwood added it as a device to avoid making it too easy for the audience to figure out that Mills's character's roommate was actually the villain of the piece—Evelyn (played by Jessica Walter), the woman stalking Dave.

"He's trying to repair his relationship with his girlfriend, so I had him take her to the Festival," Eastwood explains. "She has a roommate and talks about her, but I didn't want her talking about her too much because that is the whole trick of the

(Top L) Eastwood rehearses with his mentor, director Don Siegel, for Siegel's cameo in *Play Misty for Me*, Eastwood's first directorial effort (bar scene pictured below). (Top R) Eastwood discusses *The Bridges of Madison County* with one of the film's producers, Kathleen Kennedy, and (Opposite) with costar Meryl Streep, as they rehearse briefly.

script. I figured if we covered the jazz festival, we could submerge her talking about her roommate in the commotion of the music and the crowd. I just buried that dialogue in the festival, so that later, when Evelyn is revealed as the roommate, the audience wouldn't be going, 'It's the roommate—didn't I tell you?'"

In keeping with his resistance to the auteur label, Eastwood has never shown interest in being a writer-director like Haggis and many others. Rather, his interest lies in finding emotionally resonant stories he personally likes and which he feels can translate to the big screen. Whether those stories exist in polished screenplay form, a first draft, a treatment or outline, or as books or short stories is not important. Nor is the writer's pedigree. Whether the script and the writer come to him through other producers or agencies, or are people he has worked with before, are colleagues, friends, or complete strangers is also unimportant—all those scenarios have worked over the years.

Kathleen Kennedy worked with Eastwood on *The Bridges of Madison County* and *Hereafter*. She emphasizes that his search for material is "almost singularly focused on the characters—what makes them interesting, and what makes them evolve. He carries this through his entire process of deciding what to direct. He is always thinking about [what kind of] performance he can get, based on the characters."

Eastwood immediately realized, for instance, that *Play Misty for Me* offered an opportunity to create a truly terrifying villainess in Jessica Walter's character. The story came from an old friend—a Hollywood secretary named Jo Heims, now deceased. She pitched Eastwood on the idea of a carefree disc jockey suddenly stalked by a romantically unhinged fan, and showed him and his then producer, Robert Daley, the fifty-page treatment she had written. Eastwood immediately optioned the story from her. And then, being a major movie star, he got too busy to do much with it.

"I asked Jo if she would write the script, but I wasn't available anyway—I was working on *Where Eagles Dare* [1968]," Eastwood recalls. "While I was doing that picture, she called and said Universal was offering her more money for the screenplay and she was broke, and would I mind, if I wasn't doing anything with it, if she could sell it to them. I let her out of the option and she sold it to Universal."

Next, Eastwood worked on *Paint Your Wagon* (1969) and *Two Mules for Sister Sara* (1970) for Universal. "That's when I learned Universal hadn't done anything with *Misty*—it was just sitting on a shelf," he recalls.

The rest of the story is well known. Eastwood told Lew Wasserman, then chief of Universal Studios, that he would direct *Play Misty for Me* for next to nothing up front, and Wasserman agreed. Heims and Dean Riesner polished the script, and Eastwood launched his directorial career to solid reviews.

(Opposite) Eastwood organizes handheld camera coverage of the Monterey Jazz Festival in 1970 for *Play Misty for Me*. The unscripted sequence was possible thanks to an arrangement Eastwood made with the late Jimmy Lyons, the festival's founder. Eastwood says his team filmed at the event by "operating somewhat like a commando unit." (Above) Close shot of Forest Whitaker as Charlie Parker in *Bird*. Period footage of New York City seen through the windows of vehicles in the movie came from plates filmed in the 1940s by Frank Capra's crew.

Eastwood has frequently picked up books like *White Hunter, Black Heart* or scripts such as *Bird*, with themes or characters that greatly intrigue him, but which have languished around the industry for years. Even when studio chieftains and financiers have not been convinced, Eastwood's belief that such material can, indeed, resonate with film audiences has frequently been proven to be right. The classic example, of course, is *Million Dollar Baby* (2004). Haggis's script was well known in Hollywood, and was generally considered to be beautifully written but not likely to be commercial since, after all, as Haggis concedes, it was about "a girl boxer and euthanasia."

Thus, the project became one of very few that Warner Bros. pushed back on when Eastwood put it on the table.

"I had the green light at the studio at the time and I just didn't see [the movie being commercial]," recalls Alan Horn, former president and CEO at Warner Bros. "So Clint went around town to see if anyone else was interested, and then came back to us. I thought about it and finally said yes [Warner Bros. cofinanced the film with Lakeshore Entertainment]. Not only was it a movie we should have made—it made a lot of money and earned all those Academy Awards. Clint was right about it when we weren't sure—my hat is off to him."

From that point on, Eastwood has increasingly gravitated toward unorthodox or niche-type projects, and studios have steadily gone along. *Letters from Iwo Jima* (a coproduction with Paramount) was a foreign-language film that humanized Japanese fighters in that conflict, and *Gran Torino* was made with an unknown ethnic cast, many of whom had never acted before. Both were launched largely on faith that if Eastwood felt such stories could be made economically and find an audience, then no one at the studio had any reason to think otherwise.

Certain consistent concepts emerge in terms of the types of story elements that Eastwood might be attracted to, of course. He likes somber, dark tales with morally

ambiguous characters and, frequently, outcomes. Redemption stories, revenge stories, psychological dramas, and historical pieces are all grist for his mill, and almost everything he's done in recent years has been intensely character driven.

Gran Torino (2008) and *J. Edgar* (2011) typify his love of the character study. An unknown writer named Nick Schenk penned *Gran Torino*. Schenk had worked in a factory and driven a truck, but had never sold a feature film script until Eastwood snapped up *Gran Torino* after it had experienced a series of rejections. Clint loved the story so much that he fast-tracked it into his shooting schedule, immediately after *Changeling* and just ahead of *Invictus*, filming Schenk's original script in just over a month. His only substantive change involved moving the locale from Minneapolis to Detroit, where it made more financial sense to shoot.

J. Edgar, on the other hand, was penned by Dustin Lance Black, a rising Hollywood screenwriter who was coming off an Academy Award for writing Gus Van Sant's *Milk*. In 2011, *J. Edgar* was made as fast and for almost the exact same cost as *Gran Torino*, even though it featured opulent sets, extensive makeup, and an A-list star in Leonardo DiCaprio, who agreed to participate at a fraction of his normal rate, in order to have an opportunity to work with Eastwood.

Other projects flow in from longtime associates, as *Flags of Our Fathers*, and later, *Hereafter* came to him from Spielberg. *Invictus* (2009) was another such project— the book by John Carlin, on which it is based, had been optioned by Eastwood's friend, Morgan Freeman, who would go on to star in the movie.

"We found a screenwriter in Tony Peckham and he came up with a first draft in short order that I thought was good enough to shoot right away," Freeman recalls. "I was asked, 'Who do you want to direct it?' and I said, 'I can think of only two people—Clint Eastwood or Clint Eastwood.' No one else was even discussed. We sent it to Clint, he read it, and called a week later and said, 'I'm in.'"

(Above L) Morgan Freeman as Nelson Mandela, on location in South Africa (*Invictus*). (Above R) A young Hoover (Leonardo DiCaprio) testifying before Congress in *J. Edgar*. Note the shadow falling across half of DiCaprio's face— a common visual aesthetic in Eastwood films.

(Above L) Clint Eastwood and costar Frances Fisher. (Above R) Fisher, in character as Strawberry Alice, touched by the noirish light that permeates *Unforgiven*. (Below) "The William Munny Killings," *Unforgiven*'s original title. Concluding that the name "William Munny" would mean little to would-be filmgoers, Eastwood changed it. (Opposite) Eastwood as down-and-out William Munny with his kids.

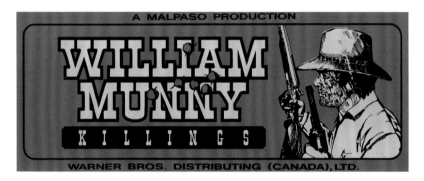

UNFORGIVEN PATH

The story of *Unforgiven*'s development is among the more unusual of these tales, even by Eastwood standards. The popular story is that Eastwood purchased the script directly from screenwriter David Webb Peoples, in the 1980s. He then tossed it into a drawer and left it there for close to a decade until he could age into the lead role of William Munny, an over-the-hill gunslinger haunted by the violent deeds of his youth.

That anecdote is true, but there is more to it than that. Eastwood not only pulled Peoples's screenplay out of mothballs years after acquiring it, he also made the movie almost exactly as Peoples had originally penned it. That decision is instructive of Eastwood's instincts—Peoples went on to be nominated for an Academy Award, one of nine nominations for the film in 1992, with four wins, including Best Picture and Eastwood's first Best Director Oscar.

"I wrote it in 1976, it languished for a while, and then Francis Ford Coppola took it over," Peoples recalls. "I did one day of rewrites with Francis, but he never could get it financed because he was having his own [financial] problems at the time. My understanding is that it arrived in Clint's office as a writing sample. He asked my

agent if the script was available, and ironically, it had just become available because Francis didn't pick up the option. Clint called and we talked briefly. The only thing he said was that it was a good script and he thought he could do a good job with it. He finally bought it outright in two payments in 1985."

Peoples remembers being disappointed to hear that same year that Eastwood was already well into production on a different Western, *Pale Rider,* presuming that, since Eastwood would never do two Westerns in a row, his movie, though bought and paid for, would never actually get made.

"Then I heard over the years that he said he was going to wait on it," Peoples adds. "But I didn't think much about it. But my wife [and fellow screenwriter], Janet, ran into Clint at the Telluride Film Festival, and she asked him straight out about it. He said 'I'm going to shoot that next.'"

Peoples had, by that point, never personally met Eastwood, and wouldn't until *Unforgiven* was almost finished.

"We spoke a few times after he started production," the writer recalls. "Much of the discussion was about the title. My original title was *The Cut Whore Killings*, which is a fine title only if you have seen the movie or read the script. Francis and I worked through I don't know how many titles and finally left it with something I never liked—*The William Munny Killings*. Clint was the one who picked *Unforgiven*. I wasn't crazy about that either, but I don't believe in being negative unless I have a better idea. After I saw the movie, and it sunk into the culture, I said to myself, 'Clint Eastwood knows what he's doing.' I now realize it's a wonderful title."

Peoples was willing, eager even, to improve it. Once production started, in addition to discussions over the title, the writer says Eastwood would "occasionally call and tell me about some casting things, and he probed a bit about what I thought about one or two points. Eventually, he asked me if I wanted to rewrite a couple of scenes. I don't remember what one of them was about, but the other one was about this idea of having the cut whore [the assault upon whom launches the story] come into the ending of the movie, and I actually thought [the addition] worked pretty well."

Peoples did that bit of tweaking and faxed the pages to Eastwood, but never heard about them again.

"When I saw him the first time he invited me to see the rough cut, I asked him whatever happened to those rewrites," Peoples continues. "He just said, 'I liked it better the way you had it at first.' That is what's so interesting about his vision for stories as an artist. Clint Eastwood has this ability to hold on to what he likes about something, and not get lost. He doesn't lose his way trying to make changes. I've learned, be careful about rewriting, you can make it worse. That's an idea that is hard for most people in the movie business. But Clint has that sense—he might

change something if he has a vision of how to make it better, but he won't ever make it worse. I admire that sense of restraint."

Eastwood calls this "trying to avoid killing it with improvements. Every time we talked about changing something [in the *Unforgiven* script], I realized and respected more and more the virtue of the script. So I eventually called [Peoples] and told him to forget all that other crap, and that I would just shoot the film the way he wrote it originally."

Eventually, Peoples came to believe Eastwood knew the essence of his story as well as or better than he did himself. He suggests this is among the director's key strengths when it comes to developing material.

"He understood the script perfectly, what every scene was about, and why it was important—even the ones I wasn't sure about," Peoples relates. "I felt there was this common way of seeing and understanding things."

More recently, in the case of *J. Edgar*, Eastwood had controversial subject matter to deal with—the issue of whether the film's subject, J. Edgar Hoover, was gay, or possibly a crossdresser. The film's screenwriter, Dustin Lance Black, revels in the fact that Eastwood left the treatment of this issue up to him, and changed virtually nothing about how Black addressed this aspect of the story as part of the larger context of Hoover's emotional arc and memories, part of a larger portrait.

"Clint treated the emotional storyline with a lot of respect and passion," Black says. "It's a cautionary tale, and he got that right away. I talked to other writers who had worked for Clint, and they all told me I was in for a treat, because he'll protect my words. He did, and that's a secure place to be as a writer."

Overall, Eastwood's movie choices are largely born out of an initial, visceral conviction that they will work if handled correctly. What movie he'll do next, what form it will take, and who will write it for him all largely flow out of early impressions.

He's fond of explaining this by saying, "Either you like it, or you don't." But when pressed, Eastwood adds, "The main thing is to recognize when you have great writing on your hands and appreciate it. There are a lot of bad movies in the world that really weren't bad ideas, but somebody wrecked them along the way. I try to avoid doing that."

"HE UNDERSTOOD THE SCRIPT PERFECTLY, WHAT EVERY SCENE WAS ABOUT, AND WHY IT WAS IMPORTANT—EVEN THE ONES I WASN'T SURE ABOUT," PEOPLES RELATES. "I FELT THERE WAS THIS COMMON WAY OF SEEING AND UNDERSTANDING THINGS."

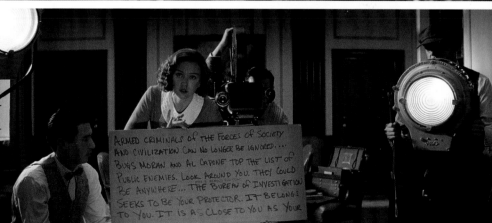

Under production designer Henry Bumstead's supervision, two significant sets in the history of Malpaso productions were designed and built: the Black Emerald Bar (Page 82), erected in Boston during the filming of *Mystic River* (shown lit up at night for an important exterior sequence), and Big Whiskey (Page 83). Here the construction crew is building the town on ranch land just outside of Longview, Alberta, Canada. They're working at near-record pace to have it ready to go in time for the *Unforgiven* shoot.

(Opposite) Jack Green's Oscar-nominated cinematography brought Alberta's wild prairie land and big skies to life throughout *Unforgiven*. (Top) Eastwood with Shane Meier as his character's son, Will Munny Jr., in *Unforgiven*—a later scene between the two was cut from the film's ending. (Above) Historically accurate film camera and motion picture lights are used as props for the *J. Edgar* scene in which Helen Gandy (Naomi Watts) holds cue cards and helps J. Edgar Hoover film an old-style newsreel public service announcement for the FBI.

"CLINT WAS SQUINTING AND STROKING HIS ADAM'S APPLE AND SAID,
'YOU KNOW, THIS IS A GOOD PLACE FOR A TOWN.'"

DAVID VALDES
CLINT EASTWOOD'S FORMER PRODUCER, 2011

CHAPTER THREE
THE RIGHT PLACES

AS HE STOPPED TO GAS UP HIS RENTAL CAR IN EARLY 2005, KOKAYI AMPAH, CLINT EASTWOOD'S LOCATION MANAGER AT THE TIME, REFLECTED ON THE FRUSTRATION OF HIS TRIP TO HAWAII SO FAR.

Ampah, Eastwood, producer Rob Lorenz, and visual effects supervisor Michael Owens had been scouting across four Hawaiian islands by car, boat, and helicopter in search of exactly the right beach location on which to film key battle scenes for Eastwood's upcoming *Flags of Our Fathers*. Specifically, they needed a beach covered with black volcanic sand, like the sand on the Pacific island of Iwo Jima, where the famous World War II battle documented in the film takes place. The production also needed a beach large and sturdy enough to stage extended battle sequences with practical effects, explosions, and the movement of authentic military vehicles.

"Iwo Jima was desolate, and had been bombarded extensively, so a lot of foliage was missing," Ampah recalls today. "The Hawaiian beaches were full of foliage, and they were not particularly wide or deep enough for what we wanted to do. Some also had nesting sea turtles on them. You obviously aren't allowed to bring tanks and equipment to such places and start setting off explosives."

In other words, "nothing we saw had the scale," Lorenz remembers. And so Eastwood and Lorenz departed Hawaii, leaving Ampah to ponder options. That's precisely what he was doing when he pulled in for gas.

"I was with the local film commissioner, telling him what I was looking for in terms of black sand beaches, and the gas station owner happened to be walking by, and he said, 'Oh, you mean like Iceland.'"

Ampah says the anonymous gas station owner "deserves a big medal" for the suggestion. When he got back to his hotel, he immediately began doing research.

"I started calling different agencies in Iceland," Ampah adds. "Then, a few weeks after I got back to Los Angeles, there was a Location Expo [trade show] going on. I brought pictures of the beach at Iwo Jima and checked around. Guys from [Iceland's film commission] were there, and they said it would be no problem. They came over to our offices on Monday and made a presentation on their beaches."

"That led myself, Rob Lorenz, and [art director] Jack Taylor to make a trip to Iceland, where we toured the beaches and found exactly what we needed [at a place called Sandvik, on the western coast, less than an hour from the capital, Reykjavik, and near the NATO base at Keflavik, which supplied soldiers as extras when production got underway, in August of 2005]. Pictures came back to Clint and [production designer] Henry Bumstead, and we were on our way. In Iceland, I explained we would be moving tanks and ordinance onto the beach, removing sand, and building a sand berm where the soldiers hitting the beach would duck for cover. I explained we would then put the beach back together again. What I learned was that the beaches are privately owned, but regulated environmentally by the government there, and that [their regulations] were something we could comply with."

(Opposite) Unit photographer captures scene underway as English Bob's carriage enters Big Whiskey (*Unforgiven*). (Above) A long-lens view of Eastwood and Meryl Streep on location in Iowa (*The Bridges of Madison County*).

tried to put into his dramatic interpretation of the events depicted in *Letters*. "The Japanese are sensitive about Iwo Jima, since a lot of people are buried there, still unaccounted for," Eastwood explains. "They asked me what I wanted to do, and I said, 'We would pretty much have to reinvade the island.' They weren't about to let us do that, but they told us we could go there and shoot a few establishing shots that would evoke the feelings the Japanese have about the island and that spiritual feeling about all the people lost there. And then we'd have to go elsewhere to shoot the rest of it, so that's what we did."

(Above L) Clint Eastwood in trenches dug on the beach in Iceland, with dozens of extras, to direct action on *Flags of Our Fathers*. (Above R) Practical effects simulate explosions while extras race around the beach during filming of the chaos of war for *Flags*. Some extras carried props with small digital cameras hidden inside, to capture additional POVs featured in the film. (Below R) Replica of a Japanese map showing the positions of opposing armies created by the Malpaso art department for General Kuribiyashi's headquarters in *Letters from Iwo Jima*.

(Opposite, L–R) Ryan Phillippe, Adam Beach, and Jesse Bradford played the three protagonists in *Flags of Our Fathers* in a stateside scene under Clint Eastwood's direction.

SITE PROCESS

The struggle to find or create authentic locales for the two Iwo Jima films typifies the importance of Eastwood's location process. Often, the selection is obvious and straightforward. *Invictus* was a South African story, so it was shot in South Africa. *Heartbreak Ridge* takes place at a military base, so filmmakers secured permission to shoot at the Camp Pendleton Marine base. *Space Cowboys* is about astronauts, and Eastwood was allowed to shoot at the Kennedy Space Center in Florida and the Johnson Space Center in Houston. *White Hunter, Black Heart* was filmed in Zimbabwe, because the movie's subject is an obsessive filmmaker in the heart of Africa. *The Eiger Sanction* was shot in 1974 on the 13,000-foot Swiss mountain of the same name—Mount Eiger—at Eastwood's insistence, simply because that is where the original novel takes place, and Eastwood felt the spectacular mountain-climbing cinematography he could acquire there would help a narrative that was, by his standards, weaker than usual.

When Eastwood decided to follow *Flags* immediately with *Letters from Iwo Jima*, that film was largely shot in caves in Barstow, California, and on a stage at Warner Bros., but it begged for footage from Iwo Jima itself. Extensive shooting on the island was simply out of the question from the start, given the reverence placed on the site by the Japanese. Therefore, the matter came down to whether Eastwood would have any opportunity to capture establishing and reference footage on Iwo Jima.

In that particular case, his personal involvement and status as, frankly, Clint Eastwood, were directly required.

Lorenz says Malpaso turned to Bill Ireton, president of Warner Entertainment Japan, for guidance through what Lorenz calls "the cultural idiosyncrasies of Japan." Ireton advised Eastwood to formally meet with the governor of Tokyo, since Iwo Jima is officially considered part of Tokyo, to discuss it. He also confided that the governor, Shintaro Ishihara, had been a novelist, playwright, and filmmaker before moving into politics.

"It was a formal meeting, attended by gobs of press," Lorenz recalls. "They exchanged gifts and, through the interpreter, Clint chatted with the governor about his background and interests, and won him over as Clint often does."

Eventually, Ishihara allowed filmmakers to briefly visit and scout Iwo Jima, and then permitted a twenty-four-hour, restricted filming visit to the island a year later, after they had filmed the rest of *Letters*. That visit would be enough to allow Eastwood to capture iconic imagery—sixty shots that magnify the authentic feeling he

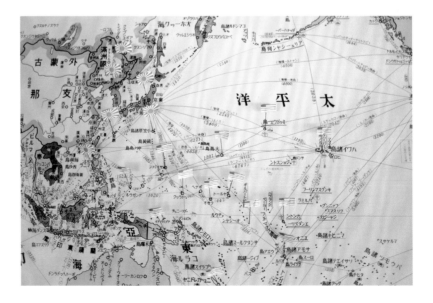

However, when story points don't direct choices, Eastwood typically relies on location managers, producers, production designers, and his camera team to do early and technical scouting work and bring him options. Therefore, current location manager Patrick Mignano and his assistants fan out to find potential settings, and then Rob Lorenz boils down the alternatives and presents them to Eastwood, who may or may not visit the location shortly before filming starts.

Many such locations are simple and modest—Malpaso routinely rents homes, apartments, and offices for films, for instance. Still, such places can be particularly important to a movie's narrative, like the two adjacent homes featured prominently in *Gran Torino*. Mignano found the two houses on a small suburban street in the city of Highland Park, adjacent to Detroit. They serve in the movie as the home of Eastwood's character, Walt Kowalski, and his neighbors, a family of Hmong immigrants. The theme of immigrants moving into a formerly white neighborhood filled with conservative old-timers like Kowalski sits at the core of the movie's dynamic. The script mandated that Mignano find a neighborhood that served this premise.

"I drove all over the city for weeks looking for those houses," Mignano says. "The requirements were two houses close to each other in a working-class neighborhood, with a garage set back behind the house where Walt lived [to keep the titular Gran Torino—his prized possession], but the garage had to be visible from the street."

The houses accommodated Eastwood's agenda for realism, mostly by being small, modest, and intimate. Their cramped nature, from a filmmaking point of view, was a plus as far as Eastwood was concerned.

"For the scene where Clint's character is sitting in the bathtub, I remember that was an extremely small bathroom," recalls production designer James Murakami. "We couldn't even fit five people in there (to film the sequence). I suggested to Clint that we could make a new, bigger bathroom off the bedroom next door by taking out a wall, but he said no, let's shoot it this way. So they ended up having to climb some scaffolding to stick the camera through the bathroom window to shoot the scene. It was harder to shoot, but Clint loves small, narrow places."

Major work was done on both houses—upgrades, as it turned out, from the owners' point of view. Under the watchful eye of longtime Eastwood construction supervisor Mike Muscarella, furniture was moved out, carpets were pulled up, walls were repainted, and doors and windows were changed. The production upgraded or restored plumbing and electrical systems in both houses, and re-sided one, as well.

"I'd like to think that, although you always hear about movie companies destroying things, Malpaso left things better than how we found them," Muscarella says of the two *Gran Torino* houses.

Eastwood says his reliance on Lorenz, as with Valdes before him, typically to handle scouting chores and bring him enough information to make final decisions, is "a system that works pretty well." But early in his tenure at Malpaso, Valdes found this approach perplexing, and it took him a while to understand it.

"The director is the only guy with the [full] vision for the movie, and we're all on that scout to help him fulfill that vision," Valdes explains. "The sole purpose of a key location scout is for the director to visit the locations with his department heads so that everyone can best prepare for that specific day of shooting in advance. Put simply, the director disseminates invaluable information [during the scout] to his key players. If he doesn't attend the scout, then we don't know what the shots will be until the day of shooting. And then we [can lose] precious time on that expensive shooting day by moving trucks that might be in the shot, not having enough background actors, not having prerigged lighting, et cetera. It was crazy for me [in that regard] in the beginning at Malpaso."

Valdes chuckles today that Eastwood's willingness to delegate leadership of location scouts to him "made me the target of countless jokes by trying to surmise what Clint might want to do at each location. Even to this day, thirty years later, I have never heard of another director who doesn't go to location scouts with his department heads."

However, many years later, Valdes now views the situation differently, and feels Eastwood taught him a valuable lesson.

"I grew to understand and eventually appreciate his unique methodology," Valdes explains. "I now believe that scouting a location in advance gives Clint a certain preparation that he doesn't want or need. Clint is like the characters he plays—a man of few words. He isn't the kind of director that tells you why he's opted to go with a twenty-one-millimeter lens on a Panaflex [camera] that is mounted to an apple box on a twelve-foot ladder to capture the master shot. He just instinctively knows that it's the best angle. And I think he hasn't given too much [advance] thought on how he's going to shoot the scene anyway. That's because he trusts his gut on the day, implicitly. And his gut is unbelievable in always making the best choice. I feel like I watched and learned from a Jedi Master who had not only learned to master the technical side of filmmaking, but who had also learned to surrender to his intuitions.

"What I think he loves most is walking onto a set for the first time with the pressure of a hundred cast and crew looking to him for answers," he adds. "I think he basks in that pressure and the pressure of never having seen the location in advance. And because he believes in himself so intuitively, he knows that his first impressions are the best impressions. Those first impressions are what he wants to paint on his cinematic canvas. He'll improvise and riff and let his senses be assaulted by the new environment, the light, the weather, the terrain, new cast members, and so on, knowing he will capture something fresh and unique that all the preplanning, prescouting, and prethinking would have killed weeks before if he had attended the traditional key location scout like I wanted him to do."

Today, on scouts, Rob Lorenz is the one in the position of assessing Eastwood's location needs. Lorenz says Eastwood "has worked with everybody who goes on location scouts for so long, and has such a shorthand with them, that many of us can go somewhere and quickly assess what will or won't work for him. So, typically, I conduct all the scouts, flying to different countries and cities with appropriate [team members], assessing them, and bringing Clint back the information. From that point on, usually, it's pretty straightforward."

However, Lorenz also points out that Eastwood loves to take advantage of opportunities when they present themselves. "When we were in Paris to do promotions for *Gran Torino*, for instance, we had a free day, so we got into a car and drove around looking at some locations we were considering for *Hereafter*."

From there, Eastwood and Lorenz flew directly to South Africa to begin filming *Invictus*, and then stopped in London on their way back to Los Angeles for more *Hereafter* scout work. But the person typically scouring the globe is Lorenz. He recalls one particularly busy jaunt in 2008, on which he accompanied Eastwood to the Cannes Film Festival to debut *Changeling*, then headed to South Africa to scout *Invictus* locations, and then went to Michigan for final work on *Gran Torino*.

"It gets a little crazy sometimes," Lorenz chuckles. "While doing one project, we're always circling others, so I rack up the frequent-flier miles."

That craziness extends into the lives of Eastwood's location managers, as well. This is largely because the problems for a location manager posed by Eastwood's working method are diametrically opposite of the problems most directors pose. Rather than needing to juggle the schedule around to stay at locations longer than planned, Eastwood's location managers frequently find themselves juggling the schedule to move out of one site and into another quicker than originally anticipated.

"The biggest thing I had to get used to was preparing for Clint to get ahead, since he works so fast," Kokayi Ampah recalls. "Whenever you prepare a location, you need to also prepare for the possibility you might need to come there a day earlier than planned. If you are not ready for that possibility, it can throw you off.

"Rob Lorenz, when he was the assistant director—he and I learned the lesson early on. We would constantly go over the schedule and guess where Clint might get ahead. That way, we could have my department and the art department prepared to have something ready for him to shoot if we got finished earlier than scheduled. We always knew what locations could be made available early and which ones couldn't, and we always had a plan to put something else in place."

Still, as with other aspects of his work, Eastwood's primary consideration is whether a site or a stage will serve his story's emotional arc. Backdrops like the plains of Alberta (*Unforgiven*), the scenic coastline of northern California (*Play*

Misty for Me), working-class neighborhoods in Boston (*Mystic River*) and Detroit (*Gran Torino*), New York City in the 1940s (*Bird*), and Washington, D.C. (*J. Edgar*) were all essential elements in the success of the movies. How to acquire or create those backdrops, however, entirely depends on a project's particulars.

Another factor is that Eastwood has shot four decades worth of movies on all sorts of subjects all over the world, and as part of his search for authenticity, he tries hard to make each location look unique, which isn't always easy. When feasible, Eastwood tries to find totally new places, of course. Exceptions happen for perfectly logical reasons—almost everyone shoots vintage railway scenes at the historic Sierra Railway in Oakdale, California, for instance. On *Changeling*, the production needed a California-based site to film sequences relating to the infamous Wineville Chicken Coop Murders of 1928—a true event in which young boys were murdered in a remote region of Riverside County, outside of Los Angeles. Eastwood's team sought the site of the actual murders by researching historical archives in Riverside. Eventually, they found a house with an intact chicken coop that may have been the actual site, or merely one of the same era, according to Rob Lorenz.

In any case, "that site was not suitable cinematically," according to Mignano. Instead, filmmakers recalled a remote stretch of road in Lancaster, California, where they had previously filmed a stateside (Texas) sequence for *Flags of Our Fathers*.

"The location worked great as Texas for *Flags*, but a couple years later, when we were doing *Changeling*, everyone kept saying the chicken coop area had to be similar to that place we shot in Lancaster," Lorenz recalls. "Finally, we all just agreed— why not just go back there and shoot again, from different angles? And so it became the murder site used in *Changeling*."

(Opposite) Eastwood collaborates with camera operator Stephen Campanelli (L) and cinematographer Tom Stern on a *Gran Torino* scene. (Above L) He consults with Stern and (Above R) with visual effects' supervisor Michael Owens (C) and second unit director Richard Bowen on location in Iceland during production of *Flags of Our Fathers*.

BIG WHISKEY AND BEYOND

For major location decisions, Eastwood strives to avoid terrain seen in his previous films. The director certainly had this concern while trying to figure out where to build the town of Big Whiskey—the fulcrum of the story in *Unforgiven*. Eastwood was determined not to have the film's backdrops resemble the other iconic Westerns he had done as both an actor and director.

"I did think about that—that was one reason I picked Alberta," Eastwood says. "John Ford always used to go back to Monument Valley [Utah], and some of his films have the Monument Valley look. I have a different philosophy. I didn't want [*Unforgiven*] to look like any other Western I had done. I like them all to have a unique look of their own, when possible. We shot *High Plains Drifter* at Mono Lake [California], and *Josey Wales* was shot in Utah, Arizona, and California—there are a variety of looks in that film. But I thought Alberta would be something different for this movie. I always felt that part of the Rocky Mountains was interesting country."

(Below) Running a roughed-up English Bob (Richard Harris) out of town in *Unforgiven*. (Bottom L) Clint Eastwood as William Munny rides out of Big Whiskey at the film's conclusion. The sequence was shot in the freezing cold on location in Alberta at the end of a marathon day necessitated by the looming threat of a massive snowstorm—a storm that began minutes after this scene was filmed. (Bottom R) Eastwood consults with Harris (L) and Saul Rubinek (also on *Unforgiven*).

So filmmakers took the Warner jet to Calgary and were met by Alberta's then film commissioner Bill Marsden and location manager Murray Ord, who immediately guided them to the premier of Alberta's personal helicopter, so they could mount an aerial tour. Eastwood, Valdes, and production designer Henry Bumstead searched for hours over picturesque Alberta, with Eastwood taking the copilot seat for an extended period. Eventually, they found what they were looking for on land that was part of the private Bar U Ranch, just outside of Longview, Alberta.

"Bumstead and I were right over it, and we both looked at each other and said that looked like the place at the same time," Eastwood recounts. "We landed the helicopter and went down there, followed the roads around, and tried to lay the whole thing out."

"Clint was squinting and stroking his Adam's apple and said, 'You know, this is a good place for a town,'" Valdes recalls. "Bummy said it was gorgeous and pointed out there was not a bad angle anywhere in the place. I couldn't help but wonder where the hell we were, and if we could ever find this location again from the ground. We proceeded to gather rocks to make a small mound, so that our location manager could find it the next day. This was before GPS, and our location manager took three days before he found our mound of rocks."

In a 2006 interview shortly before his death, Bumstead said that he and Eastwood started planning the layout of Big Whiskey as soon as the helicopter touched down.

"We decided which way to run the main street," Bumstead said. "I was lucky to build two Western streets for him from scratch—the first was *High Plains Drifter* [1973]. I always run a Western street east and west, so that we have light in the morning down the street and backlight in the afternoon. That's real production design—when you start with bare ground."

How the essence of a location like that matches the nature of a story is quite important to Eastwood. For instance, he declined studio suggestions that he could shoot *Mystic River* more cheaply in eastern Canada, because the original novel by Dennis Lehane was set in Boston, and he felt strongly that Boston's working-class neighborhoods should be prominent. Then, once committed to Boston, the production searched high and low for a dive bar to shoot in, as detailed in the script. The bar, however, had to be along the water.

"Eventually, [Bumstead] told us we would never find the right bar and we'd have to build one," Lorenz recalls. "We were driving around looking for a spot, but Bummy said we should look from the water. So the police gave us a boat tour, and eventually, we found a place to build the bar with a beautiful background of the city."

The City of Boston helped them secure the spot—an empty industrial lot on Border Street in East Boston—and Bumstead's team built the entire bar, dubbed the Black Emerald, from the ground up.

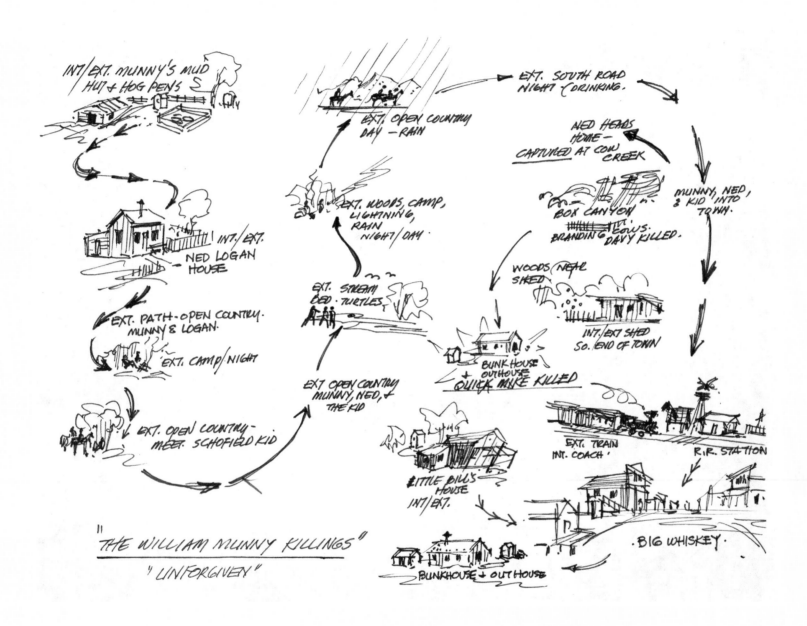

INT/EXT. MUNNY'S MUD HUT & HOG PENS

INT./EXT. NED LOGAN HOUSE

EXT. PATH-OPEN COUNTRY. MUNNY & LOGAN.

EXT. CAMP/NIGHT

EXT. OPEN COUNTRY- MEET. SCHOFIELD KID

EXT. OPEN COUNTRY DAY - RAIN

EXT. WOODS, CAMP, LIGHTNING, RAIN NIGHT/DAY.

EXT. STREAM DED. TURTLES.

EXT OPEN COUNTRY MUNNY, NED, & THE KID

EXT. SOUTH ROAD NIGHT (DRINKING.

NED HEADS HOME - CAPTURED AT COW CREEK

MUNNY, NED, & KID INTO TOWN.

BOX CANYON BRANDING LOGS. DAVY KILLED.

WOODS NEAR SHED

INT./EXT SHED SO. END OF TOWN

BUNK HOUSE + OUTHOUSE QUICK MIKE KILLED

LITTLE BILL'S HOUSE INT/EXT.

EXT. TRAIN INT. COACH

R.R. STATION

BIG WHISKEY.

BUNKHOUSE + OUTHOUSE

"THE WILLIAM MUNNY KILLINGS"

"UNFORGIVEN"

This hand-drawn ink on paper sketch (8½ x 11 inches) by production designer Henry Bumstead depicts the trail of characters related to the film's William Munny killings (*Unforgiven*). The drawing is from the collections of the Margaret Herrick Library (Academy of Motion Picture Arts and Sciences).

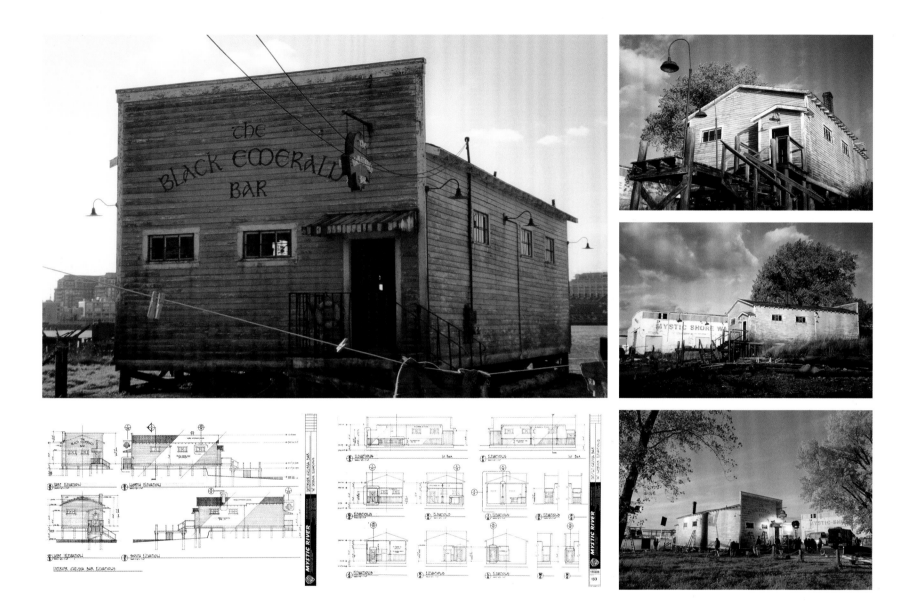

(Opposite) Academy Award–winning production designer Henry Bumstead (*The Sting, To Kill a Mockingbird, Vertigo*)—who was also the designer of the town featured in *High Plains Drifter*—returns to work on *Unforgiven*. Here (L–R), first assistant director Scott Maitland, Clint Eastwood, cinematographer Jack Green, and Bumstead examine his drawings for Big Whiskey, as Malpaso launches into building the fictional town on prairie land in Alberta, Canada. From this film onward, until his death, Bumstead collaborated exclusively with Eastwood, except for one outside film and one Malpaso film not directed by Clint.

(Above, Top L) Exterior front view of the Black Emerald Bar, built from scratch for *Mystic River* under Henry Bumstead's supervision, on an empty waterside industrial lot the production procured from the city of Boston. (Right three photos) Exterior rear and side views of the bar, which—as the art department's original schematics (Bottom L) illustrate—was designed to be entirely functional inside and out. Malpaso received offers to purchase the bar after shooting finished, but since it was not built to code, it had to be torn down. The bar's sign and other pieces have periodically shown up in online auctions over the years.

(Page 96) *J. Edgar* involved a massive practical set created by production designer James Murakami. Here, a view from high above Stage 16 on the Warner Bros. lot in early 2011 showing the full length of it, built to imitate the Department of Justice building's interior, including J. Edgar Hoover's office, a lobby, a crime lab, and a long corridor built to scale. This set is where much of *J. Edgar* was filmed—probably as ambitious a stage shoot as Eastwood has ever conducted.

THE BIRD SOLUTION

Despite his affinity for shooting on location, however, Eastwood routinely builds environments when situations require it, and he is equally comfortable on a sound-stage as he is on location. In fact, he shoots extensively on stages, and is famous for dressing local spots in and around the greater Los Angeles area to represent other geographic regions entirely. Production designer James Murakami says that, these days, Eastwood splits most movies up about fifty-fifty location/stage. He points out that while building opulent sets can get quite expensive, they normally allow filmmakers to control conditions more completely.

Thus, Eastwood's choices for where to shoot, where to be authentic, where to approximate or replicate a location—on a stage or in a computer—are intensely flexible. Rob Lorenz says Malpaso has a "rule of thumb" that it will try to shoot at a practical location any time the company can capture scenes in three days or less. In the case of *J. Edgar*, so much of the movie took place in the Justice Department and offices of the FBI, where it was impractical to bring a movie crew anyway, that it made more financial and logistical sense for Murakami to build sets on stages at Warner Bros. The rest of the movie was shot in and around Los Angeles, with a one-week trip to Washington, D.C., to film exteriors.

Bird had the slimmest of budgets (less than $15 million), and therefore it simply wasn't practical for the production to travel to Kansas City or New York for extensive shooting, although much of the story takes place in those cities. Thus, filmmakers had no choice but to creatively reproduce them on stages at the Warner Bros. back lot, and at select locations around Los Angeles.

David Valdes emphasizes that "Clint is always cognizant of what something is going to cost, and if there is a way to save money by not going somewhere, he wants to do it. On *Bird*, in particular, we got really clever. Clint decided he would use all those old tricks that people don't use much anymore."

Much of that film was shot on New York Street on the Warner lot, and did indeed benefit from many of those "old tricks." In particular, then production designer Edward Carfagno reached back to early in his career and came up with an offbeat suggestion to solve one of the most basic problems facing the production—filmmakers needed to create environmental footage to be seen through car windows.

"We needed [scenic shots while driving] of 1940s New York backgrounds, and this was before we could cheat it digitally," Valdes explains. "Ed Carfagno was about eighty years old at the time, and he went all the way back to the old studio system. He recalled a day in New York in the 1940s when Frank Capra had just finished a movie but was still under contract to the studio. He said that Samuel Goldwyn ordered Capra's crew to shoot moving process plates of the New York streets where all the

(Top) A period image from the 1930s from *J. Edgar*—an image that liberally mixes real-world elements such as the vintage automobile plates (Bottom L) and close building facades from the Warner Bros. back lot with digital elements, such as the background images, signage, lights, and more. (Bottom R) Franklin Roosevelt's inauguration parade—an entirely digital creation. Seen here from J. Edgar Hoover's office window.

great jazz places of the era were, along with Broadway and Times Square. Ed told us he had 'a feeling' that Capra had captured the kind of stuff we needed. We knew that could save us a bundle, because we could use [those plates] to do the driving shots on stage with a rear-screen projection process. But first we had to find the plates."

Carfagno's feeling was soon validated when Valdes and editor Joel Cox tracked the Capra plates to MGM Studios. A sympathetic person there—"a huge Clint Eastwood fan," according to Valdes—dug them out, and Malpaso was able to restore them. That became the imagery that flashes past period car windows in the movie, using the aforementioned, old-school rear-projection technique.

"Clint was quite pleased—the plates had the name 'Capra' on the head of the clapper," Valdes relates. Cox adds that the production was "very fortunate to find that footage. They had everything we needed—left, center, and right plates, so we could shoot across the car and have the street come out correctly behind it. In the old days, all studios shot processed plates of various things and hung on to them, but by this time, most of the studios were getting rid of that stuff because of storage costs."

KODAK SAFETY FILM 5075

"IS THE WHOLE SPIRIT, CUMULATIVELY, AND THE EFFECT OF IT ON AN AUDIENCE,
GOING TO BE IMPROVED BY BEING PRECIOUS ABOUT GETTING MORE TAKES? . . . OR DO WE TRUST
THE DIRECTOR'S VIBE? IF WE ARE GOING WITH HIS JAZZ, AND IT BECOMES CATCHING LIGHTNING IN A BOTTLE
ON TAKE ONE, THEN I KNOW I BETTER BE READY ON TAKE ONE."

SEAN PENN, 2011

CHAPTER FOUR
WATERING THE FLOWER

CLINT EASTWOOD'S CRANE RISES DRAMATICALLY INTO THE SKY, AWAY FROM THE SCENE, DESPERATELY TRYING TO ESCAPE IT. EVEN AS IT MOVES AWAY, THE CAMERA LAYS BARE SEAN PENN'S TRANSFORMATION INTO A DEVASTATED JIMMY MARKUM—A RAGING VOLCANO OF TEARS AND VIOLENCE WHO NEEDS DOZENS OF POLICE OFFICERS TO PREVENT HIM FROM HURTING SOMEONE, BOTH IN THIS SCENE FROM *MYSTIC RIVER* AND IN ACTUALITY.

Penn remembers that, as painful as it was to play the emotionally draining scene, his comfort level in being able to do what he had to do, when his character learns to his horror that his daughter has been murdered, was high. Penn knew where he "would have to go" to channel the excruciating rage, pain, and disbelief the script called for, and just as importantly, Clint Eastwood knew, so he carved out a path for Penn to make that journey.

The scene, which lies at the heart of Penn's Academy Award–winning performance, was shot in an abandoned bear den in the overgrown and abandoned Long Crouch Woods portion of the old Franklin Park Zoo in Boston. According to producer Rob Lorenz, Eastwood knew he wanted the crane shot early on, but the rest of how things played out pretty much "evolved" from where the script had it. The basic blocking called for Penn, consumed with grief, to try to race to his daughter's body, while a couple of police officers hold him back.

"I said to Clint, 'You know, this is going to get physical,'" Penn recalls. "I am not saying I would take down [the actors playing] the two cops, but somebody could get hurt. I asked him, 'How are we going to pull that off?' Because I couldn't go to the place I had to go emotionally without that happening, from what I was reading in the script. This is often the case in film, where the demand for physical reality cannot be held to a principle of 'stage fighting.'

"Clint just told me, 'Don't worry about it.'"

What Penn means is that Eastwood fully understood that he was anticipating a complete surrender to his emotional and physical state, in order to adequately channel his character's grief, and was promising Penn he would create conditions to allow him to do that without anyone getting hurt. Eastwood simply added

numerous extras as police officers, and instructed them to do whatever was necessary to restrain Penn.

"I told the [extras], hold him down, just hold the guy down—it's your responsibility," Eastwood relates. "I told them to hang on to him. He was kicking and screaming and really going. I shot a few extra angles, just to protect it all, and we did it very fast. I knew [the scene] would take Sean's vocal cords right out, so I wanted to make sure we got everything, and it worked great."

[Opposite] Sean Penn, in character as Jimmy Markum, lets loose with rage after learning of his daughter's death. Penn was concerned he might inadvertently harm someone as he summoned the rage, but Clint Eastwood arranged with the extras playing officers to ensure that wouldn't happen. [Below] Markum with his wife, played by Laura Linney (*Mystic River*).

(Above L) Sean Penn and Kevin Bacon while filming *Mystic River*—they are among the many high-profile actors who actively sought opportunities to work with Clint Eastwood. (Above R) Armie Hammer (L) and Leonardo DiCaprio film a crucial confrontation in *J. Edgar*. DiCaprio says Eastwood "pushed" emotion out of him in the scene, and credits Eastwood's experience as an actor for his success in guiding other actors to critical acclaim.

Penn adds that Eastwood's plan worked, because "there was not a part of my body that was not locked up by an additional cop. I was able to cut loose, and no one was going to get hurt. So, in other words, I was free to go for it. That was simple, clear thinking on his part. Another director might [worry] about the time to choreograph the thing and make it look real. Clint just said he had it covered—no problem."

Some actors refer to this as "creating conditions" that permit unencumbered performances to blossom. Gene Hackman, who has been on as many sets as anybody, including two films and one Academy Award (for *Unforgiven*) with Eastwood, calls this "the creative atmosphere" that, ironically, allows Eastwood to move swiftly and efficiently as ever, while "making you feel like it is all about your character. He gives us time to explore the character and try things. That is not always totally true literally, because you don't always have all the time in the world. But you feel like it is true—you have the sense that it is true. And that is why working for Clint, as an actor, is a godsend."

That is not to say that Eastwood is beyond pushing emotion out of his actors— he's just subtle about it. Leonardo DiCaprio recalls how Eastwood motivated him to go further in one of the most emotional scenes in *J. Edgar*. It was the scene in which his character, J. Edgar Hoover, gets into a fistfight with his companion, Clyde Tolson (Armie Hammer)—a mishmash of fists and fury that concludes with Tolson aggressively kissing the conflicted Hoover.

Shortly after the shoot wrapped in mid-2011, DiCaprio called the scene another example of Eastwood "creating a magical moment—just being in a room with actors and watching what's going on, and from his own experience as an actor, having great instincts about knowing when to suggest something and when not to."

"In particular, I remember at the moment [after the kiss, when Tolson storms out of the room], Clint was leaning against the wall," DiCaprio added. "He said, 'Tell him you love him.' It sort of took me by surprise, because there is nobody there at that point—I'm talking to a door. So it took me a second to respond to it. Most of the movie, I had done so much preparation, and knew exactly what I was going to do for each scene, but not for this line. So Clint repeated it again with more intensity—'Go on, tell him you love him.'

"It was hard for me, and really wrenching for my character to say that. I didn't want to say it—Hoover was a guy who did not express that kind of love. And so the line came out of me almost like a balloon seeping a little bit of air, like something he didn't really want to release. And doing it that way creates a great moment— Hoover saying something to Tolson after he is gone that he would never say to his face. Clint knew it would be hard for me, and that is why he pushed me to do it."

More frequently, Eastwood's guidance is even simpler, designed merely to point the actor in the right direction, rather than forcing him this way or that. For Forest

(Above) Clint Eastwood takes a quiet moment in the Black Emerald bar set that Malpaso built for *Mystic River*. (Opposite) Eastwood discusses a scene from the film with Tim Robbins (C) and child actor Caden Boyd.

Whitaker, who electrified when Eastwood cast him as Charlie Parker in *Bird*, it was just four words that changed the direction of one particular scene.

"I remember distinctly we were shooting the scene in which I walk into the auditorium and the [Buster Franklin] character, played by Keith David, was playing on stage," Whitaker relates. "It was a time when rock music was coming in and I was feeling lost as Charlie Parker. Clint told me, 'Hold your head up,' as I walked

into the auditorium. By doing that simple gesture, it changed the face of the scene, because it made me, as the character, try to maintain myself with a sense of dignity, even as I was losing my identity about my place [in the music world].

"You have to understand, there are synergetic things that occur between a director and an actor, when the director can see something about to emerge in the actor. Clint knows that by delaying something or slowing something down, it can bring that performance. It's very unpredictable, but he's expert at it."

CREATE THE ENVIRONMENT

Eastwood's strategy for luring consistently top-line performances has been described frequently as "simple," "straightforward," "few takes," "no rehearsal," "spontaneous," and all the rest. There is truth to all those descriptions, but if one wraps them into one idea, "trust" emerges. Trust on Eastwood's part in the actors to present their character in whichever way their hard work tells them will work best; trust on the actors' part when Eastwood suggests they try things, without making them feel like there is any sort of edict falling on them; and trust that the crew and support team will work at such a high and focused level that Eastwood and his actors need not, in the midst of the performance, think about imperfections, lighting, logistics, or any superfluous details.

(Opposite) *Bird* star Forest Whitaker shares a moment with director Eastwood, whom Whitaker credits for showing faith in his ability to handle the role. (Above) *Bird* costars. (Right) Eastwood watches as music chief Lennie Niehaus has Damon Whitaker demonstrate his saxophone technique. Damon, brother of star Forest, played the young Charlie Parker.

Eastwood's script supervisor, Mable McCrary, calls this way of working "rich," and says "it's all about respect." McCrary calls the script "the seed" and says, "The actors then make it a flower—they color in everything," with Eastwood and his crew, naturally, providing the water that makes it all grow.

Eastwood's actors agree. Forest Whitaker suggests Eastwood will let them try just about anything, as long as the attempt comes from devotion to the role. In *Bird*'s climactic sequences, for example, Charlie Parker comes to the home of a friend, faints, is examined by a doctor, looks back on his life, and eventually dies. For those scenes, Whitaker tried everything in his power to make himself look and feel like he was, in fact, on the brink of death.

"I decided not to sleep for days before those scenes," Whitaker relates. "I solicited a friend to help me keep awake all weekend. When we shot it, I went in there and lied down on the couch, and actually fell asleep. Clint started filming me sleeping, and then [an actor playing the doctor] came over. I remember looking up at him and saying, 'Who are you?' I talked to him for a bit before I realized they were filming and I was like, 'Sorry, Clint.' He said, 'No, that's perfect, let's go back to where [he woke up] and do it again.' He liked that and helped move me through the scene. He creates that atmosphere and likes to see what you do with it."

While creating the kind of free-range atmosphere on set, to permit actors to experiment in the ways that Whitaker did during production, however, Eastwood largely stays out of their preparation—beyond preliminary guidelines and offering practical help—unless asked. Hilary Swank, for instance, had to put herself through a remarkable transformation to become the boxer Maggie Fitzgerald for *Million Dollar Baby*. She remembers that, when Eastwood offered her the part, his only specific advice was, "You better start training."

"And I did, the next day," Swank recalls. "He talked about getting out of my way and letting me do it, but in his own way, he does gently guide and direct you. You don't really know he is doing it until you see the film and his fingerprints are there in how you created the character. After I started training, I called and told him I was learning to box and training two and a half hours a day, but that I was dropping

weight and needed to put some back on. He immediately connected me with his trainer, Grant Roberts, and I started working out with him two hours a day on top of boxing training. If you have trouble, he helps you, but he lets you do all your own prep."

Actors routinely talk this way about Eastwood's philosophy and method for empowering them to find, develop, and execute the characters themselves. Eastwood freely admits that, as a longtime actor, this is, in fact, his goal—to free actors and rid their process of some of the "rambling" and "talking" that can encumber things.

"I'm looking for the environment that I liked when I saw someone do it right, and I try to avoid what I didn't like when I saw someone do it wrong," Eastwood says. "A lot of times, I would see directors talking a lot, rambling on endlessly, and I asked myself, 'Why does this guy talk so damn much?' I began to realize he is talking himself into working through it—he is either insecure or he is trying to get somebody to second the motion in terms of what he believes should be done, or he is just talking to himself enough until he starts to believe it. But I found the guys I used to work with, the old-timers, they knew exactly what they wanted and they depended on you [the actor] to do it. You are the actor, which is what you are paid for—you are hired, you come in, you do the job, you give the performance. If actors present something that is wrong, you say to them, 'Let's calm down and try something else. Or play the guy with a little more zip, or be a bit more studious.' That's one thing, but why would I want to start talking to them and jumble up their focus and their whole nervous system, and not give them a chance to [find it] themselves? I want them to be spontaneous more than anything."

(Above) Clint Eastwood and Hilary Swank during the *Million Dollar Baby* shoot.

STAY OUT OF THE WAY

Eastwood is famous for conducting few formal rehearsals on set. When they do happen, he will frequently film them and use that material, doing so sometimes without even pursuing any additional takes beyond the rehearsal footage. Rob Lorenz says this approach is about "keeping the momentum going, keeping things spontaneous, natural, and alive" on set. For some actors, this method can take time to adapt to, but it's better than going in the direction of what Eastwood often calls "analysis paralysis."

"Overanalyzing or overpreparing slows down the whole process, and everyone then loses focus," Lorenz explains. "When things are moving quickly, you have to stay alert, your adrenaline is flowing, and you stay in the moment. We have found over the years that this works for cast and crew. The actors are constantly energized by what we are doing, and wanting to stay on top of their game."

This is not to say that Eastwood's cast members do not rehearse together—they just rarely spend much time doing it on set on shooting days, or with Eastwood present. Instead, they prepare on their own, any way they want, with the understanding that they will be ready to go by the time they show up on set.

A quintessential example of this came during filming of *Mystic River*. On that project, Penn and his colleagues got together and held stealth rehearsals in their hotel whenever possible.

(Above L) A quiet moment between Swank and Eastwood in the shadows of the Henry Bumstead–designed Hit Pit Gym, where (Above R) the costars also worked out. Swank says Eastwood strongly influenced her, and she considers him a father figure. (Opposite) Eastwood choreographs the final boxing match in *Million Dollar Baby* with Swank (L), and actress Lucia Rijker playing her opponent.

"I organized that," Penn says. "I went to Clint and said to him, 'Would it be all right with you?' Unlike most directors who might be threatened by that stuff, he was very encouraging. So what we did was, every Friday throughout shooting of the movie, we would get whatever available cast was still in town together. We would wrap [shooting] on Friday, and before we all went into the weekend, we would meet in a conference room at the hotel and do a full page-one read-through, including scenes that had already been shot, just to reconnect the dots.

"I invited Clint, if he felt like coming. But he is the boss, and doesn't have to be present for every board meeting. So he allowed us to do that, and it was productive. It's not about there being no direction going on—it's about a bunch of professionals really knowing their stuff and saying, 'If I make a move over here at this time, will it get in the way of your [move]?' It was a way for us to get rid of a lot of bumps that don't need to be there [on shooting day]—things that are discussed by actors on a set, anyway. We got that clutter out of the way so that when we came in, it was almost like, if you look at all the cast as a single performer, we were doing our homework as a single performer would in his hotel room before coming in the next day. That way, we didn't have to bother the director with questions that we could easily answer ourselves."

BETTER BE READY

There have been, of course, instances where actors struggled to adapt to the Eastwood way, at first. Eastwood's well-documented dustup with Kevin Costner on location in Texas during the filming of *A Perfect World* has been interpreted as relating to this issue, although those who were there insist the argument had to do with Costner's desire to give direction to crew and extras, and not about Eastwood's pace. In any case, today Eastwood says, rather diplomatically, that "the argument was no big deal," and that Costner "just had a slower windup than some other actors. He preferred to crescendo into it. But we got along fine, and he did a good job."

Veteran performers like Gene Hackman and Morgan Freeman say they ideally prefer Eastwood's pace.

"I come ready anyway," Freeman states. "Most movie parts are cut and dry. A stage play that is two or three acts, you are used to four weeks of intense rehearsal, but that is primarily to learn what you are doing [on the stage], since you need to do the entire performance at once. With a movie, you do a page at a time. You read the script and prepare yourself and go do it. That is how Clint likes things, and me too. In fact, I don't remember us ever sitting down for a full script reading on *Unforgiven*."

"All you ask for as an actor is to let you do your work," adds Hackman. "You hired me because you thought I could do the job, so just let me go out and do it. I didn't

think much about how Clint works the first time I worked with him. I just knew I had to be ready to go, and that's how I want to do it anyway. I think it's a mistake for young actors to be watching and analyzing their performance constantly. I never watched video of my performance [on set]. That doesn't make me special or

(Opposite) Eastwood explains to camera operator Campanelli (L) and cinematographer Stern how he wants to film an exterior shot (*Mystic River*). (Top) Clint Eastwood and star Kevin Costner on location in Texas for *A Perfect World*. (Bottom L) Naomi Watts as a younger Helen Gandy in service of J. Edgar Hoover during a scene in their darkened offices in *J. Edgar*. (Bottom R) Morgan Freeman in a replica of Nelson Mandela's study during a quiet moment in *Invictus*.

anything—it just means I have a clock in me that taps me on the shoulder and tells me if I'm doing too much or too little. If you go and watch your performance, you are then copying yourself or somebody else—a shadow on the screen that might look and sound something like you, but is not doing what you want to do. For me, that would not feel right."

Meryl Streep, however, has been known to ask for repeated takes on some projects. Yet she insists that working Eastwood's way was, in fact, the right approach to lure out the Academy Award–nominated performance that she gave in *The Bridges of Madison County*.

"It was right up my alley, to be honest," she says. "I really like that way of working. I didn't have a word for it at the time, but then Clint told me, 'I like to keep momentum. Momentum is everything.' And he was right—the movement of the film, the gestalt of it, depends on moment to moment. In the case of *The Bridges of Madison County*, he shot the film more or less in the order of the story on a tight schedule, so it made sense to maintain that sense of momentum. I've been on lots of films where there is a lot of fat, but Clint doesn't tolerate fat. If you go slower, it's hard to gather all the pieces back together when they have all oozed off into a big break or a post-lunch slog. That doesn't happen on his sets."

Streep cautions that this "does not mean that Clint is undiscerning. There were, in fact, a couple times where he made me do ten or twelve takes until he got what he wanted. But that was highly unusual."

Ken Watanabe came to Eastwood for *Letters from Iwo Jima* after years working in Japanese cinema and, before that, as a live-stage actor. Therefore, Eastwood's method also resonated with him, even if the level of efficiency was surprising at first.

"I didn't mind it at all," Watanabe says. "Stage acting has months of rehearsal, but the performance itself is just one time with a total focus on your character, so you have to be ready. But I do remember a scene where my character [General Kuribayashi] gives a long speech in a cave to his soldiers. It required me to go down some steps, make part of the speech, turn, do more speech, and say 'Banzai' three times, and then go up the steps. It was pretty complicated, but that was all done in a single take—no rehearsal at all, except on my own. But when Tom Stern had the camera and the light set up—we were ready to go. We did it once and that was it."

Veteran actors, in particular, seem to relate to the distinction that Eastwood makes between giving their own individual "best" performance for any given take or sequence and making sure the entire take, comprehensively, is the best it can be, including but not limited to their own performance. Thus, as Sean Penn explains, Eastwood's "first take" impulse is a well-reasoned, deeply thought out strategy that is about far more than merely "working fast."

"Clint will do as many takes as you want, but you [arrive on set] knowing that he is ready to go, and knowing everyone will bring their 'A' game on the day," Penn explains. "So if he is shooting something with, say, two or three actors in the shot, and he is doing a lot of stuff with Steadicam, well, yes, you can get another take if you want one and possibly improve your performance. But are you going to improve the body of that original recording all the way around? Is the whole spirit, cumulatively, and the effect of it on an audience, going to be improved by being precious about getting more takes? And if not, and if you think the [other actor] is better than I am in take one, even though I'm usually stronger in take ninety-three—is the scene going to be stronger? Or do we trust the director's vibe?"

[Below L] *The Bridges of Madison County* could easily be categorized as Eastwood's most romantic film, as illustrated here with costar Meryl Streep. [Below R] An emotionally charged close-up of Meryl Streep as Francesca. [Opposite] Clint Eastwood directs Ken Watanabe in the tunnel headquarters set built on a stage at Warner Bros. (*Letters from Iwo Jima*).

"IT WAS RIGHT UP MY ALLEY, TO BE HONEST. I REALLY LIKE THAT WAY OF WORKING. I DIDN'T HAVE A WORD FOR IT AT THE TIME, BUT THEN CLINT TOLD ME, 'I LIKE TO KEEP MOMENTUM' . . . AND HE WAS RIGHT—THE MOVEMENT OF THE FILM . . . DEPENDS ON MOMENT TO MOMENT."

—MERYL STREEP

(Opposite) Clint Eastwood organizes a New York City street scene on the Warner Bros. back lot (*Bird*). (Top) Morgan Freeman (L) and Matt Damon before the big match (*Invictus*). (Bottom) Damon as South African rugby star François Pienaar in *Invictus*. The partial crowd behind the actors would be digitally filled in later in postproduction.

Matt Damon, with two movies working for Eastwood under his belt, underscores that this notion of momentum is not merely about the actor's performance. It is about the set's full energy—actors and crew combined. His point is that "no one gets a better ten hours out of a crew than Clint."

"I've been on sets where it is just soul-destroying, how much time is wasted," Damon says. "Where you are just sitting there all day, doing the same scene over and over because the director is not decisive enough, so he wants enough stuff to make all those decisions later [in editing]. There is this whole group of directors who shoot and shoot and make all decisions later. It's true you can discover things in the editing room that surprise you, and I don't mind shooting a lot in that sense. But shooting from angles you know you could never possibly use to sustain a scene doesn't make much sense. Clint knows the difference in that regard."

Indeed, Damon recalls a time during the shooting of *Invictus* in which Eastwood was filming rugby sequences and, in a few minutes of incredible efficiency made possible by the talent of camera operator Stephen Campanelli, managed to shoot a series of brief cutaway shots simultaneously that, traditionally, would eat up hours or days.

"They wanted to do a shot of me, and got the rugby players lined up and the crowd screaming," Damon recalls. "After a few seconds [filming Damon], Campi takes off running with his Steadicam, while the crowd keeps cheering. Clint takes off running, following him with his little handheld monitor. Campi manages to line up one of the [extras playing a Nelson Mandela bodyguard] scanning the crowd and shoots him for about eight seconds. Then he takes off running again, and does several more. I watched them shoot eight cutaways in one two-minute take. If they put that on a call sheet, another director would schedule a day and a half for all that. As he walked past me, I said, 'Clint, you just shot eight cutaways.' And he said 'Yah.' He got all that energy in the first take. Clint knows there is no reason to shoot two minutes of me just standing there, so they used the time more efficiently."

CAST IT WELL

Of course, Eastwood's consistent success with actors wouldn't be possible without an equally vibrant casting methodology. He is fond of saying "casting is half the battle," and that the most important thing on a movie is to "cast it well." Those statements are heartfelt—Eastwood's ability to lure the right actors is the foundation that makes his directing style work.

For the most part, Eastwood has a two-track approach to the casting process. For high-profile lead roles, he usually considers people he is familiar with, or whose performances he has enjoyed in other films, and then, frequently, he will approach them himself. For other principal or minor roles, he relies on his casting director to bring him videotapes of performers, and makes choices based on those tapes. He prefers videotape to live auditions, largely he says because he "never enjoyed the audition process" early in his acting career. By sparing actors the stress of being evaluated in person, he feels he can see more natural examples of their work on tape.

Eastwood has worked with some of Hollywood's top casting directors, including in recent years Ellen Chenoweth and Fiona Weir. But his casting partner for much of his career was the late Phyllis Huffman, a close friend who died of cancer in 2006.

Huffman was involved as a casting executive and eventually casting director on twenty feature films that Eastwood acted in, directed, or both. Eastwood credits her with finding many of the iconic faces that populate his films, such as the critically acclaimed choice of Diane Venora to play Chan Parker in *Bird*. In a 2004 interview with the *Los Angeles Times*, Huffman spoke about Eastwood being typically decisive as soon as he saw Venora's tape.

"I sent [Venora's] tape back to him, and he took one look at her and said, 'That's it,'" Huffman said. "That was the end of that. He is not a shopper. He knows what he likes when he sees it."

(Above) Clint Eastwood with actress Laura Linney on the *Absolute Power* set. (Page 116) An American soldier navigates through the night fog on Iwo Jima during *Flags of Our Fathers*. (Page 117) High above the Library of Congress at night, as Leonardo DiCaprio and Naomi Watts (in the distance) enter to film a 1920s-era scene for *J. Edgar*.

Sadly, Huffman died the same time Eastwood lost another longtime friend and collaborator, production designer Henry Bumstead. He says today, "I went through a lot of life with her. Her [first] husband was murdered and a lot of stuff was going on for her. We went through a lot of it together. I miss her a lot. When she passed away, we got the best casting people who were available. They set an atmosphere, get people they think are ripe, and submit their tapes, and then it's our job to make the right choices."

Rob Lorenz adds that, except for major actors whom Eastwood already has his eye on or a relationship with, he generally shies away from getting to know prospective cast members until he's hired them.

"If you meet and talk with too many people, you get influenced by the fact that you have something in common, or friends, or other things," Lorenz explains. "Clint had to go through auditions and face rejection, and he doesn't want to do that—to get to know them and then have to reject them. So he generally doesn't meet them in person [during casting]. He feels that by looking at the tape, he can keep it objective and fair. The actors are reading the same scene, so he can compare apples to apples and select from that. Some people make decisions about somebody for the wrong reasons. Clint eliminates that from his process, and that is a big reason his films are so well cast."

But that said, for star roles, if Eastwood has someone in mind, he will doggedly pursue them. Gene Hackman recalls having a casual relationship with Eastwood for years because they would periodically cross paths. He also recalls, like many across Hollywood, having read an early version of the *Unforgiven* script when it was still called *The William Munny Killings* and was owned by Francis Ford Coppola.

By the time Eastwood acquired it, Hackman says he had "just about forgotten about it, but then Clint called. He didn't go into great detail about it. But he asked me to read it again and I did, and then I agreed to do it on the phone. I remember we talked a bit about what my character [Little Bill Daggett] would be like, and we agreed it would be somewhat similar to the police chief in Los Angeles at the time [Daryl Gates]."

Meryl Streep, meanwhile, had virtually no interest in *The Bridges of Madison County*, until Eastwood personally turned her around. Eastwood consistently fought for Streep to be considered for the role, despite studio pressure to find a younger, foreign actress to play Francesca, a transplanted Italian war bride.

Eastwood insisted that Streep was the age of the actual character in the story, forty-five, and close enough to his age at the time to make their romance believable. He eventually got his way, but even then, he had to sell Streep on the idea.

"We first spoke on the phone when Clint wanted to send the script," Streep recalls. "I had already sent word through my agent that I was not interested because I had begun to read the [original] book, and decided it was not anything I was interested in. But Clint got my phone number and called me at home. He said I should read the script written by Richard LaGravanese, because he had a different take on it and was using the book only as a jumping-off point. So I said 'OK, you can send it,' and he said, 'It's already at your front door.'"

(Above L) Costars Ed Harris and Clint Eastwood in a scene from *Absolute Power*. (Above R) Final movie art poster created for Eastwood by his longtime collaborator Bill Gold.

Eastwood first tried to lure Sean Penn into acting in *Blood Work*. Penn looked at that script and "decided on the surface that it was not something I would jump into at that time. But we agreed to meet, and I flew up to Carmel and met him for dinner. We had a very good meeting, although it was my decision at that time not to make that movie. I hoped that [decision] would not be alienating, and that he would still be open to considering me for things. Sure enough, on *Mystic River*, he sent me the script, and on this one, it connected. I called him and said I'd kill to do it."

Forest Whitaker, by contrast, had never performed a lead role in a major feature film when *Bird* came along, so Eastwood received his audition on tape, with dozens of others. He liked what he saw and called Whitaker in for a chat.

"We talked mostly about jazz and music, and I never did read for him," Whitaker recalls. "We just talked a bit about the character, and I also remember I asked him if my brother might be able to play the younger Charlie Parker [which Damon Whitaker did do]. And then I left. I called my agent and told him I thought I had the part, but to please find out for sure."

But, of course, Eastwood isn't only casting stars—he's casting entire pictures. Lorenz says Eastwood "is keen in using clever little techniques" when it comes to selecting actors for smaller roles. "He wants people the audience can distinguish from other people," Lorenz explains. "He won't hire two detectives with short, dark hair and mustaches because he knows that can confuse people. By the same token, if an actor has a really good, distinctive look the audience might remember, but is not right for the role he read for, Clint will still try to find a way to use that person. He will often gather a group of people he thinks are good actors that he really likes, and then sometimes will move them around and fit them into roles so they contrast with each other. But he wants them to counter each other, especially in scenes with two people in a room. It's uninteresting if they both approach it the same way, so he makes sure they each have a different style to bring a certain chemistry to it. If he has someone with a quiet, deliberate delivery, he will look to balance that with someone who is more animated."

[Above] Eastwood confers with actors Forest Whitaker and Diane Venora on the set of *Bird*.

"TURN ON A LIGHT.

IF IT DOESN'T LOOK GOOD, TURN IT OFF OR MOVE IT AROUND."

BRUCE SURTEES,
EASTWOOD'S ORIGINAL CINEMATOGRAPHER, 2011

CHAPTER FIVE
THE DARKNESS

LOOKING BACK ON IT, JACK GREEN FEELS THE RIBBING HE GOT FROM BRUCE SURTEES THE FIRST TIME THEY WORKED TOGETHER WAS JUSTIFIABLE. AT THE TIME, WHILE SHOOTING *FIREFOX* IN 1982, GREEN WOULD PERIODICALLY CHOOSE A CAMERA ANGLE THAT WOULD HIGHLIGHT THE ACTORS' BRIGHTLY LIT SIDE.

That led Surtees to start calling Green "the moth" because moths are attracted to light. Green had operated camera on earlier Eastwood pictures, but *Firefox* marked the first time he operated camera on a film shot by Surtees. Since Surtees did not choose his own camera operator, they had no preexisting bond.

By then, Surtees had already traveled far down the road of bold, edgy, dark, noirish lighting choices, and was being called "Prince of Darkness" by Eastwood and others. He wasn't the first cinematographer to earn that nickname, of course. The legendary Gordon Willis was called that by fellow legend Conrad Hall (a mentor of current Eastwood cinematographer Tom Stern) for years, and others have received the moniker, as well. But certainly the name perfectly matched Surtees's lighting philosophy.

Surtees told Green that there were worse things in life than photographing the part of the face of an individual in a motion picture where the light was not falling.

"He kept telling me, 'Jack, you are like the moth. You always want to go to the moth side, where the light is, while I [Surtees] want to go to the dark side,'" Green recalls. "'Don't make me relight here. Moths are always attracted to the light, but I'm not.'

"And he was right. Later in my career, I could get upset at camera operators for making me flip lights around too much. But a good camera angle is still a good camera angle, and that takes precedence. Sometimes, you flip the light around, but much of the time, just let the shadow go there. Bruce taught me that."

And it wasn't only Green who got the lesson. Numerous Eastwood team members say they were profoundly influenced by the fearless way that Surtees would light movies, and certainly it's safe to say Eastwood was also. "The moth side" evolved into a term they all use to this day, decades after Surtees first uttered the phrase, and many of the people who use the term never, in fact, worked with Surtees.

(Opposite) Eastwood offers direction for a scene (*Firefox*). (Below) A vintage Model T is used in filming a *J. Edgar* exterior scene. Such vehicles were procured for the production from various collectors on the East Coast. Behind the vehicle, first assistant director David Bernstein stands next to producer Rob Lorenz (C), among others.

But for Eastwood, the concept happened to square perfectly with his own impulses anyway. Long before he began directing movies, and even before the period that he acted for and collaborated with his mentor, director Don Siegel, who originally hired Surtees, Eastwood was already well attracted to low light, shadows, noirish looks, and most importantly, deep, rich black colors. He was already a fan of Kurosawa's methods of contrasting light and dark with minimal light sources, and was raving by then about noirish lighting styles in movies like the 1949 Carol Reed film *The Third Man*.

(Opposite) Meryl Streep waits in the shadows during a scene from *The Bridges of Madison County*. (Above) Eastwood explains a shot to actress Sydney Penny during the making of *Pale Rider*. He has a particular affinity for directing child actors and has done so frequently over his career.

And that's why Surtees refused to concede that his aesthetic preferences provided any sort of direct influence on Eastwood, even if others believe it to be the case.

"Back then, Clint knew what he wanted, and he still does," Surtees said. "I didn't influence him. He was always very visual. He has a feeling for these sorts of things. If Clint Eastwood mainly only shoots in back light or cross light, it's because it's more dramatic to do it that way. He doesn't shoot much front light at all. He just knows what looks good. This kind of lighting isn't reflective of reality necessarily, but it does look good, and I'm sure that's why he does it."

But Eastwood himself says the aesthetic, and Surtees's way of executing it, "certainly made sense to me." And it still does. He's used the style for decades, with no sign of easing the visual attraction to low light and shadows. In fact, 2011's *J. Edgar* was probably one of Eastwood's most deliberately noirish-lit feature films ever—a feat spearheaded by Tom Stern, who served for years as Surtees's chief lighting technician.

"I guess, somewhere along the line, the idea of not putting the 'moth side'—the side where the light is—on the outer side of the [frame] came to be the way we did it," Eastwood explains. "One side has flat light and the other side has depth to it, so you put the light side away from the camera and the shadow side toward it. Bruce was fearless about doing it, and he was doing it in a day when film stock wasn't as fast as it is today. Film stocks are much better today, you can do wonders with them to make darks darker, and then you can do even more in postproduction in the computer. But the film needs the right speed when you shoot it, so that you can better darken certain parts of the screen and make the blacks blacker. Bruce just lit that way and wasn't afraid of it."

DEEP, RICH BLACKS

That this look should sustain itself and evolve so successfully from one Eastwood cinematographer to the next shouldn't be surprising, considering that they all worked together when Surtees was the cinematographer, Green the camera operator, and Stern the gaffer. In fact, Stern says Surtees was "an incredibly brave artist who influenced me a great deal." He refers to the aesthetic with a formal term— chiaroscuro, which is an Italian word coming out of the hand-drawn art world that means "light-dark," as in highlighting the contrast between light and dark.

"Bruce imbued that in me [when Stern joined Malpaso as gaffer on *Honkytonk Man*]," Stern says. "I always have it in mind when I'm doing a Clint movie. I've been playing with it for thirty years, so it isn't surprising I know how to do it pretty well. Like when a guy is totally in the dark, and comes out into the light, or maybe you just catch one eye [in light]. It's the kind of stuff that would classically get you fired at any major studio because some people consider it bad lighting. Their view was, when you don't fully see the guy's face, you aren't seeing the star, and they felt that was bad. But Clint is more of an Everyman, with healthy self-esteem, and he doesn't think his audience are idiots. He wants them to expect they will use their imaginations to become engaged. If you are halfway through the movie, you don't need to see his entire face. You already know who he is. He might start talking and then emerge from the shadow into the light. It's a perfectly natural thing. We've been doing it for years, and I expect we always will."

Indeed, Stern's own gaffer, Ross Dunkerley, says there is, in fact, an intentional goal within the Eastwood camp to shoot virtually every frame this way, when feasible.

(Above L) Eastwood, alongside actor Richard Dysart, considers options for filming a scene from the climax of *Pale Rider*. (Above R) Dysart during a vintage train scene, filmed at the historic Sierra Railway in Oakdale, California, near Sonora—the same location used later for train scenes in *Unforgiven*.

(Above L) Eastwood directing Forest Whitaker on *Bird*. (Above R) The film's final poster art, designed by longtime Eastwood collaborator Bill Gold, based on a test image captured by Jack Green.

"Every sequence we shoot, as much as we can, we try to stay off the moth side," Dunkerley says. "If the light is hitting the actor from camera right, then we want the camera to be slightly to the left, to photograph more of the dark side of the face than the light side of the face. Clint, Tom, myself, and [camera operator Stephen Campanelli] try to do that for everything. Granted, it's not perfect. Depending on how light falls for a [wide] master shot, there might be a portion of the shot that falls on the moth side, but if you watch Clint's films, at least eighty percent of the time, if not more, we are staying off the moth side—and on the shadow side. You might say this is 'quintessential Clint' from a visual point of view."

Dunkerley points to the scene in *Mystic River* when Sean Penn's character, Jimmy Markum, kills Tim Robbins's character, Dave Boyle, on a riverbank at night, as a typical example.

"We had zero fill [light usually used opposite a key, or main, light to lower contrast] for that sequence," Dunkerley says. "Everything you see on the screen is either light or black, no in-between. That's what we love—where you can show a visual contrast to match the dramatic contrast of the scene."

There are, of course, dozens of other examples from over the years. The Eastwood film that perhaps extends the low-light aesthetic further than any other work he's done is 1988's *Bird*, shot by Jack Green. The story's nature, about the dark and troubled psychological battles of jazz legend Charlie Parker, combined with the

era—mainly the 1940s—and the fact that numerous scenes take place at night in poorly lit jazz clubs, all led Eastwood eagerly down the path of darkness as never before. Some critics at the time, in fact, felt the movie was under-lit, although Eastwood suggests that if they felt that way, "they probably hadn't been to many jazz clubs."

By contrast, Eastwood and Green grew up going to such clubs in the Bay Area. Because of this, Green says, *Bird* was the only film he shot for Eastwood in which the director called him in before production to have an extended discussion about the nature and design of the film's visuals.

"That was the only film style discussion we ever had," Green relates. "Before and after that, Clint always let the film style come out of the story within his normal desires and way of working. But on *Bird*, he had an opinion and called me into his office and discussed how we both grew up going to the same jazz nightclubs. He wanted an edgy look like those clubs. So I offered to shoot a test. We had Forest Whitaker [the film's star, playing Charlie Parker] come in with a saxophone, Tom Stern [then Green's gaffer] came in, and I was my own assistant and camera operator. I asked Tom to give me only an edge [side of the face] light on Forest, and a little piece of a white card to [bounce light] into the saxophone."

That test, according to Green, became the template for the eventual one-sheet marketing poster for *Bird*, showing Whitaker playing a glinting saxophone in near darkness.

"In the screening room the next day, as we were looking at it, Clint elbowed me and said, 'You got it, bingo,'" Green recalls proudly.

So the style of *Bird's* visuals was built based upon this foundation, and then honed with loving reference to old black-and-white photographs out of vintage bebop and jazz magazines.

"That's exactly how those clubs were lit in those days," Green adds. "That's what we wanted. As a matter of fact, I tried to talk Clint into just shooting it black-and-white. He wouldn't do that, but [during the photo-chemical color-timing laboratory process in postproduction], we tried to put blacks even more into the shadows. They call that ENR [excess noise ratio, a process that saturates film images and makes blacks richer]—it gave us a 'contrasty' look that [was reminiscent] of a black-and-white look."

(Opposite) Sean Penn, as Jimmy Markum, kills the man he erroneously thinks murdered his daughter (*Mystic River*). The scene was shot with a single light to intentionally promote murky shadows over detail.

Eastwood confirms the pursuit of a black-and-white aesthetic.

"I wanted to shoot like it was black-and-white," Eastwood states. "It was shot on color film, but with a black-and-white feeling. Those old black-and-white pictures had such wonderful looks. You think of *The Third Man*, which [director] Carol Reed did with Orson Welles—that's wonderful. I thought, give me that in color. A film with bold lighting like some of the old black-and-white films had. Sometimes, when you shoot in color, you don't get the drama. *Bird* came before we could desaturate the movie as much as we can today with digital tools, but we could print it desaturated [in the lab]. Most of the work, though, was done in the lighting setup."

On that film, Eastwood, Green, and Stern were essentially boldly waving the flag that Surtees had planted at Malpaso years earlier. And, not coincidentally, it's a style that was born in the black-and-white era.

"I come out of the days of black-and-white," Surtees said. "In those days, they were pioneers—real photographers. My dad [cinematographer Robert Surtees] worked with some of the great cameramen in that period. They used smaller lighting units, and they spotted light around. They had no color on the film, so they had to be better at lighting than they are today. Today, they have fluorescent lights and light banks and things—it has changed. But in the days before color, the lighting was better, and we were trained at the studio as assistant cameramen with lots of the top guys, so I learned how to light. I was an assistant to [legendary cinematographer] James Wong Howe, and I picked up what he was doing. Some of it is a lost art. Some people call it 'hard lighting' but it isn't really. You have big shadows, so you have to diffuse light so one light doesn't pop into another.

"I took all that to the Eastwood films, and Clint understood it. He had worked on black-and-white projects and had watched everybody work. He understands—it's not a big secret, although people act as if it is. Turn on a light. If it doesn't look good, turn it off or move it around."

Eastwood movies are filled with prototypical examples of how low light levels and shadows playing across the faces of lead characters can look natural and real, while having a telling impact on the drama of the moment. This ambiance can be seen boldly in the parlay scene between Eastwood's character, Josey Wales, and the Indian chief Ten Bears, when they have their climactic meeting in *The Outlaw Josey Wales*. Throughout virtually the entire encounter, Josey Wales's face is overtaken by shadows from the brim of his hat as they meet under a fading afternoon sun. Ten Bears, whose face is covered in blue war paint, is likewise framed in a dusky manner in close-ups. No thought of giving either character

(Opposite) Actor Adam Beach in a stateside scene from *Flags of Our Fathers*. The color scheme was different for such scenes, compared to the film's battle sequences.

125

front light was undertaken, according to Surtees, who shot the film. "Heck, both of them are in backlight—figure that one out," he said with a chuckle.

Even more evocative of how this aesthetic is used to heighten dramatic story points are the sequences that take place inside Greeley's Saloon in *Unforgiven*, particularly during the film's climactic gunfight. Jack Green says he decided early on that he should light the saloon entirely with kerosene lamps, as befits the era. Green recalled Surtees telling him years earlier that, in order to prepare for scenes in candlelight for *The Beguiled*, the Don Siegel film starring Eastwood, he placed himself into rooms lit only by candlelight.

"For the general look of Greeley's, we knew the light would be practical kerosene lamps, because that's all they had back then," Green explains. "In preparation, I asked [production designer] Henry Bumstead to get the biggest kerosene lamps he could find, and he found beautiful, huge lamps with six-inch-diameter wicks. We had five of them, so that was five lights with a six-inch-diameter burning flame. When we were getting ready to shoot in Greeley's, Tom Stern [Green's gaffer] and I went in there and sat down for awhile at night with nothing but those lamps

burning. We'd spend about thirty minutes in there adapting our eyes to the dark, and then discuss a lighting scheme that wouldn't get in the way of that. We also had people sit in there with cowboy hats on, so we would understand how shadows would work in that light. We realized the lamplight alone would not be enough for our film lenses to pick up details, so Tom and I came up with the idea of a lighting setup that was largely just the kerosene lamps with a few very specific, small accent lights in particular places—accent lights that pretty much matched the lamplight, but just slightly brighter. They were enough to give us the small amount of light we needed to light the angle that [Eastwood's character] would be firing his gun from [as his gun barrel first announces his presence by entering the frame to start the shoot-out]."

At the root of why this lighting aesthetic resonates with Eastwood is the fact that he has an abiding and enduring love for deep, rich blacks as the foundation for his

(Opposite) Eastwood as William Munny in *Unforgiven*, in a close-up that typifies his lighting style—keeping light off "the moth side." (Above) After taking a beating in Greeley's Saloon—a set lit largely with kerosene lamps. (Page 128) Eastwood reviewing lines with actress Sydney Penny (*Pale Rider*). (Page 129) He conceives a shot on set, as he frequently does (*Bird*).

imagery. He has felt this way for as long as anyone can remember, and there are both visceral and technical reasons why he believes it enhances his ability to tell stories.

"I heard him say it to Bruce Surtees many years ago," Tom Stern explains. "It wasn't that hard to understand. He loves blacks. That's why I am now the custodian of the blacks for Clint. We are just trying to make the blacks blacker and blacker.

"The reason he likes them is twofold. The first reason is that, if you have a choice to play a piano with sixty-six keys, would you prefer that to a [typical] piano with eighty-eight keys? For him, the blacks give him, as we describe it technically, a greater dynamic range [the range of luminance that can be captured on film]. And secondly, the more aesthetic reason is that blacks are a place of imagination for him—as in mystery. Look at the one-sheet for *Unforgiven*—the viewer has to imagine his face. And what you can imagine is great—it enhances the storytelling. In that sense, he likes it dark because he doesn't like to direct down to the audience. Look at his films, and you will find a lot of things that can be viewed at different levels."

Stern also points out that, since *Flags of Our Fathers*, Eastwood has become expert in using newer postproduction digital processes to enhance and deepen blacks using the computer in ways he never could before—a technique for color-timing films known as the digital intermediate (DI) process, which is now nearly ubiquitous in the industry. Indeed, on both Iwo Jima films, Eastwood had Technicolor colorist Jill Bogdanowicz radically desaturate combat imagery using the DI process to dramatically drain color out of battle sequences, contrasting them with more colorful stateside scenes, and highlighting as never before his beloved blacks—particularly the island's famous black sands.

(Above) Scene from *Letters from Iwo Jima*.

(Opposite) Clint Eastwood and Ken Watanabe (*Letters from Iwo Jima*). (Above) Actors Adam Beach, Jesse Bradford, and Ryan Phillippe as the lead characters in *Flags of Our Fathers*, photographed in typical noirish low light by Eastwood's team.

"He's very aware of this technology, and he has really embraced it," Bogdanowicz says of Eastwood's adoption of the DI process. In fact, to this day, when he wants Bogdanowicz to push desaturation further on a scene, he urges her to "go Iwo Jima" with it.

But Eastwood freely admits he had to be talked into trying a DI on *Flags* by Tom Stern and Michael Owens in 2006. Even by then, a large swath of the movie industry had already abandoned traditional photochemical laboratory processes that had ruled for a century in favor of the DI. But Eastwood resisted until *Flags* came along—its visual effects were so extensive that a large portion of the movie needed to be digitally painted anyway, so he made the move.

He has taken every film since to Technicolor, where Bogdanowicz and Stern help him complete his dark color palette in a far more comprehensive way than was possible earlier in his career. Today, Eastwood loves the DI because of the computer's ability to hone in and massage color not only in frames overall, but portions of frames—increasing creative possibilities in Eastwood's mind.

"I finally decided the time had come," Eastwood explains. "[*Flags*] had so many looks and visual effects, and we could color correct [to make it all consistent] as we went along, rather than having to color correct the whole run of the film [in a photochemical process] and then go back and say 'change this' or 'change that.' We can change each part as we go along, and then when we have it as we want it, we can put it on film."

THE ONE CAMERA

Stephen Campanelli, or "Campi," as he is known on Eastwood sets, has been Clint's "right arm," according to Eastwood himself, for more than seventeen years. Campanelli is Eastwood's primary camera operator, and like Jack Green, the man who brought Campanelli into Eastwood's world, and who previously served as Eastwood's camera operator, he has an intimately close creative relationship with Eastwood. That's because Clint, unlike many film directors, does not believe in a hierarchical communication system—he feels no need to first ask cinematographer Tom Stern to check with Campanelli on how a just-concluded shot worked out. Instead, he interacts with Campanelli directly, and frequently.

Eastwood usually follows the action live while standing as close to his actors as possible, both eyeballing them and viewing them on his wireless handheld monitor to study framing and composition as the shot is happening. Whether the shot was in focus is up to Campanelli and his first assistant operator, Bill Coe, to make a final call on, and whether the lighting had any issues is Stern's arena.

Furthermore, shots on an Eastwood set are never played back on a video monitor, since Eastwood implicitly trusts Campanelli's word on whether he thinks it all ended up right on celluloid. If Eastwood likes a take, and Campanelli assures him he "got it," the Malpaso crew usually moves on. This reliance on Campanelli's eye and instincts is key to Eastwood's shooting process and preferences.

"The operator is your right arm when you are directing," Eastwood says. "He's the one framing everything and looking through that viewfinder—if there is a problem, he is the one who should see it. It's the three of us who talk—myself, Campi, and Tom Stern—because Tom makes sure the lighting is consistent. They make suggestions and then I decide. But Campi is an excellent operator, and he's particularly great with the Steadicam. He has the ability to do things few [camera operators] do. If actors go beyond the [planned] shot into something else, he can improvise, and I want him to improvise.

"I tell him, 'If you see anything really interesting, go to it,' and he'll adapt from what we started with. If something changes in the scene, if someone steps the wrong way or something, he'll reframe for it, which is a lot better than yelling 'cut' and doing the whole thing over. Sometimes, his reframing is equal to or better than the original plan anyway. I want him, like everybody, to use his inner self, and not be locked into an exact architecture."

Coe suggests that this methodology is all about allowing Eastwood "to support his actors. People have to understand that it's not all about the camera work or the lighting for him—it's about creating shots to tell the story, while being nonintrusive to the actors."

Campanelli adds that this philosophy works because Eastwood has formed an unusual bond with his camera team.

"It's a close bond," Campanelli says. "If I say I got it, he moves on, unless Tom says there was an issue with lighting. If Tom says that, Clint defers to

him and we do another one. But he'll first ask, 'How bad was it?' If we can fix it [in postproduction], he still might move on. This is all based on efficiency, and Clint's belief that the magic is in the performances." That bond across the set is so organic and well practiced that, frequently, what Eastwood team members call "unspoken communication" or "shorthand" takes over.

"With Clint, we speak the same language—sometimes, it is almost as though we are an old married couple," Campanelli only half-jokes. "We even finish each other's sentences. Everybody on set has this eye contact stuff going on, or sometimes a little sign language. Most sets traditionally have a lot of yelling and screaming. But with Clint and Tom and I, it becomes a triangle of nods and winks. Maybe a thumb up or down."

An interested party who has learned to read those winks and nods in recent years is first assistant director David Bernstein. In his capacity as first AD, it's his job to run the set, communicating with each department about who is needed, and when, and making sure there are no communication mishaps or avoidable interruptions.

And yet, Bernstein has never been asked to call "action" on Eastwood's set, nor has he ever yelled "quiet on the set" or any of the other typical things first ADs normally shout out. Instead, Bernstein simply whispers into a tiny handheld microphone to department heads and other interested parties wearing surveillance-style earpieces, so they can hear him disseminate information without disturbing the set's calm. Cell phones are always off, no one wears an open walkie-talkie, and no one ever yells.

In many ways, Bernstein says, "I've had to unlearn all the behavior I was used to [as a first AD], because the norm on [an Eastwood set] is different."

"I don't yell 'roll,' 'cut,' 'background action,' or any of that," he says. "The job is all about being present and in the moment for what is happening at the camera, while holding yourself as invisibly as possible. The thinking behind why Clint does it that way makes a lot of sense. People get tense when you tell them to stand by or roll camera. But if you whisper to one person on a walkie-talkie that we are rolling, and on the periphery, they use hand signals to tell everyone else. As to why my second AD letting other department heads not in close proximity know what is happening quietly, it creates the environment he wants for actors."

The other unique thing about Eastwood's shooting style is that he works almost exclusively with a single camera, outside of specialized effects or stunt sequences. As to why Eastwood eschews multiple cameras, which are rather common for many directors, the answer, once again, revolves around his desire to marry creativity and efficiency.

As mentioned earlier, Eastwood feels he gets a better performance from actors who play only to a single camera. But, additionally, there is also the issue of light—a big issue for Eastwood. Lighting for shots from multiple angles usually isn't as pretty as when it is tailored to a specific camera angle.

"There are advantages to multiple cameras," Eastwood says. "The big advantage is that everything matches up—if one person scratches his forehead, he does it at the exact same time [from each angle]. But the problem is that sometimes you sacrifice lighting in order to get a shot that has everything matching up. I'd rather take a little extra care to try and get it to match up with separate takes [from different angles] and get a little better lighting on them. That way, you also don't have another camera sitting in the way, and you don't have to avoid that other camera, the other camera operator, the other focus puller. So you have more flexibility to move. If the actor moves one way, you don't have to worry about a camera in the background."

But why no video playback—something that is fairly standard across the industry? For Eastwood, it's "an extra thing" that disrupts the flow.

"We had crude video playback on *Play Misty for Me* and a little bit on *High Plains Drifter*," Eastwood says. "But most of the time, I felt like it got in the way. It was an extra thing. It got cumbersome. Actors were always wanting to come over and look at themselves, and would start discussing what we should or should not have done, and I felt like they weren't looking objectively at themselves. We also had assistant directors looking at it and saying, 'Oh, there's an extra back there. Who turned left when I told him to turn right?' After all, how did all those good pictures get made in the old days without instant replay? They got made because directors knew how to make decisions.

"And so everyone starts building reasons why a shot doesn't work. I don't think that way. I like to look at things and think about why they do work, not why they don't. People get too anal about these things, and when they do, they can miss the spirit of the whole thing. I feel if you make a decision, you should be able to live with it, and if you can't live with it, you shouldn't be directing films."

(Opposite L) Stephen Campanelli, wearing his Steadicam rig, films Clint Eastwood performing a *Gran Torino* scene. (Opposite R) Campanelli consults with Eastwood and Tom Stern on *Million Dollar Baby* and (Above L) Campanelli films *Hereafter* and *Invictus* scenes. Campanelli says he, Eastwood, and Stern communicate with "nods and winks." Campanelli won the Society of Camera Operators Award for his Steadicam work on *J. Edgar* in 2012. (Above R) Producer Rob Lorenz at Eastwood's side on set (*Hereafter*).

(Page 134) Eastwood ponders camera angles and light in Big Sur, in preparation for a major romantic interlude scene in *Play Misty for Me*. (Page 135) Easwood preps to shoot a scene near the *African Queen*, the boat that plays a key role in *White Hunter, Black Heart*.

"THAT WAS THE CLOSEST ESCAPE WE EVER HAD."

CLINT EASTWOOD ON FINISHING THE UNFORGIVEN *SHOOT
IN THE FACE OF AN OVERPOWERING STORM, 2011*

CHAPTER SIX
WE'LL FIGURE IT OUT

DAVID VALDES PUSHES HIS EGGS AROUND HIS PLATE AND GRINS BROADLY WHEN ASKED HOW CLINT EASTWOOD DEALS WITH ADVERSITY DURING PRODUCTION. "WELL, HE DOESN'T PANIC, THAT'S FOR DAMN SURE," VALDES SAYS. "I CAN TELL YOU A STORY ABOUT ADVERSITY, IF YOU LIKE."

The tale etched into Valdes's mind involves crossing the finish line a hair ahead of a crippling Chinook winter storm that swept across the Alberta prairie in October of 1991, as production of *Unforgiven* was winding up. Valdes had heard stories of the infamous Alberta weather, and arranged with a local weather service to give him advance warning of any threatening conditions. With just two weeks of production left, including the crucial finale sequence yet to be filmed, reports of an impending snow assault got Valdes's attention. When he relayed his concerns to Eastwood, his boss responded as he often had over the years in such situations—what Eastwood calls "Malpaso weather" and "Malpaso luck" would prevail in the end.

When Valdes pushed his concerns further and discussed potential scheduling options with Eastwood, he says Eastwood calmly continued shooting as planned, figuring there was no point in worrying just yet about a possible event five days into the future that he couldn't control. "He said, 'Don't worry, we'll figure it out—we always do,'" Valdes remembers.

It wasn't the first time Valdes had received an optimistic Eastwood response in the face of actual or potential problems. For seemingly a lifetime, Eastwood had been surmounting challenges and cooly adjusting his schedule and approach as conditions warranted on dozens of films. Valdes remembered experiencing this attitude for the first time in Idaho, when Eastwood flew off a horse and separated his right shoulder while trying to film his character riding through the mountains of the Sawtooth National Recreation Area during production on *Pale Rider*.

"We had completed all our main unit photography in Idaho, and on that particular day most of the crew were flying to Sonora [California] for the last few days of shooting," Valdes says. "But about five or six of us stayed behind with Clint to get some second-unit shots."

Eastwood had selected a beautiful, remote mountainous area outside of Sun Valley that had recently received a light dusting of snow.

"It was freezing, but we got the camera gear out, and then Clint rode out about fifty yards, getting ready for the shot," Valdes adds. "We shot him riding his horse back and forth at different gaits when suddenly, on a particularly fast trot, his horse stepped in a hole. Suddenly time stood still—it seemed like an eternity."

"We were shooting the ending," Eastwood picks up the story. "We were up on this hill, the colors were changing—it was beautiful, but starting to get to be winter. We went up into the mountains to get this shot of me riding down to the campgrounds. I told them, 'I'll ride out here and you just keep the camera rolling. I'll turn around, and come back.' That's what I was doing, having the horse lope along, which was my mistake, because by this time there was snow falling and ice on the ground. The horse went into a ditch, head over heels, and I was a cruise missile for a second or two."

(Opposite) Eastwood shares a moment with longtime collaborator Buddy Van Horn, who was directing him at the time in *Any Which Way You Can* (1980). (Above) Eastwood with African actor Boy Mathias Chuma, who played Kivu in *White Hunter, Black Heart*.

WE'LL FIGURE IT OUT

Eastwood was driven to Sun Valley, over an hour away, to find a hospital. It was there that an orthopedist told him he needed to keep his arm immobilized in a sling, hanging without movement for weeks to avoid permanent tendon damage. By this time, most of the crew was already in Sonora, expecting to resume shooting the next morning.

"I asked him what we should do, and Clint said we should get on the [Warner Bros.] plane and get to Sonora," Valdes recalls. "I couldn't believe that he actually thought we could shoot the next day as planned when he had a dislocated shoulder. When I said he would have to draw a gun with his [injured arm] in the next scene we scheduled, he looked at me and said the same thing [he would say years later in Alberta]—'Don't worry, we'll figure it out. We always do.' And, of course, he did."

"I just did everything left-handed," Eastwood says, smiling. "I drew the gun, made a purchase, everything with my left hand."

Valdes suggests that decades of this inherent calm under fire, combined with good luck and great instincts, had kept Eastwood from being overly concerned about the looming storm during the *Unforgiven* shoot. Valdes, however, kept receiving the most god-awful weather reports.

"One day, the guy tells me six inches of snow is coming, and the next day he says, 'I made a mistake, it will be at least a foot of snow,'" Valdes says. "I went to Clint and told him that this was serious—that we had just two days before the mother of all snowstorms buried us along with most of Alberta. And we still had five days of work to complete—crucial work, like the ending of the film." Once again, Eastwood promised him they would "figure it out."

As the weather report degraded even further, Eastwood and Valdes eventually devised a radical plan to compress five days of shooting into two. Valdes suggests, "There is not a director alive who would have listened to, much less attempted, such an impossible plan. But Clint is Clint—nothing is an obstacle. In fact, I think he views obstacles as opportunities." As they had on *Pale Rider*, Valdes had scheduled vintage train sequences for *Unforgiven* to be shot in Sonora, where filming was scheduled to wrap. Production designer Henry Bumstead proposed breaking down the bunkhouse sets (and anything not physically connected to the town of Big Whiskey), packing them on trailers, and driving them immediately down to Sonora. The seasoned Malpaso team would then work around the clock to shoot the ending of the movie in the rapidly closing window available to them.

"It was a crazy plan," Valdes says. "Instead of wrapping at sunset on the first day, as previously planned, we shot into the night until one o'clock in the morning, to get half of the final bar sequence completed with Gene Hackman [whose health precluded him from working all night]. So that first day became a hideous eighteen-hour shooting day. And then we sent everyone back to the hotel and told them to get three or four hours of sleep, and then come back to the set at six A.M."

Labor rules call a schedule that requires less than nine hours of rest a "forced call," meaning everyone involved would be getting paid in the neighborhood of three or four times their hourly salary as a penalty. "We knew it would be costly, and there was still no way to guarantee we could finish all the work, but it was the only option we had," Valdes relates.

(Opposite) Eastwood filming a *Pale Rider* scene as the Preacher character—he would later separate his shoulder during filming and switch his gun to his left hand. In another moment during filming (Top), Eastwood prepares actor John Russell, as the deadly Marshall Stockburn, for the scene in which Stockburn makes another character "dance" in a hail of bullets near the climax of that film. (Bottom) Scenes from the climactic portions of *Unforgiven*.

Catering chief Tony Kerum greeted the frazzled crew as they dragged themselves back to the set in the darkness of the wee hours of the next morning to offer them a quick meal before their Herculean effort resumed.

"Everyone ate in darkness," Valdes adds. "And then, Clint essentially did the impossible. He shot the seven-page scene in which the Schofield Kid [Jaimz Woolvett] character talks about how terrible it is to kill a man [originally scheduled to take up two days] non-stop. We finished that scene at dusk, fed the crew quickly, and then shot with multiple cameras the remaining bar scene [the shootout in Greeley's Saloon where Eastwood's William Munny character kills Hackman's Little Bill], and Munny's final departure from Big Whiskey in the pouring rain. As Clint's horse continued to slip and slide on the wet, icy street, the sky started to lighten and the first snowflakes started to appear, almost as if on cue. I went up to Clint knowing that he had shot nearly twelve script pages in twenty-four continuous hours with less than four hours sleep, and still, he didn't get all the shots he wanted. He looked down at me from his horse and said it again—'Don't worry—we got some good stuff. We'll make it work.'"

Eastwood calls that day "the closest escape we ever had." When he addressed the crew about the next day's schedule, he says he informed them "'there is no tomorrow. We are shooting today and tonight and we'll keep shooting until we are finished.' And we did it. It was hard and ice-cold, and we still had things to do [in Sonora]. But the crew moved great. The only problem was at the end, when we did the rain sequence, the [artificial] rain would freeze by the time it hit the ground. That turned the whole street into a huge ice block and, of course, the horses couldn't walk on ice. So we kept running a little tractor over it, plowing the ice under and doing shots. By the time we shot the part where [his character] rides off and finished, it was almost sunup—about five thirty in the morning. On my way down the hill to the house where I was staying, I watched the aurora borealis—the northern lights. It was beautiful. I got up around midday, and there were a couple of feet of snow on the ground. We got out of there just in time."

That was hardly the first weather-related emergency Eastwood productions have grappled with over the years, of course. As Eastwood says, despite efficient production methods, "things come up" from time to time, and when they do, his veteran team finds solutions.

There was the time, for instance, that "cutting rain," as Valdes called it, ruined a planned day of exterior shooting during production of *A Perfect World* in 1993. On that occasion, Eastwood changed course and directed the company into an alternate strategy.

(Opposite) A quick, and rare, rehearsal with actor Jeff Fahey before filming a scene from *White Hunter, Black Heart* on the banks of Lake Kariba in what was then the new nation of Zimbabwe (1989).

(Above L) Clint Eastwood discusses with cinematographer Jack Green the plan for shooting on the actual *African Queen* steamboat built for *White Hunter, Black Heart*. The boat would sink a short time later in the rapids of the Zambezi River, but all personnel escaped safely. (Above R) The cinematic launching of the *African Queen* steamboat is captured for a key moment from *White Hunter, Black Heart*.

"Once again, Clint said to me, 'What do you think we should do?'" Valdes says, smiling. "That time, although I had never said it before, I said I thought we should send everyone home and call it a day. He paused for a moment and then asked, 'What do you think we could shoot on a stage?' I pointed out we didn't have a stage. We did have a warehouse back in Austin, though. So Clint paused again, stroking his neck, and said, 'Let's do some of the driving stuff—a 'poor man's process' [shooting a stationary car by moving lights around it and rocking it, to make it appear it is driving at night], with Kevin [Costner] and the kid [T.J. Lowther] driving around in the car.'"

Valdes insists "rain was practically ripping metal off the roof of his bus," but Eastwood's crew made it to the warehouse and, "within two hours, not only was the equipment on stage, but we were spinning lights, and having brushes going past the lights to give the appearance the car was driving outside at night."

"Sometimes, you have to think quick on your feet and make changes when necessary," Eastwood says. "If you are wedded to an idea and are stuck with it, you can spend an entire day sweating over it. Some [directors] will do that. I remember Robert Mitchum telling a story about how [director] David Lean, on the picture *Ryan's Daughter*, wanted a certain look on top of a mountain, and he sat there for two weeks until light came out at just a certain angle, and then he did that one shot. He knew what he wanted and he wasn't going to adapt. He was going to wait for it. That's a luxury I have never been able to afford, and besides, my nature wouldn't allow me to wait anyway."

Eastwood's nature, however, also requires him to seek realism and beauty in film locations when feasible, and to be aggressive in those locations once he gets there. In the case of *White Hunter, Black Heart*, however, he was without much of his usual

crew—filming in a rugged environment near Lake Kariba in Zimbabwe with only his camera unit, Valdes, and a foreign support team. He has fond memories from that shoot of figuratively stalking the famous Chura bull elephant—a real-life creature captured in some of the movie's filmmaking photography as the central obsession of the film's lead character, John Wilson, Eastwood's John Huston–based film director.

Famous for being easy to spot in a certain region near Lake Kariba for many years, the Chura bull was distinctive for its unusually long tusks—a fascination for Eastwood. So authorities carefully escorted his crew to photograph the creature for its role in the movie's climax.

"His tusks were magnificent—the longest I've ever seen," Eastwood recalls. "Authorities were always following him through this national park with automatic rifles because he was the target of poachers. So they knew where he was, and we got approval from the head of their national park system to photograph him. The animal was always escorted by two younger bull elephants that protected him, and they were the ones you worried about—if you got too close, they would charge you.

"We went out to film it, and they thought we would just get a long shot of the elephant. But I said I had to be photographed stalking him [in the distance]. We got the shot OK, but the guy with the automatic rifle was always ready in case one of those elephants would charge. It was an interesting experience."

A far more harrowing experience on that shoot involved scenes of his character piloting a small steamboat down the rushing whitewater of the Zambezi River—a workable, full-size replica of the model boat used in Huston's *The African Queen*.

(Above) Elephants filmed in Zimbabwe as Clint Eastwood's crew pursued the legendary Chura bull elephant. (Opposite) Later, Eastwood with actress Catherine Neilson during filming of *White Hunter, Black Heart*.

The production had the boat built in England and shipped to Zimbabwe, but it was built for calm waters or a water tank. Eastwood wanted POV shots of his character piloting it near rapids, below Victoria Falls.

"We got a couple of beautiful shots and all looked well, but we couldn't get all the shots because the boat started sinking," Eastwood recalls. "It kind of went sideways in the rapids and water started coming in."

Jack Green was steadfastly doing his duty, filming Eastwood at the helm of the boat, when he started to feel water around his ankles. That was alarming enough, but with a battery pack strapped to his waist by a twenty-pound belt, and a forty-pound camera in his hands, it was even more disconcerting.

"I felt the boat turning, and I'm trying to keep filming Clint as he delivers dialogue," Green relates. "But once we got into a narrow eddy, and [a support team in rubber boats] came alongside, we threw the camera gear into one of them, and then I jumped into another with everyone."

Eventually, the abandoned boat started to sink. While the filmmakers watched from the Zambia side of the river, Eastwood's African Queen went down for good.

"We had to be helicoptered out," Eastwood adds. "We went back later and shot close-ups in a rubber boat. But my big boat is still at the bottom of the Zambezi River. The helicopter needed two or three trips. I was sitting there on a rock, trying to be the last man—the captain going down with the ship—and I'm thinking this is kind of peaceful. Then, all of a sudden, I noticed a pack of baboons staring and yelling at me from the cliff up above. But we got some good shots and everyone was OK, which was the main thing."

Eastwood and his colleagues look back wistfully on such adventures today. But the director becomes quite reserved when recalling the ultimate mishap of his filmmaking career—the tragic death of English mountain guide/camera operator

David Knowles, on the first day of shooting *The Eiger Sanction* on Mount Eiger in Switzerland, in August of 1974.

The incident was documented by Knowles's colleague, Mike Hoover, not long after it happened. Hoover was a professional mountain climber and cinematographer, whose Oscar-nominated short film about climbing, *Solo* (1972), was greatly admired by Eastwood. He served as the film's principal mountaineering cinematographer, and also as technical advisor on the project, responsible for, among other things, training Eastwood to climb, so that he could do his own stunts.

Hoover had to film some POV shots of fake rocks falling from the top of the Eiger for the movie's rockfall scene that day, and Knowles volunteered to help him out. After acquiring the shot, the two men were organizing their equipment when a real, freak rock slide occurred. The result, as Hoover documented in a personal account in the August 1975 issue of *American Cinematographer* magazine, was that Knowles was struck and killed, while Hoover suffered pelvic and rib fractures. Eastwood and producer Robert Daley decided immediately to cancel the project, but Eastwood says today that Knowles's climbing colleagues asked him to reconsider.

(Page 144) Actors gun down the Spider Conway character during the filming of *Pale Rider*. (Page 145) Gaffer Alan Martin (without shirt), cinematographer Jack Green, and Clint Eastwood prepare a shot during the making of *White Hunter, Black Heart*.

(Opposite) Eastwood, as Dr. Jonathan Hemlock, hangs on a cliff face during the shooting for *The Eiger Sanction*. (Bottom L) During production for *White Hunter, Black Heart*, actors George Dzundza (L) and Timothy Spall, and a trained monkey, wait between setups for filming to resume. (Bottom R) Eastwood reflects on the day's production. (Above) Eastwood and actress Marisa Berenson on location in Zimbabwe.

"I told them, I'm going to pull the plug," he quietly relates. "After David was killed, I felt just terrible. It wasn't that anyone did anything wrong—they were all doing well. But the Eiger is all limestone and it isn't as solid [as other mountains]. So, certain times of day, if the weather changes and it gets warmer or cooler, you can get a lot of rockfall.

"Dougal Haston, a Scotsman, was our head climber and mountaineer. When I told him I was shutting down, he said to me, 'Give us a week to organize, and we'll be ready to go again. We know the risks in this business. We are all prepared for [this sort of thing].' He said the climbers didn't want to quit. I figured, if they wanted to go on, then OK, so we went and made the picture."

Hoover's article firmly supported the decision, stating, in his view, there was no reason not to go on. "We all knew that serious accidents were a real possibility before we started," he wrote.

Eastwood shot some footage in a hotel, away from the mountain for a week, and said he would wait for Haston and his team to signal him one way or the other. They called and asked to resume, and so production on the mountain went on.

Looking back on it today, Eastwood explains why he originally wanted to shoot on the Eiger. "In the old days, you would have had to shoot it with papier-mâché rocks, but I figured, no, we should do it on a real mountain with real climbers.

"After David's death, we went back on the hill and finished, but it's something I wouldn't do again. It's a dangerous place. There is a reason so many people have been killed on that mountain. There are too many unexpected things with limestone. It's not like Yosemite or something that is solid granite. But there is no way you can do movies with stunts or adventure or action without having some risks, because [by definition], you are doing things out of the norm. You try to make it as safe as possible. For me, the greatest thing was when Dougal told me they weren't blaming anybody. Those guys were all Scotsmen, terrific guys, and they told me they are in the game because of the risks, the challenges of overcoming nature."

(Opposite) Filming a dummy hanging off a ladder (below) during the making of *The Eiger Sanction* are mountain cinematographer Mike Hoover (sitting on ladder), and Clint Eastwood (in blue).

ONE DAY ON IWO JIMA

The significance of the exceedingly rare opportunity to set foot on the Japanese island of Iwo Jima to shoot establishing imagery and intimate shots of lead actor Ken Watanabe for *Letters from Iwo Jima* was not lost on Clint Eastwood, Rob Lorenz, Melissa Lorenz (who served as second assistant director during the Iwo Jima shoot), cinematographer Tom Stern, camera operator Stephen Campanelli, prop master Mike Sexton, and camera assistants Bill Coe and Bobby McMahan, along with Warner Bros. executives Bill Ireton and Richard Fox, when they visited the island in April of 2006. After all, they were being given a tiny window to get rare footage in what is, in Stern's words, "a sacred and spiritual place," during perhaps the most unusual location shoot of their careers.

But no one on the trimmed-down Eastwood team that made the trip could relate to the experience quite the way Watanabe did. Sipping a cup of green tea, Watanabe momentarily goes quiet, struggling for words to explain what that day meant to him.

"I was afraid to land there," he says. "I mean, there are something like twenty thousand soldiers' souls remaining under the ground there. As we were getting ready to land, Clint called me over, and we could see Iwo Jima from the plane. Then I stepped into the cockpit and could really see the island. I couldn't stop crying.

"When I stepped on the soil, I got warm feelings. I don't mean it was hot—just warm feelings. It wasn't until I stepped there that I felt what we were doing

was not a problem, that it was acceptable, respectful. We went and prayed at the cemetery on top of Mount Suribachi, praying for soldiers of both countries who died there. Mike Sexton had flags for both countries, and I told him to hold the Japanese one and I took the American flag, and then we took pictures. That's when I completely recognized that the project had meaning for both countries, to really understand the sad history of that war."

Eastwood and Lorenz had briefly toured the island, almost exactly a year earlier, to secure permission to return for an abbreviated shoot at the end of production on *Letters*. Eastwood was grateful for his precious twenty-four hours on the island.

"So many people died there, so to do [heavy filming] would be considered a spiritual invasion," he says. "They wouldn't let us shoot in the tunnels on Iwo Jima because of that. But we found a silver mine [in Barstow, California] that was very close to the real tunnels, and we were able to shoot that stuff there. So I figured we could shoot some exteriors on the island. We shot [Watanabe] coming up the beach, tying in Mount Suribachi in the background, and then we shot in old gun emplacements. We were lucky to be able to have that opportunity."

The imagery they captured that day provided some sixty iconic shots for *Letters*, as well as the closing shot of the Iwo Jima memorial for *Flags of Our Fathers*.

Filmmakers managed to arrange for Stern, Campanelli, and Lorenz to spend the night on Iwo Jima, although there are no official accommodations

to speak of. The Warner Bros. jet that brought them there needed two trips to bring everyone over anyway, so Eastwood and Watanabe slept in Tokyo and came over early the next morning, while the camera team and equipment was off-loaded the night before. That allowed Stern to start filming at dawn, even before Eastwood and Watanabe arrived.

"It's a difficult place to work, to say the least," Stern says. "There is a home defense air force base on the island, and on the base, there was a construction presence. We weren't allowed to mix with the Japanese military, but we were able to stay with the construction people in converted ocean containers that had been transformed into dormitories. We received permission to start shooting the next day at four in the morning—to capture film of the dawn and things like that. Clint and Ken Watanabe came in a little later, and we started shooting Ken's scenes, of course, but most of the time, I was getting mood stuff. We shot all day, and then we got off the island that night."

(Opposite) Clint Eastwood walks the black sand beaches of Iwo Jima during his brief visit there. (Top R) Ken Watanabe takes notes while filming establishing scenes like the one below right in *Letters from Iwo Jima*, during the brief shoot on the island. Eastwood visited a memorial to war dead during that visit (Bottom L). Most of the film was shot in California (Above L), with sand later desaturated on the computer.

CARS

After jazz music, if there is one thing Clint Eastwood loves, it's automobiles. He owns dozens, and his personal interest frequently translates into a deep involvement in choosing, evaluating, or consulting on the kinds of cars used in his movies. From the Jaguar XK-150 his character drove in *Play Misty for Me*; to the old Lincoln convertible limousine that is central to the road trip in *Honkytonk Man*; to the iconic 1972 Ford Gran Torino that gave birth to the name and concept in *Gran Torino*, a vehicle now on display at a small automotive museum on the Warner Bros. lot; to the procession of pickup trucks seen in several of his movies; to rumbling tanks, trailers, tractor-trailer rigs, and more, motor vehicles have been a strong thematic element in Eastwood movies from the beginning.

Larry Stelling, Eastwood's current transportation coordinator, has been with Malpaso as a mechanic, picture car coordinator, and transportation captain since *A Perfect World* in 1993, and as transportation coordinator since *Flags of Our Fathers* in 2006. He is responsible for arranging on-location transportation for cast, crew, and equipment, as well as helping the production find, use, maintain, and dispose of vehicles seen in Eastwood films.

Stelling says that, as with everything else, Eastwood is particularly economical with vehicles in his movies. "The same Chevy pickup truck we used in *A Perfect World* was used [a couple years later] in *The Bridges of Madison County*," Stelling says. "Clint is always saying, if we can, let's use what we've got."

Cars were prominent in *A Perfect World*. Stelling remembers the convict's car in the movie—a 1957 Ford. "We had three of them, one of which the special effects crew adapted so the driver could sit in the trunk and drive the car [using] cameras [to see]," Stelling says, referring to the scene in which the vehicle lurches out of control, churning downhill. That picture also featured Eastwood's character, Red Garnett, chasing the convicts in an Airstream trailer that Stelling says was specially built on top of a Chevrolet Blazer chassis and motor.

For *Gran Torino*, Eastwood insisted Stelling specifically find a 1972 Gran Torino, as the script called for, and he did find it, through an auto magazine ad, in a small town in Utah. "Usually, we try to find a hero car and one or two backups, but Clint said it wouldn't be used that much, and we just needed one," Stelling recalls. "The car was already restored the way you see it in the movie."

More recently, for *J. Edgar*, Stelling rented dozens of vintage cars from private collectors in both Los Angeles and Washington, D.C.—finding them through car clubs he contacted over the Internet.

"Some owners were concerned about having their cars out in [inclement] weather," Stelling relates. "For the scenes in Washington, D.C., our first day, we showed up at seven A.M. on a Sunday morning outside the Department of Justice, and sure enough, there was light snowfall. We had mostly Ford Model Ts from the 1919 period, and then Model As and others from around 1930.

"The Model Ts have narrow tires, and in bad weather, that can be a problem. I was worried we were in trouble and [the car owners] wouldn't show up, but ninety-five percent of them were there. Needless to say, it helped that it was a Clint Eastwood movie, and more importantly, that Clint was interested in their cars. He would walk around and talk to them about their vehicles and make it fun for them to meet him."

(Top) A youthful J. Edgar Hoover (Leonardo DiCaprio) during an exterior scene filmed in the greater Los Angeles area to resemble Washington, D.C., in the 1920s (*J. Edgar*). (Bottom L) Actress Judi Dench next to a vintage Ford Model T (*J. Edgar*). (Bottom R) Clint Eastwood as Walt Kowalski (*Gran Torino*).

(Opposite, Top L and R) The 1972 Ford Gran Torino used in Eastwood's film. Transportation coordinator Larry Stelling found the vehicle through an auto magazine ad, in a small town in Utah, already restored and suitable for filming. Today it sits in a small museum exhibit on the Warner Bros. lot. (Opposite R) Bee Vang, as the character Thao, drives Walt Kowalski's Gran Torino, a gift from his late friend, at the film's conclusion.

(Opposite R) The 1937 Lincoln Convertible Limousine used in *Honkytonk Man* ranks among Eastwood's favorite cinematic automobiles. (Opposite, Bottom R) A vintage GMC panel truck leads the Bronco Billy caravan. Carefully selected vehicles are frequently featured prominently in Eastwood films. (Opposite, Bottom L) Vintage vehicles during the Charlie Parker funeral scene at the end of *Bird*—a detail typical of Eastwood's period work.

(Page 154) Sound effects recording team of John P. Fasal (L) and Alan Murray capture antique car sounds for *Changeling*. (Page 155) Eastwood first directed himself in *High Plains Drifter* in a variation of the Man with No Name character he had played in three Sergio Leone movies as The Stranger. Pictured here in a quintessential pose.

"[HENRY] ALWAYS KNEW WAYS TO GET US OUT OF CORNERS. HE HAD HIS IDIOSYNCRASIES,
BUT WAS A REALLY CLEVER GUY WHO REALLY UNDERSTOOD FILMMAKING."

CLINT EASTWOOD,
ON HIS LATE FRIEND AND PRODUCTION DESIGNER, HENRY BUMSTEAD, 2011

CHAPTER SEVEN
BUMMY COLORS

ALTHOUGH HENRY BUMSTEAD PASSED AWAY AT THE AGE OF NINETY-TWO IN 2006, SHORTLY AFTER HELPING TO DESIGN *LETTERS FROM IWO JIMA*—HIS ELEVENTH CONSECUTIVE CLINT EASTWOOD PICTURE AS PRODUCTION DESIGNER—EASTWOOD AND HIS COLLEAGUES CONTINUE TO OPERATE, IN A SENSE, AS THOUGH HE WERE STILL AROUND. "WE ALL FEEL THAT WAY," COSTUME DESIGNER DEBORAH HOPPER INSISTS. "HE'S STILL HERE."

Still, 2008's *Changeling* became the first Eastwood production since *The Rookie* (1990) made without Bumstead's official participation. When watching *Changeling*, if you look closely early in the movie, you will see a restaurant named Bummy's Cafe flash by, in tribute to him. But Eastwood's transition from Bumstead to current production designer James Murakami actually began during *Letters from Iwo Jima*, when Eastwood and Bumstead, whose health was failing by that point, brought in Murakami to help art direct that film. Murakami had worked with Bumstead periodically over the years as an art director on various projects, including Eastwood's *Unforgiven* and *Space Cowboys*, so he was chosen to fill that role on *Letters from Iwo Jima*. Murakami says, "The joke was that they wanted an art director of Japanese ancestry," and indeed, his personal knowledge of Japanese culture proved invaluable. But he was also a highly respected art director, who already had history with both Bumstead and Eastwood.

"We were doing a Japanese story, and Jim had worked with us in the past, so there was a working relationship there," producer Rob Lorenz relates. "He understood Clint's style, and they were comfortable with each other, so we brought him on. The movie ended up being a transitional period for Clint to become more familiar with Jim and vice versa. So, by the time the project was done, there was a big comfort level there."

Lorenz at first asked Murakami if he wanted a production design credit on *Letters*, but Murakami deferred to Bumstead. As Bumstead's health declined, however, Murakami's duties grew. As the project concluded, Eastwood insisted on bumping his credit up to co-production designer, with Bumstead concurring, and Murakami has been part of the Malpaso team ever since, taking over the department upon Bumstead's death.

(Opposite) Production Illustrator Joe Musso's colored storyboard from the IKON Satellite Sequence (*Space Cowboys*). (Above) Clint Eastwood and longtime friend and collaborator, production designer Henry Bumstead, in Boston (*Mystic River*).

And yet, Murakami freely admits that he continues to run the Malpaso art department much as Bumstead had, and that he follows many of the creative templates his predecessor left behind. All of which is fine with the rest of the team, considering how beloved Bumstead was, and also how successful. After all, he had worked with many legendary directors on great films, in a career that stretched back to 1948. He owned two Oscars (for *To Kill a Mockingbird* in 1963 and *The Sting* in 1974)

and four total nominations, including for his work on *Unforgiven* in 1993. That was his first film back with Eastwood since he served as art director on *High Plains Drifter* in 1973 before going off to collaborate with George Roy Hill and others. From *Unforgiven* until his death, Bumstead was one of Eastwood's closest collaborators, advisors, and friends.

In a 2006 interview shortly before his death, Bumstead joked that he was surprised he didn't win an Academy Award in 1993 for his work on *Unforgiven*.

"I thought for sure I'd win," he said, chuckling.

He hardly needed the award. It's just that he and everyone associated with him understood the degree of his team's accomplishment in designing and erecting the fictional town of Big Whiskey from the ground up in just thirty-two days, on ranchland in Alberta, Canada.

It wasn't the first time he had built Eastwood a Western town. In 1973, he supervised construction of the ramshackle town of Lago for *High Plains Drifter*, only to see Eastwood's special effects team burn it to the ground in the film's climax. But this time, for Big Whiskey, Eastwood was plotting to start shooting in August, just twelve weeks after finding the town's location, leaving Bumstead with the unenviable task of constructing, in a few weeks, an entire Western town that creatively fit the script's demands, and logistically would work for filming in a grueling locale. The film's producer, David Valdes, recalls the conversation between Eastwood and Bumstead—Bummy to his colleagues—on the flight home after scouting the location.

"Clint said he wanted to be shooting within twelve weeks," Valdes recalls. "Bummy said 'What? We just discovered it today.' And Clint said he would shoot some of the badlands stuff first, and maybe move to the town last, so maybe he could get about thirteen weeks. As soon as we landed at Burbank Airport, Bummy told me we had to go back to Alberta right away and get started. At that point, we didn't even know whose land it was. We shortly got it sorted out, and Bummy put it on full burners and, boom, started building Big Whiskey. It sounds crazy, because Bummy couldn't bring any of his American [construction] crew, and was forced to hire Albertans he had never met before, but he managed to build the entire town in thirty-one days. Another impossible feat accomplished, and we stayed on track to begin shooting in August."

Bumstead built an iconic, practical town with several buildings that featured usable interiors and prominent exteriors. Jack Green, the film's cinematographer, says he worked closely with Bumstead as he designed Big Whiskey. To this day, Green claims he has never seen a more impressive feat of efficient craftsmanship on any film he has worked on.

(Opposite) Clint Eastwood in an astronaut suit (*Space Cowboys*). Costume supervisor Deborah Hopper had to have the suits custom made with cooling systems so the actors could tolerate wearing them on set for long periods. (Top) Henry Bumstead (second from left) with other Academy Award winners in 1962, when he earned an art direction/set direction Oscar for *To Kill a Mockingbird*, and again (Bottom L, on the right) after winning another Oscar in the same category for *The Sting* in 1974. (Bottom R) Bumstead discusses a drawing with Alfred Hitchcock, another of his high-profile collaborators, for whom Bumstead worked on four movies.

"Think about it—in just a month, they built the entire town, including painting, streets, the eight-mile road that served as the service road [from the highway to the Big Whiskey site], everything," Green relates. "He had great construction people, don't get me wrong. But it was a marvelous achievement. Only someone of Bummy's experience and skill could have pulled that off."

(Above L) An architectural scan of the physical, hand-painted backdrop representing the second-floor Carriage House view of a courtyard and square in Savannah, Georgia, chosen by Jack Green during production on *Midnight in the Garden of Good and Evil*. (Above R) From the same film, Eastwood's dramatization of the famed real-life murder that spawned the book upon which the movie was based. Here, actor Jude Law during the murder sequence.

Bumstead was wonderfully proficient with the practical aspects of production design—where to hide cables and generators to supply power to the set, for instance. In this case, he put the generator in the town's livery stable.

"Bummy taught me a lot of tricks," Valdes recalls. "One of the first things was, when you build a Western town, you circle the town with cable for the electricians. It's more expensive, but more efficient, and he taught me when and why it would make sense. He also said you always hide the generator in the barn, because there is hardly any action in or near that building in a Western. He strategically designed every building in Big Whiskey to not only appear as part of a period Western town, but also as a structure that could protect the set dressing, props, electrical equipment, grip equipment, camera equipment, and even one structure that hid our Andy Gump toilets."

Jack Taylor worked as Bumstead's art director for twelve years. He talks about his former boss reverentially, and calls him a mentor and "a second father." Taylor suggests that the notion that Bumstead could begin planning intimate design details as early as the location scout, as he did on *Unforgiven* (which Taylor did not work on), was hardly unusual. He taught Taylor early on that one of a production designer's most important jobs is to personally help choose locations.

"He'd tell me [the producers] wanted us to go scout a location, and before we would scout it, I would go over our breakdown list with Bummy and tell him, 'I think this section should be built [on stage] and this should be on location,' and he would talk to me about it," Taylor explains. "But he wasn't influenced by jumping to conclusions. He'd say something generally, but then he was very big on wanting to visit the location, to let the environment be our filter for the script. Lots of times, things on location are not the way you see them in the script, and you end up making changes."

Taylor points to the way Bumstead worked on *Midnight in the Garden of Good and Evil*, to illustrate how location and stage work were inexorably linked in Bumstead's mind. The location shoot was in Savannah, Georgia, where the story takes place. The production photographed some spectacularly eccentric architecture, including the original Mercer House, where the real-life murder depicted in the film occurred. Despite the opportunity to film there, much of what the filmmakers saw had to be separately replicated on stage at Warner Bros., due to the limited time frame of the location shoot.

"We shot the interior of the Mercer House, but [the family member] in charge of the estate, while she allowed us to film in rooms on the ground floor and the lobby and exterior, would not let us film in the room where the actual murder took place," Taylor recalls. "But she let us in to measure it, and so Bummy was able to reproduce it on a stage."

Taylor adds that "it was a real quick shoot" in Savannah, and therefore, "we also had to build the courtroom and numerous sets on the lot. Henry and I took the set list and split it. He came right from Chicago, where we were working on another film, to Savannah, where he met Clint, and they went through and [quickly] picked locations and took photographs of them. We then built them [on stage], but because

(Below, L–R) Clint Eastwood, John Cusack, and Kevin Spacey discuss a scene during filming of *Midnight in the Garden of Good and Evil*. (Opposite) Clint Eastwood hoists a handheld camera to film random footage of wreckage left behind from the fight to the death that climaxes his directorial debut, *Play Misty for Me*.

Henry went to Savannah himself, he knew specifically that we were going to shoot certain house exteriors only, while we would have to build interiors for other ones, so he got me [busy] designing it all. Then Bummy went back to Savannah, while I oversaw the drawings. Every couple weeks, he would fly back here on a weekend, go through the drawings with me, and fly back [to Savannah]. I stayed [at Warner Bros.] until the whole company made their move back from Savannah, and by then, everything was ready."

Eastwood refers to the things Bumstead preached as his way of making sure "he would never put you in a corner with his design. He always knew ways to get us out of corners. He had his idiosyncrasies, but was a really clever guy who really understood filmmaking. He had worked with all the greats, and he understood how things fit together."

Rob Lorenz adds that Bumstead spent decades at the top of Hollywood's art and design elite, due to an unusual "cinematic eye that allowed him to read a scene and draw the set in his mind. It was obvious to him, and he was good at it. Add that to the fact that he was of the same era and near the same generation as Clint, and you can see why they were in sync for so many years."

And that influence still reverberates today. Murakami, in fact, says his creative approach often evokes Bumstead's, which is logical, considering those tastes match Eastwood's preferences to begin with.

"I pretty much operate things the same way," Murakami says. "He had what he called 'Bummy colors.' I've sort of taken after it. It's the idea of staying in design with neutral colors, so you don't have to worry much about clashing colors [with wardrobe, etc.]. It also works better for Clint's [palette], since he emphasizes deep blacks anyway. These things won't usually clash with that. Our painter still has Bummy's color charts, and we refer to those all the time. You start with basic colors, warm and cool, beiges, browns, grays, and that just makes things easier— you are safer than trying something more specific, like a lot of red or dark greens or certain kinds of blues. With a neutral color, you can add to it depending on the story, but I pretty much keep with Bummy's feelings colorwise."

(Opposite) To capture a dramatic shot of Sydney Penny's character calling out in anguish to the Preacher character in *Pale Rider*, filmmakers placed her on the turret of a Chapman camera crane, with stunt coordinator Buddy Van Horn holding her in place, and used a long lens to film her above the waist, pressed against the Sawtooth Mountains from on high.

(Page 164, Top) A rough computer-animated rendering, created by visual effects supervisor Michael Owens's team, of the American armada landing on Iwo Jima. (Page 164, Bottom, L–R) A sketch drawing of the landing, a live set of a bombed-out Japanese hillside gun emplacement filmed in Iceland, a live-action plate of actors, and a raw plate of a military vehicle. (Page 165) Detailed Landing Craft paint schematics from the Malpaso art department detailing the look and style of military vehicles used in *Flags of Our Fathers*.

FORM OF LETTERS AND NUMERALS

SINGLE STROKE GOTHIC VERTICAL LETTERING

ABCDEFGHIJ
KLMNOPQRS
TUVWXYZ
1234567890

WIDTH OF LETTERS TO BE 2/3 OF HEIGHT
WIDTH OF LETTERS "M" AND "W" SAME AS HEIGHT
WIDTH OF LETTER "I" AND NUMERAL "1" TO BE 1/6 OF HEIGHT
STROKE TO BE 1/6 OF HEIGHT
SPACE BETWEEN LETTERS AND NUMERALS TO BE 1/6 OF HEIGHT
SPACE BETWEEN WORDS TO BE 2/3 OF HEIGHT

VERTICALLY APPLIED LETTERING:
SPACE BETWEEN LETTERS AND NUMERALS 1/6 HEIGHT
SPACE BETWEEN WORDS SAME AS HEIGHT

Vehicle Unit Designations:
C10
C23
D15
D18
Paint unit designation on vehicles as directed

NOTE:
All lettering of vehicles to be F. S. 33655 yellow (flat)

NOTES:
1. Vehicle Interiors to be Marine Green – F.S. 34052
2. Camo Colors to be applied with Brushes.
3. Each Vehicle should be variations on basic pattern.
4. Dust Age, Weather Age per Art Director.
5. Vehicle Base Color shall be SPRAYED.

Camoflage Patterns and Colors

- Dark Tan (flat) F.S 30219
- Field Green (flat) F. S. 34097
- Military Brown (flat) F. S. 30117
- Interiors Only — Marine Green (flat) F.S. 34052
- Assault Beach Green F.S. 34138

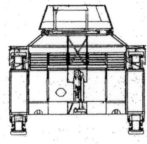

SECTION

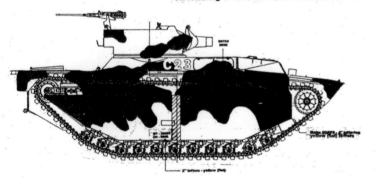

RIGHT SIDE

FRONT

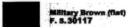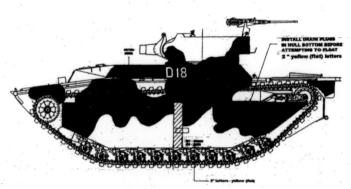

LEFT SIDE

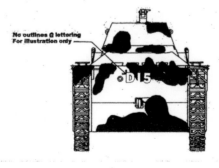

BACK

No outlines @ lettering For illustration only

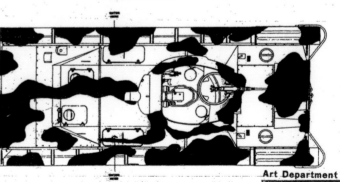

TOP VIEW

Art Department
Released

LVT - (A) 4 U. S. Marines
Plans & Elevations — Camouflage, Colors, Graphics

FLAGS OF OUR FATHERS

155240

408

LVT(A)-4 AMTANK

Taylor elaborates on this color scheme, suggesting that a designer of Bumstead's caliber was able to maximize the value of what is, in actuality, "a limited palette of colors on set."

"The art directors and cinematographers years ago developed a whole palette of [color] values that were complementary to skin tones, and Bummy used that for a long time," Taylor explains. "Henry left me his little swatch books that he always used if he was working a set. They had little dove and adobe grays [various shades and formulations based on gray]—either warms or cools, depending on the [color values]. There were what we call 'uniwhites'—white [tones] of different [color] values and all these other colors that always look good on film. He would always stay with those books, but used them to play with other textures and colors."

Eastwood clearly misses Bumstead. He suggests he "apparently has a thing for older art directors," after the years he spent first with another legend, Edward Carfagno—who worked on nine films in the 1980s involving Eastwood, until he was about eighty-two years old—then, eventually, Bumstead, and now Murakami.

The "brilliance" of Bumstead, as Eastwood describes it, was in his full cinematic envisioning of how best to combine his artistic vision with Eastwood's story requirements, logistical and financial limitations, and working method. Bumstead, in fact, claimed in that 2006 interview that Eastwood used to tell him he should direct movies himself.

"Clint told me I could probably direct better than ninety percent of the guys out there, because you do need to know how to lay out a set, and how to shoot on it," Bumstead said. "And it is true that, to be an art director or production designer, you have to be a director more or less. You can't lay the set out if you don't understand how it will be shot. You have to know, Will they come in through the door on the left? The right? The rear? Often, you decide that [as the designer]. But I laughed when he said that, because I told him I doubted I could get the kind of performances out of people that he gets. I would certainly know where to put the camera, but performance? That's another thing."

[Opposite] An ILM Miniature of Space Shuttle Cargo Area created for *Space Cowboys*—the film that brought Eastwood into the modern visual effects era. (Top L) IKON Satellite Set Unit on Warner Bros. Sound Stage, built to match the miniature. (Bottom L) An art department storyboard sketch of the IKON set showing the arrival sequence (a proposed shot) of the Soviet Satellite. (Above R) Art director Jack Taylor's color swatches—dog-eared from decades of constant use. Samples based upon the so-called "Bummy color" scheme.

ECONOMY OF DESIGN

Still, although production design, by definition, is an artistic endeavor that boosts Eastwood's entire creative process across the board, much of the job involves managing money, resources, people, and expectations—a skill Eastwood excels at and expects his department heads to excel at, as well. Those who worked with Bumstead, and now with James Murakami, say that what Murakami calls "the Malpaso way" of doing design economically lies at the heart of Eastwood's success building believable environments.

Murakami explains that the idea is to "use your money so you see it [on screen]. You have to think about the money—Clint does, and we have to also."

On 2011's *J. Edgar*, the production was on a razor-thin budget [$35 million], and yet, Murakami was in charge of building opulent sets to realistically mimic J. Edgar Hoover's office and portions of the larger Department of Justice (DOJ) building in Washington, D.C. The production visited the real DOJ building, and did measurements there to guide construction of the central corridor and Hoover's office on stage at Warner Bros. as close to scale as possible. And yet, filmmakers couldn't perfectly mimic everything in the real world, given their budget and timeline.

"What impressed Clint when we visited was the size and height of the corridor and offices [at the DOJ building]," says Murakami. "He said he wanted us to reflect that. But there were budgetary limits. On the ground floor, the real building has a bank of six elevators, which would be costly to do. So we went with one elevator. We felt it was important to get Hoover's office correct, and then we took liberties with other things. We cheat some things, but do the things Clint feels are most important as close to reality as possible."

(Above) J. Edgar Hoover (Leonardo DiCaprio) and Helen Gandy (Naomi Watts) tour the deserted Library of Congress at night.

Following that logic, Eastwood normally tells his team not to spend too much time designing accurate ceilings and floors. After all, "that's what viewers see the least," Murakami points out. "But if it is in the shot, then you have to be more careful."

Indeed, during a crucial *J. Edgar* scene in a period hotel room, Hoover (Leonardo DiCaprio) and Clyde Tolson (Armie Hammer) engage in a fistfight during a critically emotional moment.

"They tumble on the floor, and then the shot looks up at the ceiling, so Clint reminded us to make sure the floor and ceiling were accurate," Murakami adds. "I gave him a good ceiling with beams and, originally, some nice tile on the floor, Spanish style. But we pulled out the tile and replaced it with double-padded carpeting to make it more actor-friendly."

Of course, there are other issues beyond what the viewer sees. Crafting places to hide lights and cameras, and room to maneuver, are all important. So is safety and comfort, Murakami emphasizes. The fact that Eastwood is an actor himself, Murakami says, means he wants to make sure designs consider actor safety and comfort. Thus, the floor on which DiCaprio and Hammer tussled had padding built into it at Eastwood's recommendation—hence the term "actor-friendly."

Murakami's art director, Patrick Sullivan, says he and Murakami "learned the hard way" to make these kinds of accommodations on their previous film, *Hereafter*.

(Above L) Leonardo DiCaprio in script review. (Above R) Clint Eastwood and screenwriter Dustin Lance Black review dialogue for a scene during filming in 2011 (*J. Edgar*). (Opposite) Leonardo DiCaprio consults with Clint Eastwood during filming (*J. Edgar*).

(Above L) Clint Eastwood with legendary actor Eli Wallach, who had a cameo as a liquor store owner in *Mystic River*. (Above R) Sketch supplied by former art director Jack Taylor of a parade float that was created for the film. (Below R) Design plan for the layout of a fictional boxing arena with ring and audience staging designed to be built inside the Los Angeles Olympic Auditorium (*Million Dollar Baby*).

"We built a rooftop set for the scene in which people pull [actress] Cécile de France out of the water and onto the roof," Sullivan says. "They had to pull her over an edge, and we built the edge, a little step actually. But it wasn't padded. We could have put a piece of foam there and painted it the color of the building, but we didn't think to do it.

"Clint told us, 'That wasn't too actor-friendly.' We scrambled to [add padding] along the edge and it worked out fine. But the point is that he didn't want a real sharp edge there—he didn't want her feeling any pain going over it. As an actor, he is very aware of such things."

These practical considerations are nothing new when it comes to production design at Malpaso. Frequently, Eastwood's company multipurposes locations to save time, money, and headaches. Jack Taylor says the idea is to "try to consolidate the company in one location so you can do multiple things." Therefore, especially in the cost-conscious Eastwood world, "the way to save money is by finding locations you can shoot on in confined areas. You can make an entire day of filming go fast that way."

Mystic River and *Million Dollar Baby* are two cases in point. According to Taylor, both movies extensively repurposed single locations as multiple sites, thanks to clever design and construction work. *Mystic River* is perhaps best known designwise for the functional waterfront bar dubbed the Black Emerald, which Bumstead's group built from the ground up—interior and exterior—in Boston. But just as important was the strategic use of two empty warehouses to hold sets for several scenes.

"The [warehouses] had room for modern offices for us, but we also realized we could build sets for interiors of some [houses] in the movie," Taylor explains.

"Those houses were small and cramped, and we couldn't always bring the full company into them. So we decided we would build those at the warehouses, especially the scenes with the staircase in a house, and the Boston police station viewing rooms, incarceration rooms, offices, and we even housed our art department there."

And then, a year later, for *Million Dollar Baby*, Malpaso took the concept even further. Since more than twenty boxing sequences were staged throughout the movie in what are supposed to be a wide range of venues all over the world, Taylor went through the script and created a book of details for each fight. Then he and Bumstead discussed how they could dress a few key sites—ranging from the old Sun Chemical building to the Hollywood Athletic Club to the Olympic Auditorium in Los Angeles—to represent different venues.

"At one location, we figured we could shoot two or three different boxing sequences," Taylor says. "One was supposed to be in Germany, and other places. We would discuss it and say, well, if we shoot from this direction, bring in bleachers, banners, and advertisements and a boxing ring with red, white, and blue ropes and a tan covering, we could shoot for one auditorium. And then we could shoot it from a different direction with a different audience and different bleachers, changing the ropes, the tarp covers, the ads, and the colors, and get entirely [different] boxing sequences in the same day, in the same place. In one of those places, we made a big space in a hallway into a dressing room for London, and then, around the corner, we made one for New York City. That's how you save money. You don't have to do them all in different places."

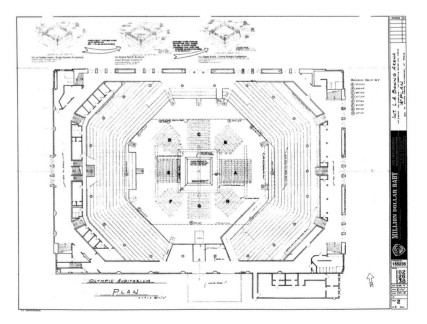

THE FINE ARTS

The volume, degree of labor, and loving craftsmanship expended by Deborah Hopper's costume department on each Clint Eastwood movie could theoretically get overlooked, since, after all, the work is intentionally understated, according to Hopper. She is the first to point out that Eastwood's movies are always character driven, and as such, "It is not about the clothes. If viewers are watching clothes, I'm not really doing my job."

Hopper's work, and the work of colleagues like prop master Mike Sexton, makeup department head Tania McComas, and several others is central to Eastwood's stories, particularly since Eastwood makes so many period films where inaccuracies can be magnified.

COSTUMES

On *J. Edgar*, Hopper's team costumed 1,800 extras in accurate period clothes, ranging between the years 1915 and 1972. In that film, Leonardo DiCaprio underwent eighty costume changes, while aging from a young man to his death, and all of them, along with Armie Hammer's costumes, were made to order from scratch.

The costume design process on most Eastwood films begins with a discussion between Eastwood and Hopper to examine characters and the film's color palette. She then prepares costume storyboards for him to review,

including photographs, sketches, and fabric swatches. Once the cast is available, Hopper arranges costume fittings, photographing everything, and submitting those photographs and materials to Eastwood. The final decision-making process is then based on choices both of them feel will enhance the story, rather than distract from it. But, as Hopper points out, Eastwood's subjects range "from space to boxing to military to Westerns."

Space Cowboys required astronaut costumes for four tall actors—Eastwood, Tommy Lee Jones, James Garner, and Donald Sutherland. NASA doesn't provide suits, and Hopper says costume houses didn't have replicas for actors that tall. She therefore had suits specially manufactured that were lighter than the real ones, and lined with portable cooling units to make them bearable to wear on a movie set.

Six years later, the two back-to-back Iwo Jima films posed probably the biggest challenge ever for Hopper's team.

"We had to make all the Marine uniforms," she says. "They had a special [cotton] twill fabric for them, and we made about seven hundred for that movie. We had teams of costumers fitting ten thousand extras in four locations—Iceland, Washington, D.C., Chicago, and Los Angeles. We also had to match the most iconic image in America's wartime history (the raising of the flag at Iwo Jima)."

Next, on *Changeling*, Eastwood made valuable suggestions for Angelina Jolie's wardrobe, according to Hopper. "He knew it was the 1920s, and so he

said her character should not wear a lot of jewelry or gold," she explains. "He also said he didn't want a lot of costume changes for her, because people at that particular time, around the Depression, would not have a huge wardrobe. We repeated many of her clothes, and she wore the same coat throughout the whole movie."

(Above) Ultra detailed props and clothing procured or built for *Million Dollar Baby* and *J. Edgar*.

(Top L) 1920s-era typewriters refurbished by Eastwood prop master Mike Sexton's team, and (Bottom L) period shoes selected for *J. Edgar* by costume designer Deborah Hopper, in consultation with Clint Eastwood. Hopper's team dressed over 1,700 extras for the film—head to toe—with period clothing made from scratch. (Top and Bottom Center) Ornate lamps, furniture, paintings, photo frames, and other items were carefully researched and selected for the film to match period looks and photographs of homes and hotel rooms. (Top and Bottom R) The boxing office at the fictional Hit Pit Gym, built for *Million Dollar Baby*, and boxing equipment strategically placed in the gym.

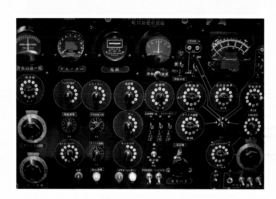

MAKEUP

J. Edgar brought great attention to makeup work in an Eastwood film since it jumped around in time. In that film, three actors—Leonardo DiCaprio, Armie Hammer, and Naomi Watts—were aged using practical makeup techniques to tell a story that covers decades.

Complicating matters was the fact that the production had little time for testing. A single day of makeup tests was done for DiCaprio, while the other two actors' full makeup was not developed until production was launching. DiCaprio's personal makeup artist, Sian Grigg, handled his prosthetic work, while Eastwood makeup department head, Tania McComas, handled the other two actors. And Eastwood's longtime hair department chief, Carol O'Connell, returned from a two-film hiatus to handle the extensive hair and wig work. It was a complicated effort, considering the fact that the actors—particularly Hammer, who was only twenty-four years old when the film was made—were far younger than their aged characters. Thus, some shots required digital touch-up work.

"That was tough—definitely not a typical Clint Eastwood movie," McComas says. "It was long hours, and very difficult for the actors in the makeup chair. The smart thing was Clint organized it so all the shooting involving old-age makeup was done at once, over the last couple weeks of the shoot. We had to do life casts on their faces, sculpt them, make molds, and then make prosthetic pieces from those molds and apply them piece by piece. There were also contact lenses, dental implants, and wigs, of course."

Before *J. Edgar*, probably the most makeup-intensive Eastwood film was

Flags of Our Fathers, McComas suggests, simply because it was a war picture. And so, on the beaches of Iceland, she ran around lugging "boxes of silicon wounds."

"Clint would be shooting fast, his normal pace, and when there was an explosion and we needed wounds for a shot, we would run on set, open the box, and ask Clint what wound he preferred," she says. "There is pressure because he's staring, wondering how fast you can apply it—normally we got it down to five minutes or less in most cases. We definitely learned to think on our feet on that one."

PROPS

When a point of clarification came up on the *J. Edgar* set, during filming of a restaurant scene, everyone turned to Mike Sexton for answers. A line called for J. Edgar Hoover to ask a waiter to bring "a bottle of your finest Dom," as in Dom Pérignon champagne, for a toast. But the scene took place in 1933, and there was some debate about whether Dom Pérignon was available in restaurants at that time. Sexton, Eastwood's prop master since *Midnight in the Garden of Good and Evil* after taking over from his mentor—longtime prop master Eddie Aiona—is the production's research guru on such matters.

Just like vintage typewriters, guns, rugby balls, boxing gloves, and other things, Sexton knew his champagne history. His final word: "My research said Dom was not available in restaurants that year." And so the line was changed to "your finest champagne."

"(Eastwood) wants me to do proper research on each script," he adds. "I go places—garage sales, antique stores. I research photos, and on the Internet, I buy stuff on eBay—anything I can do to find things, get colors right, and the textures of things. If there is a scene of a guy eating, we research the guy. What colors did he like? What did he eat? Getting it right is important, and also prevents actors from thinking about props."

Sexton frequently buys props from suppliers and has them refurbished or repaired, since antique devices have to look new or recent in a period piece. But he will put a team together to make things that can't be procured any other way, as with the ladder prop from the Lindbergh baby kidnapping storyline depicted in *J. Edgar*. Sexton located a source at the New Jersey State Police Museum dedicated to the Lindbergh case, and they had the actual ladder.

"They let me photograph every inch of it, including placement of nail holes and knots," he says. "We got identical nails and brought the photos to our prop builders and said it had to look identical."

(Top L) Typical Eastwood low lighting and shadows in a nightclub scene from *Bird*. (Top Center) A piece of Hilary Swank's wardrobe from *Million Dollar Baby*—her boxing robe with the engraved Irish motto "Mo Cuishle" (it's slightly misspelled—"Mo Chuisle" is correct). The phrase's meaning is revealed in a poignant moment at the end of the film. (Top R) Ken Watanabe, in a period costume for a flashback scene in *Letters from Iwo Jima*, sitting alongside the costume designer behind the outfit, Deborah Hopper. (Bottom, L–R) Three images revealing the painstakingly researched and built props and set pieces that are part of the illusion crafted for *Letters from Iwo Jima*.

AGING LEO

These images show some of the stages Leonardo DiCaprio went through during the 4½-hour process it took each day to apply the prosthetic makeup necessary to transform him into the elderly J. Edgar Hoover. (Top L) Makeup artist Sian Grigg (R) says the illusion started with contact lenses for DiCaprio to turn his blue eyes into Hoover's shade of brown. A special makeup effects company, Coulier Creatures, created a bald cap with punched-in hair, and DiCaprio's hair stylist, Kathy Blondell, added a toupee that radically altered the actor's hairline.

Then, he received mouth appliances—fake teeth and teeth padding (three different sets for three different ages in the film) to give DiCaprio a "bull doggy jowl," according to Grigg. An appliance was also inserted into his nose "just to disfigure it slightly," she adds. "The idea was to age Leo as far as we could, but still keep it convincing, giving him Hoover's features, the weight in his face, and his characteristic short haircut. For that, we used the silicon bald cap and silicon appliances sculpted for us by (prosthetic makeup artist) Duncan Jarman (Center R) for his neck, chin, cheeks, and forehead pieces, as well as eye bags, eyelids, lips and hands. And, finally, the toupee, eyebrows, and contact lenses were added."

(Page 174) Forest Whitaker as Charlie Parker, on a dimly lit set meant to mimic a vintage jazz club, during the making of *Bird*. (Page 175) Filming through a rain-splattered windshield to register the pain in Francesca's face, near the climax of *The Bridges of Madison County*.

"YES, CLINT SHOOTS THE WHOLE SCRIPT,

BUT I CAN TAKE A BLUEPRINT AND SEE A WHOLE HOUSE,

WHILE SOMEONE ELSE MIGHT JUST SEE DRAWINGS."

JOEL COX, EDITOR, 2011

CHAPTER EIGHT
FINDING THE MOMENTS

WHEN EDITOR JOEL COX AND WARNER BROS. MARKETING MEN JOE HYAMS AND MARCO BARLA BROUGHT A ROUGH VERSION OF CLINT EASTWOOD'S *THE BRIDGES OF MADISON COUNTY* TO LENOX, MASSACHUSETTS, IN 1995, TO SCREEN THE FILM FOR ITS STAR, MERYL STREEP, THEY RECEIVED AN UNANTICIPATED REACTION.

Streep was shooting her next film, *Before and After*, in Lenox, so arrangements were made to screen *The Bridges of Madison County* for her and her assistant in a local theater during a break in her filming schedule.

"She was shooting in this little town, and it was just two people watching the movie in this thousand-person theater, while Joe, Marco, and I waited outside," Cox recalls. "When the screening was over, Meryl got up and left. I'm thinking, 'Wow, that was bad.' But she comes back and tells us she left because she was getting emotional. She looked me in the eye and said, 'How did you guys do this? We didn't shoot a lot of takes, so how did you do this?' We talked about how we edited the movie—getting the spontaneity right, the realness of people meeting for the first time, and being vulnerable. I'll never forget her initial reaction."

Today, Streep says she was surprised by Eastwood's editing choices. Only after seeing the movie, despite having worked with him on location for six weeks (the movie was shot in just forty-two days), could she begin to fully absorb Eastwood's instinctual style.

"I was really surprised by the candlelit dinner scene between my character [Francesca] and Clint's [Robert Kincaid]," Streep explains. "When we filmed it, I thought it was the strongest, most intimate part of the movie. It's where [the viewer] learns what these two people are going to do about their romance. That made me feel like it should be shown close in, intimate, but Clint chose to look at it from far away, as though [the end of their romance] was fait accompli. He mainly used the master [wide shot of the two characters]. Maybe he had this in his mind all along even as he let me go through the emotions of it [thinking the shot would be close up]. Or maybe he and Joel made the choice in editing. But it worked powerfully."

Cox explains that, although plenty of close-up coverage was available to them, he and Eastwood were of a like mind that "it made sense to show them from some distance,

because this is good-bye for them. So we played it wide and then came in a bit when we really wanted them to hit it. Clint says you can always do close-ups, but you can also tell emotion in certain cases without having to get close, because of the lines and body language. He wanted to show distance—that it was over between them."

In that sense, the close-up is a precious jewel to Eastwood—a tool used sparingly in *The Bridges of Madison County* and in most of his films.

"I liked the feeling of it as one [wide] piece and a little bit of distance in it," Eastwood says of the editing choice in *The Bridges of Madison County*. "An awful lot of

(Opposite) Eastwood and editor Joel Cox on the *J. Edgar* set. As he typically does, Cox began cutting the film while production was still under way. (Above) A lighthearted moment illustrates the ease of the Eastwood-Streep collaboration on *The Bridges of Madison County*.

films nowadays use close-ups to a great degree. You watch television, and it is ninety percent close-ups. They are easy to shoot and easy to cut in—the close-up and the long shot are the two easiest shots to make. But it is the connective tissue in between that ties it all together. How you use those shots smooths the picture out and creates the overall impression you want to leave. There are elements of the scene you want to punctuate with the close-up—a look here or there, but you don't want to overdo it. We shoot the close-up, but we don't always use them when it comes to editing."

Cox suggests there is also a psychological dimension to how Eastwood utilizes the close-up.

"The movie is playing on a forty-foot screen and Clint wants there to be air and space, for the film to breathe," Cox says. "To [put an actor's face on a big screen] requires a good reason. By that, I mean the audience is watching the story through the eyes of the people on screen. We don't believe in tipping to the audience something before the character sees it. It's like reading a book—you don't want to know what is on the next page until you turn it. Too many [close-ups] tend to telegraph something with the character, so we tend to only use them when we want to telegraph something, or to

show a reaction. You can often understand emotion better by seeing their entire body, rather than just the face."

Over the years, Eastwood and Cox have partnered to cut together everything from formulaic Westerns, action pictures, romances like *The Bridges of Madison County*, to a foreign-language picture, and greatly unorthodox character studies, in terms of their structure, such as *Bird* (1988) and *J. Edgar* (2011). Both of those are biopics on the surface, psychological dramas below the surface, told in nonlinear fashion, jumping around in time with flashbacks, and sometimes jumbling together character memories and historic perspectives. In both cases, what is going on in the central character's head is where everything else in the film flows from. But even Eastwood pictures with more standard structures tend to revolve around the emotional and/or psychological aspects of the story and the "feeling" Eastwood wants the viewer to leave with.

(Above) Eastwood as William Munny during a train sequence for *Unforgiven*, shot near Sonora, California. (Opposite) Adam Beach in a *Flags of Our Fathers* scene shot on a remote road in Lancaster, California.

Thus, a few years before *The Bridges of Madison County*, they made a cut that surprised screenwriter David Webb Peoples in the classic Western he wrote for Eastwood—*Unforgiven*. Peoples found himself initially disappointed to learn that Eastwood and Cox had chopped out the original final scene they shot from his screenplay. As documented elsewhere in this book, Eastwood shoots virtually the entire script unchanged in most circumstances, and *Unforgiven* was no exception. Eastwood filmed the closing scene, and everyone involved was pleased with how it turned out at the time. But then, in the editing suite, he matter-of-factly removed it.

The scene involved Eastwood's character, William Munny, returning home after violent events conclude in the town of Big Whiskey, meeting up with his son, and going to unearth the reward money hidden in his barn.

"The boy asks him, 'Did you?'" Peoples relates. "And Munny says, 'Steal it? No, I didn't steal it.' And the boy says, 'No, I mean, did you kill anybody?' And Munny looks at him and says no. He's lying, of course. It's kind of a rip-off of *The Godfather*, but it was a good scene, no question. In fact, I loved that scene."

And yet, Peoples adds, Eastwood "was entirely right to remove it. These movies are his music, and that musical note wasn't exactly in the right place."

Eastwood says he and Cox felt the nature of the story precluded it from having too happy of an ending, "where he goes back to his kids and they live happily ever after. That would take away from the story. I liked it where it ends, in a mystery [as Munny leaves Big Whiskey]."

Cox adds that "Clint shoots the original story because that's his bible, the backbone of everything—our map. But sometimes, he will say to me that 'I knew when I shot this scene it was going to come out, but you never know.'"

(Above) Clint Eastwood counsels actress Diane Venora during the making of *Bird*. Eastwood credits his late casting director, Phyllis Huffman, with finding Venora to play the key part of Chan Parker.

EMOTIONAL CUTS

As good an editor as Cox is (two Academy Award nominations and one Oscar, for *Unforgiven,* in 1993), his influence on Eastwood's work largely revolves around his personal understanding of Eastwood's creative psyche. That insight has been the foundation of possibly the most important single creative partnership in Eastwood's career, enabling the nuts-and-bolts work of assembling the elements Eastwood has created during production into emotionally compelling movies with stunning consistency.

"A lot of directors just direct off the [written] page," Cox says. "Clint has the whole film in his mind when he starts shooting it. So, yes, he shoots the script, but I can take a blueprint and see a whole house, while someone else might just see drawings. So he is envisioning things, and I think I have that ability also as an editor. I see a scene and get some great ideas—not always the same ideas Clint has, but ideas to give him something to see and comment on. Then we work together to create what he wants it to be, and we've been doing that for thirty-six years."

In other words, Cox comprehends Eastwood's general direction most of the time long before they sit down to discuss it in detail. Therefore, he cuts evolving Eastwood films while they are in production at near lightning speed, compared to typical industry standards—"normally, we are editing within three or four days after they start shooting the movie," he explains. He and co-editor Gary Roach are thus

(Opposite) *Bird.* (Above) Virtually all of *Bird* was dark and moody, with most exterior scenes, like this one, taking place at night.

(Above L) Costars Clint Eastwood and his son Kyle, then thirteen, during filming of *Honkytonk Man* (1982). Kyle says his father is "easygoing" when directing children, and recalls making the movie as "a great summer. My dad and I were pretty much roommates in a big hotel room and got to hang out together." (Above R) As with many Eastwood-directed films, final poster art by Bill Gold.

left alone to build a first-cut version of the movie before Eastwood ever gets into the editing process. They essentially use the same approach Cox was taught when he first started out—they create a 'bible' of notes on each take for each scene based on their viewing of dailies, and then use those notes to form their approach to sewing scenes together. By the time most Eastwood productions finish shooting, Cox and Roach normally have a first cut ready for their boss to review. Typically, they do all that work from their editorial offices on the Warner Bros. lot, and then they travel near to Eastwood's home in Carmel, California, to work with him directly on finalizing the movie.

The only exception to this approach over the years was *The Bridges of Madison County*. Cox says that was "the one and only Clint film that I did not edit while they were in production."

"Clint was shooting it while I was editing [James Keach's] *The Stars Fell on Henrietta* [a rare non-Eastwood-directed Malpaso production that used most of Eastwood's crew]," Cox recalls. "So it was a schedule thing that prevented me from editing [*The Bridges of Madison County*] until after he was done shooting. But it was unusual to have Clint around for the entire editing process. We would talk about things, he would leave, I would block things out, and then he'd come back in. We took about seven weeks and did it together, sort of like he was a co-editor, except he never told me what to do, and always worked off the version I created for him."

The other instructive thing about how Eastwood and Cox cut *The Bridges of Madison County* was Eastwood's willingness, as a director who also starred in the film, to cut his own character out of particular moments. Certainly *The Bridges of Madison County* is the most romantic film Eastwood has ever made, and he offered some of his most emotional acting in it. However, he deleted significant chunks of that acting from the picture, all based on an agenda to "make sure the movie was built around [Meryl Streep's character, Francesca]," according to Cox.

"I remember when we did the scene [where their characters have an argument] in the kitchen, Clint allowed himself enormous displays of vulnerability," Meryl Streep adds. "And then he took them out of the movie. He can be very dismissive of his own gifts as an actor—I remember him saying some scenes he had just shot were 'adequate,' so he could then move on. But these were scenes that many actors would put into their show reels. He didn't think about any of that—he [edits the movie] to make sure the characters are serving the story and nothing else."

Joe Hyams remembers Streep bringing this issue up as soon as she first viewed the film. "They shot scenes where his character was really vulnerable," he says. "Far more vulnerable than the scene in the rain [near the end of the picture, where his character, Kincaid, is seen crying in despair]. Meryl felt there were things Clint just didn't want to show. But she was very moved that day by what she saw."

Cox adds that *The Bridges of Madison County* was among the most complicated Eastwood movies he has ever edited because of the fact that it was such an intensely romantic drama, all about emotional moments, and devoid of the kind of action that made Eastwood famous.

"Cutting an emotional film is a lot harder," Cox says. "An action film, you cut anywhere and can make action happen. You can make it tenser by ringing the cuts or crescendoing the cuts and always making something out of it. But emotional films are all about moments. And in a film like that, the most important moment may not even include dialogue. It might be only a glance. In fact, Clint and I both believe that the emotion is often more important to show visually than verbally. Sometimes, we pick a shot that does not include the best line reading, and sometimes, Clint will say to forget the dialogue altogether. He tells me to put it together emotionally, and we can always fix the dialogue [in postproduction] if we have to. Sometimes, we even take a line out, because you have to stop for a moment and show a reaction of two people looking at each other. The trick is figuring out how long that moment should be, but for us, it all comes from the heart."

(Opposite) The Malpaso crew filming a dramatic scene from *Mystic River*. (Page 184) Eastwood's team shoots a restaurant scene from *Breezy* (1973), the first movie Eastwood ever directed without acting in it. (Page 185) Clint Eastwood consults with then producer Fritz Manes during production in Europe of *Firefox*.

ENDURING PARTNER

That Eastwood and Cox are normally on the same page is no surprise. They have been working together for almost forty years, and Cox is the most senior member of Eastwood's inner creative circle. From the time he was an assistant editor at Malpaso under the late Ferris Webster, to co-editor with Webster, to sole editor, to now co-editor with Gary Roach, Cox has put an important and distinctive stamp on Eastwood's paintings.

This partnership is not unusual at filmmaking's upper echelons—many great directors enjoy long-term relationships with editors. But it is among the industry's most enduring, making Cox a central ingredient in the Eastwood filmmaking brand.

"I allow Joel, and now Gary, a lot of input, especially if I'm still working [in production]," says Eastwood. "I can't come in and look at it every day, so they might as well keep editing. They assemble it as quickly as possible, and then I'll come in and pick it apart with them. Sometimes, I'll say, 'Hey, that's great,' and sometimes I'll say, 'That's great, but it's too long, or too short' or whatever. And so I become something of a critic with them, but they do a good job building it so we can [finalize it] together. I give them a lot of freedom and a chance to give me input. I don't want editing for them to be just a mechanical thing."

Indeed, some people have suggested the editing process is Eastwood's favorite part of filmmaking because that is where he fulfills his vision. He doesn't quite explain it that way, but it is true that Eastwood sees himself, and all good directors, as editors of sorts, and all good editors like Cox as filmmakers, rather than technicians. And so he enjoys the back-and-forth interaction—what Cox calls "the free form"—that he gets in the cutting room.

"A director has to be an editor himself, because he is trying to have [the film] edited in the way he visualized it," Eastwood explains. "But I don't want to do that with a technician. I want to do it with someone who isn't afraid to suggest cuts that might even exceed what my first vision of it was. And Joel is great at that. He's also a really good music editor. A lot of times, I give him a piece of music, and he'll come back and say, 'Let me show you something I did with it,' and usually it will be really good. I joke with him now that he's more of a music editor these days. But the point is, you need creative input like that from your editor, not just a guy who can use the machines."

Eastwood's level of trust in Cox is so high that Cox insists Eastwood only made him recut a single scene in a fundamentally different way from his initial approach in all their years together. Normally, changes are mutually agreed upon, and tend to flow from the original approach, driven totally by story and rhythm considerations.

"There is a flow to a film—each one has its own speed," Cox says. "Clint says there is no [editing] rule that can't be broken, if you have a good reason to do it, depending on the story. He's even willing, if he has a good reason, to cross that imaginary one hundred and eighty degree line with two people in a scene, in which they might be looking in the same direction, but I try to avoid that myself. I want the two people looking at each other. But Clint is so visual and knows so much about the tempo of a story and the emotion of a story—he has good reasons if he does something unorthodox."

Eastwood's reliance on his editors to implement his directive that a story needs to be cut based on emotional rhythms was dramatically illustrated when Cox and Roach edited *Letters from Iwo Jima* in 2006. The movie was shot in Japanese and subtitles would be added later, meaning the editors had an English-language script and their instincts to go on during the initial cutting phase.

"We had no interpreters until we were finished [with the initial cut]," Roach recalls. "I asked Clint if we would have an interpreter, and he told us that we would just figure it out. It wasn't nearly as bad as what I'd thought. When we were done, [interpreters] came in as we got ready to add subtitles, and we had only a couple of minor mistakes, missing a word here or there [four word fixes, to be exact, according to Cox]."

Cox adds that Eastwood kept telling them that understanding the dialogue was unimportant, as long as they could get the rhythm. "Clint didn't want us to be inhibited by interpreters, to have them influence the [narrative]," says Cox. "He told me, '[The Japanese] speak in sentences, just like anyone else,' and so he felt we'd sense the rhythm. He felt it would be easier to get the rhythm down and use our instincts, and then fix anything that was off, and he was right."

While Eastwood has certain theories, as illustrated in this chapter, about things like the close-up, finding a rhythm, pacing, documenting emotion, and so forth, he is quick to emphasize that he has no single cutting style. "There is no rule about it," he insists. "That's the fun thing about movies—every film is its own deal."

(Opposite) Gelled lights, shadows, and a generally dark palette enhance a romantic feel in *The Bridges of Madison County.* (Above, L–R) Clint Eastwood, producer Rob Lorenz, actor Bee Vang, script supervisor Mable McCrary, and behind her, cinematographer Tom Stern with the rest of the Malpaso crew, filming a scene from *Gran Torino.*

MOVING UP

Ferris Webster was a well-known, award-winning editor who had already enjoyed a long collaboration with famed director John Sturges by the time he became friendly with Clint Eastwood while editing Sturges's *Joe Kidd*, starring Eastwood, in 1972. He went on to edit, or co-edit with Joel Cox, fourteen films starring Eastwood, including eight directed by Eastwood, before retiring in 1982.

Webster was highly creative and innovative in pacing a movie, but was also a raconteur, whom Eastwood calls "a crazy old character and an editor from the old school."

"I liked the way he worked on *Joe Kidd*, and asked him to carry over to *High Plains Drifter* [1973]," the director says. "I remember, he would sit there with a cup of coffee and spill it on the Moviola [an old-style film editing machine], and a cigarette, with ashes running down on the film. But he was a real character and a tremendous editor in his day. He did a great job, but started handing over some of the work to Joel over time."

Indeed, by the time he added Cox as his assistant for *The Outlaw Josey Wales* in 1975, Webster was eager to let "the kid" dive right into the process and rapidly work his way up to co-editor.

"In *Josey Wales*, there is a campfire scene where they are dancing, and Clint wanted to cut the music down slightly," Cox recalls. "He left for a few min-

utes, and I made a cut in the song at the appropriate spot and put it all back together. Clint came back and ran it and said, 'Where did you make the cut?' I said, 'I made it right there.' And he was surprised I had the background to understand and edit music. Ferris would cut music in a lump cut because his expertise was picture, not music. We'd listen to a bad cut for months until the music guys came in and adjusted it. I had a background that Ferris didn't have in postproduction with sound effects editing, dialogue editing, looping, music, and other things. Those are things technique-wise I could add that Clint found valuable early on."

But the budding Eastwood-Cox relationship was one that Webster totally supported, according to Cox, even though most editors preferred a hierarchical chain of command back then.

"He came up in the old studio system, and in those days, the director never set foot in the editing room," Cox relates. "You would meet him in the projection room and get notes, and run back and do it. So Ferris didn't want to deal with the director in the editing room anyway, which was great for me, as an assistant, to learn things. So when Clint would come in to give a note, Ferris would tell me, 'OK, kid, you do it.' He didn't want anyone over his shoulder. So he would do things, and then I would often work with Clint to make changes."

Eventually, Webster himself suggested to Eastwood that Cox was ready for the co-editor role.

"By then, Joel was an all-around guy—he would assist, edit, and then drive Ferris home or to lunch and back again," Eastwood remembers. "Ferris knew he was doing more than just an assistant's responsibilities, and so he asked me to put him on as co-editor."

As mentioned earlier, Cox emphasizes how Eastwood taught him to have confidence in his "first instincts" when cutting films. This isn't merely a reflection of Eastwood's personality, Cox suggests. Decades of conversations with Eastwood have convinced him that the philosophy comes from Eastwood's ongoing study of filmmaking as a discipline.

"He's studied the great directors, and they felt it was important to not play with a film very long [in editing]," Cox says. "The longer you play with it, it's the worst thing for emotional films. When you play with a scene too long, it starts to lag and slow down, and then you worry about needing to tighten it up. And when you do that, the magic you had at the beginning begins to go away, but you don't realize it, because you have been watching it so many times. Clint doesn't want to do that. He only watches a film three or four times in its fullness [during editing]. He tells me he wants to keep a fresh approach, which he can't do if he's watching the film every day."

Eastwood and Cox promoted Cox's son-in-law, Gary Roach, from assistant editor to co-editor, as the pair headed into cutting *Letters from Iwo Jima* (2006). Roach first joined as an apprentice in the middle of Malpaso's transition from cutting on a traditional flatbed film-editing device, where

pieces of film were literally cut and pasted together, to computerized nonlinear editing on the Avid editing platform, which eventually became dominant in the industry.

As Roach joined the team, Malpaso was making *Absolute Power* (1997), its first feature film cut digitally. By that time, a large swath of the feature film industry had already transitioned to the digital cutting platform, and today it is nearly uniform throughout the movie world. Typically, however, Eastwood was in no particular rush to make the switch, since his usual cutting process had worked fine for decades. However, by the late 1990s, the technology had simply proven itself to be superior in terms of speed, flexibility, and creativity, compared to the old flatbed method. So Eastwood green-lighted the switch, and soon fell in love with yet another way to be simultaneously fast and efficient.

"Maybe we were a little resistant at first—people like to have their hands on film and all that," Eastwood says. "But I came to like the Avid a lot, because I like to work fast and I like to print first impressions. On the Avid, you can [easily] get a first impression. You can see shots and make changes right away. You don't have to walk away for thirty minutes [while they cut and splice film], and then wonder why you made that change. In the old days, it was a much more arduous thing, and then if you didn't like it, you would have to take time to put it back the other way. On a [digital] editing machine, you can do it in seconds, and change it back in seconds and keep [every version] available to you."

Therefore, Malpaso added assistant Tony Bozanich as an Avid expert on *Absolute Power*, while retaining Cox's longtime assistant, Michael Cipriano, for traditional film assembly for dailies viewing. Thus, Cox had an opportunity to train Roach in both traditional film editing and digital editing when he came aboard. After that, for years, Cox, Cipriano, and Roach were the primary Malpaso editing crew, until Roach moved up after Cipriano departed once Malpaso converted to digital dailies around the time of *Changeling* (2008), finally eliminating film assembly entirely from its process.

"Clint had been suggesting for a couple of shows that I [start editing material directly]," Roach recalls. "But that was difficult to do because I was the only Avid assistant, and Joel was comfortable with things working that way. But, finally, *Letters from Iwo Jima* came along and there were two movies [because it was done back-to-back with *Flags of Our Fathers*], and so I got the opportunity. Joel felt I could do it and, as long as I could defend my choices to he and Clint, he was fine with making me co-editor. It's just another instance of Clint giving someone an opportunity in this business—I came in as Joel's son-in-law, but wouldn't be here if I hadn't learned to do the job."

"Clint gave me my break, and then he wanted to give Gary a break, and it seemed right," Cox adds. "It was valuable as an assistant for him to learn both film and the Avid, and the way we do things."

The Cox-Roach partnership is now so seamless that there is essentially no pattern to how they divide up sequences—it all depends on how production is going and who is available to do what at any given moment. Deep, complex, often nonlinear storytelling has become routine for them. The director claims to have no fear of experimenting in the cutting room. In fact, he even employs Cox's help in the casting process periodically, intercutting actors reading the same part, so that Eastwood can directly compare them.

"Joel kind of knows what I'm thinking a lot of the time," Eastwood says, smiling. "He's done OK, hasn't he?"

(Opposite, Top L) Clint Eastwood and actor Billy Curtis wait to film a scene from *High Plains Drifter*, and (R) a classic bar scene from that film. (Bottom L) Eastwood with the late Chris Penn as the Josh LaHood character (*Pale Rider*).

(Above L) The veteran Eastwood shares some laughs with rookie actor Bee Vang during the making of *Gran Torino*. (Top R) Editor Joel Cox received a Lifetime Achievement Award from his editing peers in 2012. Eastwood personally presented it. (Bottom R) Eastwood and costar Gene Hackman during filming of *Absolute Power*—the second Eastwood film that Hackman starred in.

(Page 190) Practical explosions and other effects were commonplace during the making of both Iwo Jima films, including this scene depicting an American air raid in *Letters from Iwo Jima*. (Page 191) Depression-era low light covers Eastwood as he performs a song in a cheap bar in *Honkytonk Man*.

"I LIKE A QUIET SCORE TO RIDE ALONG UNDER THE PICTURE,
INSTEAD OF HAVING IT RIDE OVER THE PICTURE WITH A LOT OF BOMBASTIC DRAMA."

CLINT EASTWOOD, 2011

CHAPTER NINE
WHAT MOOD SOUNDS LIKE

CLINT EASTWOOD FREQUENTLY HUMS TO HIMSELF ON SET—SIMPLE LITTLE MELODIES THAT POP INTO HIS HEAD WHILE HE'S SHOOTING MOVIES. FREQUENTLY, PIANOS ARE PLACED INTO HIS HOTEL ROOMS WHEN HE TRAVELS, AND BACK AT HIS WARNER BROS. BUNGALOW, HE CAN OFTEN BE HEARD GENTLY STROKING THE KEYS OF HIS OWN PIANO IN HIS BARELY LIT INNER SANCTUM.

Although he only started solely composing music for his films in recent years, Eastwood has always been involved in the process to one degree or another, frequently writing tunes or the foundation of tunes that wind up in his movies, and pointing his collaborators to sources and influences of music that interest him for particular projects. His familiarity with, and enjoyment of, the musical process is understandable, considering his background and love of jazz, and the advantage he has had working over the decades with some of the industry's leading composers, ranging from the legendary Ennio Morricone (who composed the Sergio Leone spaghetti Western music), to Lalo Schifrin (who wrote the famous *Mission: Impossible* theme), Jerry Fielding, and several others. Most notable, though, has been his intimate working relationship with Lennie Niehaus for almost thirty years, and more recently, with his oldest son, Kyle Eastwood.

Eastwood's involvement in the music process emanates from this background and his native interests, but also out of his determination to put, as he calls it, "my own concept" into every aspect of his movies—to set mood in a particular way.

"I grew up with Max Steiner and Franz Waxman on films like *Gone With the Wind* and *Spellbound* [respectively]," Eastwood says. "I always admired them. But in those days, they wouldn't be working much with the director because movies weren't always made just by the director—other people would edit them and producers would put them together, hiring the composer to come in and do his own interpretation. But nowadays, a director usually wants his own concept on it, and I don't want the music to fight my concept. I got lucky to have some great composers, but I also did some of it on my own because I like the idea that less is best. I like a quiet score to ride along under the picture, instead of having it ride over the picture with a lot of bombastic drama. I like to tell the drama separately, and not have the music be the drama. Maybe it can enhance drama, or be a component of it, but I don't

(Opposite) Clint Eastwood directing Forest Whitaker in *Bird*. (Above) Eastwood on set with camera operator Jack Green and his son and costar Kyle Eastwood (*Honkytonk Man*).

want it to drive the drama. With that philosophy in mind, I just started doing my own scores. You want the music to enhance the film, and the melodic line of the theme to be something you feel matches the picture."

Since *Mystic River* in 2003, Eastwood has served as sole or co-composer of original music on several films. But long before that, he was writing individual songs in films where Niehaus handled the full score, including the elegant guitar solo that serves as the main theme in *Unforgiven*—a song dubbed "Claudia's Theme."

According to Eastwood, "Claudia's Theme" is a tune he thought up while traveling to the Alberta, Canada, location to shoot the picture.

"I told Lennie I had this theme, and I wanted [late classical guitarist] Laurindo Almeida to play it," Eastwood relates. "I said it had to be Laurindo, because he had a certain sound. We went to the recording session, and Laurindo came out and started putting a lot into it. I told him, no, just pretend you don't know how to play guitar that well—make it really simple, but with that great tone he knew how to manufacture."

Niehaus, of course, will be remembered as Eastwood's closest long-term musical partner. An accomplished jazz musician, recording artist, and film composer, Niehaus first became friendly with Eastwood in the army. Years later, he found himself doing orchestrating work for the late Jerry Fielding, around the time that Fielding was composing music for Eastwood in the late 1970s.

"I would go into a session, and suddenly, I saw this guy I remembered from the army," Eastwood relates. "I said, 'Hey Lennie,' and we started shooting the breeze."

Fielding passed away suddenly, when he was only fifty-eight years old, around the time Eastwood was heading into *Tightrope* (1984). Needing help quickly, Eastwood thought of his old army pal. Niehaus remembers that Fielding was a brilliant, experimental composer, but "he would take a long time to write a two-minute cue, and was always under the wire. I think Clint liked that I could write music [fast] when I needed to."

And so, "Clint called suddenly and asked if I could help on *Tightrope*." The director had Niehaus fly immediately to New Orleans, walked around Bourbon Street with him, and asked him to flavor the *Tightrope* score with the jazz-style music swirling around them.

(Above) Directing young actors during the opening shot of *Bird*—a long tracking shot of a very young Charlie Parker riding a pony home that is reminiscent of the famous opening tracking shots in many of Eastwood's Westerns. (Opposite) Filming *Pale Rider* with actor Michael Moriarty in the wide expanse of the Sawtooth National Recreation Area in Idaho.

"He told me it was a 'little' movie—he called them all 'little' movies back then," Niehaus says. "He said it took place in New Orleans and he needed jazz and Dixieland, and some mystery music also. He asked me if I'd mind writing some ditties for it. I remember staying in the hotel and having no scoring paper with me, but I got right to writing, putting lines on blank paper. I wrote a tune in the style of an old soprano saxophone player, New Orleans style, and then some stripping music for the scene with the stripper. I ended up staying up all night and wrote six tunes for him—we recorded all six the next day."

And so it went for the next quarter century between Niehaus and Eastwood. In addition to his groundbreaking work on *Bird*, Niehaus produced a massive volume of work directly built out of Eastwood's story themes, impulses, and instincts. For *Pale Rider*, Niehaus says he built the score out of "adjectives" that Eastwood threw at him. Since Eastwood's character in the movie poses as a preacher and wears a collar, Eastwood told him he wanted a "low growl theme."

"I knew of a sixteenth-century composer named [Giovanni Pierluigi da Palestrina], who wrote music in intervals of fifths," Niehaus explains. "So I based the low part of the score on that. I got three trombones—a couple tenor trombones and a bass trombone—and a tuba for the 'low growl.' I played two bars for Clint, and he said, 'That sounds fine.' The relationship in those days was pretty loose in terms of how we put it all together."

(Above L) Eastwood discusses a shot with actress Sydney Penny, who played the character Megan Wheeler, during the making of *Pale Rider*. (Above R) Eastwood leads his camera team into the mountains to shoot sequences for *Pale Rider*. On one such expedition, he separated his shoulder.

For *White Hunter, Black Heart*, however, the director told Niehaus that he didn't think the movie really needed much music, so he asked Niehaus for a strategy. Since the piece takes place in the heart of Africa, Niehaus responded to the challenge by writing a melodic alto flute piece over ethnic percussion. Eastwood asked him to record a sample.

"Instead, I wrote for all the places in the movie I thought he would need a [musical] cue," Niehaus says. "He liked what I did, and we started recording it all at seven the next evening. At ten P.M., we were supposed to stop or go into overtime. Clint said to keep going, so we went to midnight, which is golden time [double overtime for studio musicians], and he said keep going. We went to three in the morning and got the entire score done for that movie."

Starting in 2003, Kyle Eastwood and his colleague, Michael Stevens, began composing soundtrack pieces for movies such as *Mystic River*, *Million Dollar Baby*, and *Flags of Our Fathers*, before Eastwood handed full musical chores to them for *Letters from Iwo Jima*. Kyle Eastwood is a professional bass player, recording artist, and actor. He had periodically participated in his dad's movie music when feasible—writing a song as far back as *The Rookie* (1990) and frequently doing cameos as a musician in the films.

For *Letters from Iwo Jima*, Clint Eastwood asked Kyle to handle the soundtrack after Kyle and Michael Stevens had done some orchestrating work on the theme Clint had written for *Flags of Our Fathers*. Father showed son the script for the second *Iwo Jima* movie during that period, with advice for Kyle to inspire himself with musical elements out of an old Japanese school song that was broadcast from the mainland during the Battle of Iwo Jima to support Japanese troops—a choir song called "Our Proud Island, Iwo Jima," an original version of which, at one point, is heard over radios in the movie.

"I told Kyle to dissect it and take it apart, take out notes, and do whatever he wanted with it—to play with it a bit," Eastwood explains.

"That gave us some ideas for different things," Kyle Eastwood adds. "We consciously did not want to make the soundtrack too ethnic sounding, but we had a few cues where we added Japanese instruments in, and [pieces of] Japanese military music, and we added that to trumpets, pianos, and that kind of instrumentation. We tried to apply the Asian feel more from the melodies and intervals of the music than by using too many Japanese instruments."

In 2008 and again in 2009, Kyle Eastwood took the composer reins for *Gran Torino* and *Invictus*, respectively. *Gran Torino* was particularly notable for the haunting and evocative "Gran Torino Theme," composed by Clint Eastwood and sung by recording artist Jamie Cullum, and briefly, in a raspy voice by Eastwood himself.

"That was initially an idea my father had on the piano," Kyle explains. "We recorded it and then messed around with it to incorporate it into the movie as one of the themes. Michael Stevens and I worked it into song form, wrote a melody and did a bridge for it. Then we decided to have someone write lyrics, and I had worked with Jamie Cullum before, so we took the script to him and asked him to come up with some lyrics. Jamie wrote lyrics and changed a few little melody things, so we all wrote the song together."

(Opposite) Keith David's Buster Franklin character is mobbed in *Bird*. (Top) Actors Samuel E. Wright and Jason Bernard (L–R) kid around with Forest Whitaker on set, and (Bottom R) actress Diane Venora in the stylized light seen throughout *Bird*. (Bottom L) The backlot at Warner Bros. transformed into New York City.

SNAPPY SOUNDS

What audiences hear—or sometimes, don't hear—at an Eastwood movie, of course, is part of the director's larger plan to set mood for his stories, and that plan goes far beyond the musical score. His longtime partners when it comes to designing and executing sound effects—co-supervising sound editors Alan Murray and Bub Asman—say, however, that his philosophy with sound effects is no different than it is with music, editing, or other disciplines. "It can be understated and reserved, so as not to compete with a delicate story, and [only] loud and rough to bring home a point," Murray explains.

It's an art form Eastwood is particularly adept at, according to his colleagues. In fact, producer Rob Lorenz says Eastwood has "a particular ear for the sounds in his films, much as he has a particular eye for visuals." This makes sound effects, dialogue choices, and the overall audio mood of his movies just as important as the musical score to Eastwood.

They always assumed Cullum would sing it in the movie, which he did, but Michael Stevens mentioned the idea of having Eastwood's character, Walt Kowalski, sing it, as well. They recorded Eastwood (as Kowalski) singing the entire song—"speak-singing as Walt, really," Kyle adds. "We decided it would be best to have that be the last tag of the song, to start with Walt and then segue into Jamie for the credits."

"We were recording Jamie doing it one night, and [Michael Stevens] said to me, 'Why don't you do it also?'" Clint remembers. "I said, 'OK, I'll do it as my character.' That's the way I've always sung in movies, even going back to *Paint Your Wagon* [1969]. I was singing it like the guy in the movie. We had a few laughs over it, but Kyle and Michael did some good things with it."

Since *Gran Torino*, Kyle has been busy with his music performing career, so his father has taken to largely writing his own music, and bringing in Niehaus or others to arrange or conduct whenever necessary. But regardless of whether Eastwood is writing music solo or collaborating, those who have worked closely with him insist, as his son suggests, that "he has a really good ear," and as Niehaus suggests, "he's a natural tune writer."

And Eastwood's music philosophy is clearly aligned with his larger filmmaking philosophy, according to his son.

"He shies away from the big sweeping orchestral scores certainly," Kyle says. "He prefers 'sensitive' and 'sparse.'"

(Above L and R) Filming the climactic scene in *Gran Torino* on a street in Michigan—the scene in which Eastwood's character, Walt Kowalski, confronts gang members. (Top L) Eastwood works with Jessica Walter during *Play Misty for Me*. Walter was the first of many prominent leading ladies in Eastwood's films. (Bottom L) Clint Eastwood shares a moment with Angelina Jolie, star of *Changeling*. (Opposite) Eastwood's character finally performs at the Grand Ole Opry near the end of *Honkytonk Man*, which costarred his son Kyle Eastwood (R).

(Opposite) Eastwood counsels actress Diane Venora during the making of *Bird*. (Above) Clint Eastwood, with decades of firearm experience, instructs cast members on the rifle technique he prefers, during filming of *Letters from Iwo Jima*.

"His style when it comes to sound, like a lot of things, is grittier, more natural sound," says Lorenz. "He doesn't want it cleaned up, or for the audience to necessarily hear every word. He actually prefers that some things get lost, and that the audience work a little bit to pick out what is important to them about the story. He wants to make it an experience where you have to figure it out for yourself, rather than spoon feeding it to you."

One day in late August 2011, Eastwood sat on a couch at a sound mixing stage at Warner Bros. rolling through the sound mix for *J. Edgar* with Murray, Asman, and their colleagues. Eastwood briefly debated with them whether to bring up or down the volume of the audience members in a 1930s movie theater scene, as they boo the sight of J. Edgar Hoover on their movie screen, interrupting their enjoyment of James Cagney's *The Public Enemy*. Murray offered to "thin out" the booing a little, so there wouldn't be too much noise over the recorded sound of Hoover (Leonardo DiCaprio) talking on a newsreel.

"No, it's OK—real snappy," Eastwood replied. "A little rudeness is OK. It sounds fine."

That was about as complicated as the mixing process got that day. The Malpaso team knocked out all changes in reel three, out of seven, in mere hours, and launched into reel four before the day ended. After the session wrapped, Murray and Asman took a break to reminisce about their decades running Eastwood's sound department.

"Remember how *Pale Rider* opens up with the gang of horses galloping through the valley toward the mining town? We went to a recording location around Sand Canyon, California, with a group of cowboys and their horses. I strapped a Nagra [portable audio recorder] on my back, got on a horse behind a cowboy, and held on around his waist as eight horses galloped back and forth," Murray recalls. "I'm holding onto the cowboy with one hand and holding a microphone down close to the horse's legs so we could get that sound of a terrifying stampede.

"We did crazy things like that over the years. I'll never forget for one of the *Dirty Harry* car chases, we set up a recording session with a police car going down a desert road about a hundred miles per hour. I was in the trunk of that car with a microphone aimed at the tailpipe. In those days, you physically put yourself into situations to record sound like that. Today, of course, we have wireless mics, and wouldn't have to do it that way, but still, Clint's philosophy is to do things as real as possible."

Murray and Asman have been integral to creating the diverse range of sounds heard in Eastwood films since they joined Malpaso when Eastwood was starring in Don Siegel's *Escape from Alcatraz* (1979). Since then, they have been nominated for sound editing Academy Awards on three Eastwood films, as well as for others, and won in 2006 for *Letters from Iwo Jima* (they were also nominated for *Flags of Our Fathers* that same year). They recall Eastwood's keen interest in sound from that first project together. One of the unique things the sound team did was to supply Jerry Fielding, the film's composer, with a specific library of ambient sound effects recorded on Alcatraz Island. It included various sounds of the prison's actual jail doors, prison alarms, foghorns, even seagull cries that were recorded in great detail by Eastwood's then production mixer, Bert Hallberg, who has since passed away.

"Because Alcatraz Island was such a harsh environment, Clint and Jerry both thought it would be a unique idea to incorporate those natural sounds into the film's musical score," Murray relates. "Jerry then took those sound elements and sonically altered them through pitch shifting and synthesizing to make musical notes and refrains that were added to his compositions."

(Above L) Longtime stunt chief Buddy Van Horn on the set of *Letters from Iwo Jima*, where he supervised action sequences, including this training scene (Above R), shot in the California desert.

"But given the nature of the movie, Clint, as the star, had to do a lot of the sound effects himself. His actual digging and scraping through the concrete prison wall with a sharpened spoon were all used, thanks to [Hallberg's] dynamic production sound, and then topped with sound effects and Foley [separately recorded footsteps and other sounds] for the final result."

An important constant in Eastwood sound design is an intense devotion to realism. Over the years, Murray and Asman have evolved into, among other things, research wizards. After all, period movies such as *Changeling*, *Flags of Our Fathers*, and *J. Edgar*, among others, bring with them the requirement of period sounds.

For example, they located collectors with World War II–era Mustang and Corsair airplanes to get sound of those planes into both Iwo Jima movies, and scoured the Internet to find two 1920s-era phone ringer boxes for the ringing phone exchange sounds in certain scenes of *Changeling*. For that film, they also found a cable car museum with vintage cable cars to provide the film's trolley car noises.

In *J. Edgar*, the sound of 1920s-era Pennsylvania Avenue traffic outside of J. Edgar Hoover's office presented another challenge. The two men say their research led them to a video transfer of an antique 1915 newsreel shot around Union and Market Streets in San Francisco.

"We were amazed by the chaotic traffic of horse-drawn carriages, wagons, and early Model Ts winding in and out of traffic lanes," Murray explains. "We decided that early Pennsylvania Avenue must have had the same cacophony of sounds. We then [located] authentic early Model Ts and drivers, and set up a recording session on the back lot at Warner Bros. Two recordists captured sound from a fourth-story window, while various period cars drove up and down the street. Period horns, horse traffic, and authentic hand-cranked fire and police sirens were also recorded and added to the final mix."

(Above) Prepping to shoot a vintage airplane visual effects plate for *J. Edgar*. The sequence involving Hoover on a flight to New Orleans was later cut from the film by Eastwood and editor Joel Cox.

(Below L and R) Eastwood directs scenes in the crime records and crime lab rooms featured in *J. Edgar*. (Opposite) Characters in the film examine pieces of the ladder allegedly built by Lindbergh baby abductor Bruno Hauptmann—an exact replica of the real one, according to prop master Mike Sexton.

 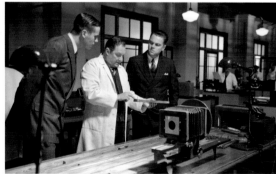

Both Iwo Jima films required, at times, extraordinary effort to make sure the sounds of guns, artillery, and military vehicles were accurate to the period. With cooperation from the Marine Corps, all period weapons—both American and Japanese guns—were digitally recorded for the show, and sessions were set up at the 29 Palms Marine Base in California to record the sounds of tanks and howitzers.

"When we did the sound mix for *Letters*, we had actors yelling instructions to each other, and we realized that, in reality, you would never hear every word they are saying because there are hundreds of machine guns going off—the sound of war," Murray says. "So Clint talked to us and we agreed that you shouldn't hear all dialogue during battle scenes—we just had to make sure the viewer got the gist of what they were saying."

The two films offered a ream of other challenges, as well. The battle scenes were continually evolving because significant portions were created with digital visual effects, so they found themselves constantly updating and evolving their sound design for those battles.

They also had to deal with the issue of Japanese dialogue in *Letters from Iwo Jima*, and the fact that picture changes would necessitate Japanese dialogue fixes to retain accuracy. "We had to have a very close alliance with [the film's star and dialogue advisor, Ken Watanabe] and his translators to come up with a way to check

(Opposite) Eastwood's Walt Kowalski in *Gran Torino*. (Above) Country music legend Marty Robbins (L) accompanies Clint Eastwood's character in a cameo role as Eastwood sings in *Honkytonk Man*. The movie features Robbins's last recorded performance—he passed away shortly before the movie's release.

with them every single time there was a picture change," Asman says. "That was one long, difficult project," he adds, referring to both Iwo Jima movies combined.

Likewise, foreign-language dialogue played an important role in *Gran Torino*'s examination of the ethnic Hmong people. The project required Murray and Asman to record group dialogue of Hmong language conversations for background use. This is called "Walla group ADR," which refers to recording entire conversations and pieces of conversations to add a murmur effect in the background for realism. In addition to the several Hmong extras whom the production used in the movie, dozens more were bused down to Warner Bros. from Bakersfield to allow the audio crew to record them for background tracks, according to Asman.

Editing and mixing sound that is rough, raw, or complicated in one way or another is nothing new for the two men. For years, production sound has been retained in Eastwood films that is less than ideal, largely because Eastwood is more concerned with the actors' performance than whether he gets a pristine recording. *A Perfect World* (1993), for instance, was shot in Texas in locations that presented far more ambient noise than was ideal.

"There was lots of wind and tons of cicada bugs in the production tracks," Murray recalls. "We would try to just make sure their sound matched from shot to shot, or

we would search through outtakes and try to fill in around the dialogue so that you feel like the bugs were part of the natural environment, and you don't hear them coming out of the center speaker with dialogue. If the editor cut from a close-up to a two shot, the pitch of the cicadas would change through the take, so our dialogue editors would try to extend dialogue from one angle to another, so that the pitch was not choppy or irregular sounding. That was just a lot of extra work that, in those days, was done with razor blades and splicers, and by searching through miles of audio tape and [magnetic audio] tracks."

And that wasn't necessarily even the biggest challenge of *A Perfect World*'s audio track. The film's star, Kevin Costner, declined to come in and perform automated dialogue replacement (ADR) work for lines that were not clear from production tracks, and as a result, Murray and Asman had to work around the problem.

"We were told no ADR was coming from Costner, so we looked through outtakes, and separate scenes to manufacture synch dialogue," Murray explains. "There were some scenes shot with a Steadicam, where the camera crew followed Costner and the boy [T.J. Lowther] on a boardwalk in front of the general store, and you would hear the crew's footsteps over the two actors' voices. In those instances, we just cut out as many footsteps as we could around the dialogue, so it sounded like only two people walking and talking. We filtered out crew footsteps during the dialogue using sound processors on the dubbing stage."

These audio challenges on *A Perfect World* were not well advertised at the time. But looking back on it years later, David Valdes, the producer of the film, suggests that "Al Murray should have won an Oscar for that movie. I know he has won one since, but he definitely deserved one for the work his guys did on that movie."

(Below L) Eastwood with actors Ahney Her (L) and Bee Vang in native Hmong costumes, and (Below R) with actors during *Gran Torino*.

BIRD MUSIC

The strategy, creative approach, and technical proficiency with which Clint Eastwood's team reproduced the musical stylings of legendary saxophone player Charlie Parker (nicknamed "Bird") by, among other things, weaving Parker's actual alto sax into the soundtrack of *Bird*, has been much analyzed in the music community since the movie was released in 1988. That approach was suggested by Eastwood, designed by Niehaus, and executed by Niehaus, music editor Donald Harris, scoring mixer Robert Fernandez, and technicians at Chace Audio, an audio postproduction facility in Burbank. It involved peeling Parker's sax out of vintage live recordings provided to the production by his widow, Chan Parker, and a few other sources, and sewing it into performances of studio musicians mimicking Parker's original backup bands. While the work was innovative and state of the art for the era, some Parker aficionados in the jazz community questioned why full and original Parker recordings were not used.

There are multiple answers to this question. Eastwood says he needed Parker's original sound from live recordings rather than better-quality studio recordings because he wanted extended, rare, and highly innovative solos from Parker in club settings—material that only existed on infor-

mal live recordings. For this, Eastwood turned primarily to Chan Parker's privately recorded tapes, and a few other similar sources. Chan Parker's material, however, was not professionally recorded, and largely consisted of Parker's lengthy saxophone solos only. The rest of his band was rarely recorded, and never professionally.

"She hung microphones on Charlie's microphones, to get the full, big sound of his solo, but the trouble was, she turned the thing off when he wasn't playing to save time on the recording tape," Eastwood explains. "So we had his solos, but we didn't have the entire tune in most cases."

Other sources were hotly pursued, of course. Among them were the so-called Benedetti tapes—amateur recordings of Parker made at small clubs in the 1940s by a rabid fan named Dean Benedetti. Benedetti's tapes had been considered lost for years after his death, but later surfaced in the possession of his brother, who tried unsuccessfully to sell them. Eastwood's then producer, David Valdes, remembers Eastwood asking him to track them down as *Bird* was ramping up. After weeks scouring the globe, they traced them to a family member's house that, ironically, was just down the street from their Warner Bros. offices in Burbank.

"I learned they lived a mile away, and when I told Clint, he immediately said 'Come on, let's go,'" Valdes recalls. "We pulled up to a little, rickety house, and Clint jumped out before the vehicle even fully stopped and quickly rang the doorbell. An elderly woman opened the door, and was shocked that Clint Eastwood was standing at her front door. She invited us in, introduced us to her husband, and Clint asked about the recordings. They were incredibly trusting, and let us take the entire box to see if we could do anything with them. I remember Clint hugging that box on the ride back to the studio. He was excited, I was excited—we felt that we had discovered a treasure."

The acetate recordings and tapes they found in that box, however, were recorded much like Chan Parker's tapes—focusing on Charlie Parker's solos only. To make matters worse, they had suffered severe water damage in a flood years earlier, and were brittle. Eastwood's team quickly determined that they were unusable for a motion picture, and he declined to buy them. (A few years later, Dean Benedetti's brother, Rick, sold the tapes to a small jazz label called Mosaic Records, and a three-year project was undertaken to restore them and publish them as a limited edition of rare live Parker performances.)

Still, Eastwood was determined to infuse the movie with Parker's original, unmatchable sound. He asked Niehaus if he could rebuild the Chan Parker

recordings piece by piece, by combining original Parker solos with modern artists mimicking his band. "We decided to give it a try, figuring that if we couldn't, we could still go with a sound-alike later," Eastwood says. "But Lennie Niehaus made it work."

Niehaus took the recordings to Chace Audio to isolate Parker's saxophone, hired musicians to replicate the original bands in concert with the Parker saxophone, and had his music editors put it all together.

This laborious work over many months happened before the digital era, so it was "somewhat pioneering at the time," as Eastwood puts it. Niehaus recalls spending weeks with a recording engineer, telling him when to press which button to remove which part of the track without, as much as possible, diluting the power of Parker's horn.

"They had machines that could isolate the piano, the bass, and the drums, so we could take out the highs and lows on the recording," Niehaus recalls. "But it wasn't perfect—when Max Roach was doing the drumming, he used to play what we called 'bombs,' with loud, hissing cymbals. The more they pressed the buttons to remove that, the more they were losing Bird's beautiful sound. So where it was impossible to remove the 'bombs,' I would

write down [what they were playing] rhythmically, and get a new musician to play an exact cover of that to remove what was leaking in from the original track. So we'd make Max's drum softer, and then I'd have someone play a fill over that. It was easy to take out the bass because it is on the low end of the register—lower than the alto sax—and the piano was sometimes real high. But it was real labor to get the drum right."

All this work made *Bird* a highlight of Niehaus's career. Given how important the subject matter and the music were to Eastwood and to Niehaus, himself an accomplished alto sax player, it was effort fondly and proudly recalled many years later.

"*Bird* was influential to how I play the saxophone myself, and I really wanted to do the best we possibly could," Niehaus says. "It was a lot of work, a big challenge, but satisfying."

(Opposite L) Iconic image of Forest Whitaker emulating Charlie Parker in *Bird*. Music supervisor Lennie Niehaus taught Whitaker to play the saxophone and generally imitate Parker's style. (Opposite R) Eastwood discusses with actress Diane Venora the horseback serenade scene from *Bird*, which was filmed on the Warner Bros. back lot.

(Below L) Whitaker as Parker in a jazz club scene with Samuel E. Wright as Dizzy Gillespie. (Below Top R) Eastwood on set with bass player (name unknown). (Below Bottom R) Eastwood confers with composer, collaborator, and friend Lennie Niehaus during the making of *Bird*—a film on which Niehaus made a central contribution.

(Page 208) Extras play rabid rugby fans during the filming of *Invictus*. Filling a stadium with extras was cost prohibitive, so Eastwood had visual effects supervisor Michael Owens digitally replicate the actors to create a full stadium and a believable crowd. (Page 209) Stunt man George Orrison, doubling for Eastwood, navigates a motorcycle stunt in *The Gauntlet*.

"[CLINT] SWORE HE WOULD NEVER,
EVER DO A VISUAL EFFECTS FILM AGAIN IN HIS LIFE."

JACK GREEN, CAMERA OPERATOR,
ON EASTWOOD'S REACTION TO MAKING FIREFOX, *2011*

CHAPTER TEN
JOINING THE REVOLUTION

THE THUNDERING, ACADEMY AWARD–NOMINATED TSUNAMI SEQUENCE THAT OPENS 2010'S *HERE-AFTER* WOULD HAVE BEEN UNTHINKABLE IN A CLINT EASTWOOD MOVIE A FEW YEARS EARLIER. BUT BY THE TIME HE GOT AROUND TO MAKING *HEREAFTER*, EASTWOOD HAD CONFIDENCE HE COULD USE VISUAL EFFECTS MORE OVERTLY THAN IN THE PAST, AND THAT HIS VISUAL EFFECTS SUPERVISOR, MICHAEL OWENS, COULD DESIGN AND EXECUTE THE TSUNAMI SEQUENCE WITHOUT BOGGING DOWN EASTWOOD'S BRISK PRODUCTION PACE.

The sequence's very existence descended directly out of previous success weaving major visual effects into *Flags of Our Fathers* and *Letters from Iwo Jima* in 2006, *Changeling* in 2008, and *Invictus* in 2009. Rob Lorenz, Eastwood's producer, says that following *Flags of Our Fathers*, the director seemed to "loosen up and begin to appreciate modern visual effects."

"He began to trust them, and allow more of the burden to shift to visual effects to make realistic sequences, extend sets, fix problems, all those things," Lorenz adds. "I don't think he would have taken on *Hereafter* [years earlier] because he might not have been confident in pulling off [the tsunami] so easily. But he did so well on other films working with Michael Owens, and likes and trusts him to execute these things."

Indeed, Eastwood now declares that digital effects "are a great tool—we can do wonderful things with them. As a director, it's an excellent way to put together all the elements you need effectively. Now that the technology has improved, and it's become easier to make it work, I enjoy using them."

Eastwood's enthusiasm is a far cry from his reaction the first time he dipped his toe into such technical waters. In fact, those who worked closely with him on *Firefox* in 1982 have the same basic memory of Eastwood's reaction to the visual effects process on that project, which happened at the dawn of the effects genre's movement into the modern era, on the heels of *Star Wars* a few years earlier, but long before the current digital revolution.

That reaction at the time, according to Jack Green, who was a camera operator on *Firefox*, was not positive. "He swore he would never, ever do a visual effects film again in his life," Green recalls. "It was a tough shoot for a lot of reasons."

(Above) Filming a big action scene with explosions and other practical effects (*Firefox*). (Opposite) A visual effects shot from *Flags of Our Fathers* illustrates how completely Eastwood embraced the use of computer-animated imagery as a tool by this stage in his career. Only the actor and parts of the horizon are real in this shot.

(Opposite) Replica of the fictional MiG-31 Firefox jet at the center of *Firefox*. Models and replicas were used for the grounded plane, and visual effects legend John Dykstra created dogfight sequences. (Above L) Actors left to right: James Garner, Courtney Vance, Tommy Lee Jones, Donald Sutherland, and Loren Dean on location at Kennedy Space Center during *Space Cowboys*. (Above R) Clint Eastwood works inside the Space Shuttle cockpit—a set designed to be rocked using electronically controlled hydraulics to mimic motion of the spacecraft.

"We were in a foreign country [Austria] with crew who did not speak English, and that kind of adjustment slows you down a bit. But then, he had all these visual effects shots to deal with. All of Clint's energy goes into keeping a fast pace, so that creativity is not slowed or interrupted in any way. I remember him saying that the [visual effects] process slowed the company way down, and that troubled him."

Firefox was originally scheduled to be made earlier, but was pushed back in order to make time to resolve a host of visual effects issues posed by the story of an American pilot stealing a high-tech Russian fighter jet. To figure out how to design and execute *Firefox's* climactic dogfight scene between two such jets, the production eventually turned to one of the original *Star Wars* effects wizards—the legendary John Dykstra. He and colleagues at his company, Apogee Inc., built the dogfight's visuals in a way that was quite cutting-edge for the pre-computer graphics (CG) era, with a technique Dykstra dubbed "reverse blue-screen photography." That's really a fancy name for a method of painting models of the planes with phosphorus paint, and photographing them with strong light and then ultraviolet light to create different elements—called mattes—that could be stitched together effectively with photography of a bright blue sky with puffy white clouds and other environmental images.

Creating that method was necessary because Eastwood insisted the *Firefox* planes be shiny and reflect sunlight, which meant that many of the earlier techniques Dykstra and his colleagues had already perfected on *Star Wars* and subsequent films would not work. Dykstra's effort made the visual effects believable for the era, but they were also slow and laborious to execute. When the shoot finally came along, Eastwood, as the star of the picture, also had to spend hours being photographed in various positions in a cockpit on a stage that was rotated by a gimbal system, further slowing his typical process.

SPACE COWBOYS

It was understandable that Eastwood wanted to avoid visual effects after that, and besides, he wasn't running across many psychological or emotional dramas that required them anyway.

But finally, along came *Space Cowboys*, from Eastwood in 2000—a tale of aging astronauts thrust into an improbable, last-chance space mission. Eastwood loved the buddies-in-space concept, and craved the opportunity to work with peers and friends like costars James Garner, Tommy Lee Jones, and Donald Sutherland, so he gave it a shot. By this time, the computer-generated visual effects revolution was underway, and new methods of creating realistic outer space imagery had come along.

"This wasn't shooting rockets around like Buck Rogers," Eastwood says. "Everyone has seen pictures or video of space. We are at a point in history where everyone has seen the Earth from the point of view of the moon or the shuttle. [Visual effects] are hard to do when you do things that people already know. So that was our challenge."

(Below) Filming Clint Eastwood and Tommy Lee Jones in a *Space Cowboys* scene. Rob Lorenz, then first assistant director, is center, next to James Garner.

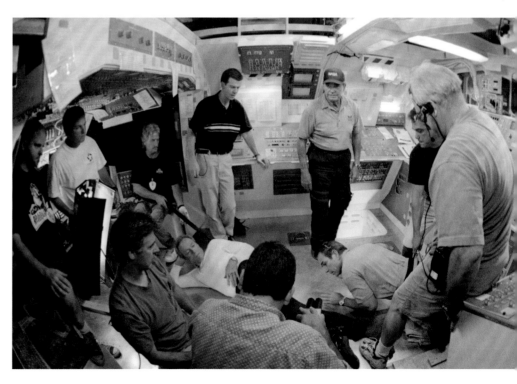

For this, Eastwood turned to Industrial Light & Magic (ILM), and hooked up with Owens, who was then on staff at ILM. Unbeknownst to either man at the time, Owens would evolve into a central collaborator whose work has become crucial to Eastwood's recent films. Indeed, Owens now serves as Eastwood's visual effects supervisor and directs second unit as needed to acquire visual effects plates and other supplemental elements.

"At the time, they thought they had about thirty to forty visual effects shots," Owens says of *Space Cowboys*. "Because the crew makes movies in such an organic and natural way, it was hard for them at the time to imagine things that were not in front of them—what could be in the shot. Whereas, that's what I do all day long. So Clint and I discussed it, and I pointed out a couple sequences in the script that needed fleshing out. I said, 'I know you don't like to do storyboarding, but I could do it for you—one simple scene, and see what your thoughts are.' Clint said, 'Great,' and I pre-visualized [with simplified computer animation] a five-minute sequence. He immediately saw how there was more going on than he initially thought. He told me to go ahead and open up more sequences, so I created those and showed them to him. Next thing you know, he's interacting his thoughts off storyboards and pre-visualization, discussing spatial things for outer space that are more than you can simply stage."

After this introduction, Eastwood's openness to a process he previously avoided was remarkable. Owens eventually created full animatics (animated templates) of approximately the last quarter of the movie to give the sequences movement and depth, adding music and dialogue to them so they could serve as a blueprint for shooting the live-action pieces, and to give Eastwood and editor Joel Cox material to use for illustrating those effects as they cut the movie. This was important since Cox edits while Eastwood shoots, and needed to show him how things were evolving long before final visual effects could be realized.

Owens admits that, despite enormous progress in the visual effects field since Eastwood made *Firefox*, "the process was still more laborious for him because of technical issues and not being able to see everything in a shot at the time you are shooting [the actors]. But I tried to design it so it was fairly minimal for him. And then he let me direct, as he did in later movies, those nondramatic shots that had technical requirements to make visual effects sequences work correctly, checking in with him constantly, of course."

Portions of *Space Cowboys* were, in fact, more time-consuming than Eastwood likes, but not so much so that he could not see the potential of this kind of work being able to support the making of wider stories.

[Opposite] A contemplative Clint Eastwood waits for the next setup during the Vienna shoot of *Firefox*.

(Above) The opening scene of *Space Cowboys*, depicting young astronauts ejecting from test aircraft, is filmed on a stage. Special effects foreman Steve Riley holds an air cannon to produce a wind effect for the scene.

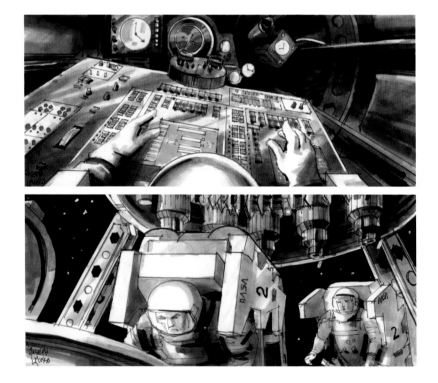

(Above) Production illustrator Joe Musso's colored storyboards (*Space Cowboys*).

(Opposite Top) Marine landing sequence for *Flags of Our Fathers*—live action combined with extensive visual effects. (Opposite Bottom L) Actor Ned Eisenberg (R) as Army photographer Joe Rosenthal, shown snapping the famous photo of the flag-raising on Iwo Jima. Clint Eastwood's prop team made sure the actor used an actual Graphlex Speed Graphic camera like the one the real Rosenthal used on Iwo Jima.

FLAGS OF OUR FATHERS

From that point on, Eastwood found himself interested in learning more about the visual effects process. He quickly grasped that although he had little interest in doing heavy visual effects–oriented films, such techniques could save money and time as technology and computer processing power improved, allowing him to create environments and locations, or extend sets and locations digitally, rather than having to take up valuable production time filming or building all of those pieces practically.

On *J. Edgar*, for example, despite filming in southern California, where several racetracks were available for horse-racing scenes, Eastwood opted to build rudimentary bleachers in the parking lot at Warner Bros., to serve as the foundational element of Owens's visual effects work on those scenes. Owens's team then digitally built period versions of the Del Mar and Pimlico racetracks, as they looked a quarter-century apart, to fit around actors Leonardo DiCaprio and Armie Hammer and numerous extras for two important sequences in the movie.

(Above) Storyboards by production illustrator Joe Musso for *Flags of Our Fathers*.

(Opposite Bottom Center) Black sand, shadows, and desaturated colors were all used by Eastwood as aesthetic storytelling devices for the battle scenes in *Flags of Our Fathers*, including this one with actor Jesse Bradford, flag in hand. (Opposite Bottom R) Marines storming the beach—an elaborately designed sequence shot on a beach in Iceland, with the digital addition of the American armada in the background (*Flags of Our Fathers*).

"That's typically how we use visual effects—for set extensions," Rob Lorenz explains. "We built the stands and then Michael Owens extended the stadium [digitally], and when we did reverses, he put in plates that have the horses racing. We didn't have to go to a racetrack. Modern tracks would have to be altered digitally anyway to look like tracks [of that era], so this was just as good and saved us some time."

While that illustrates Eastwood's typical use of digital effects, Eastwood simply could not have made some of his recent films, financially or logistically, without such techniques. In particular, the two *Iwo Jima* films, *Changeling*, and *Invictus* required extensive visual effects, although viewers likely never realized it. *Flags of Our Fathers* was probably the picture that made it clear once and for all to Eastwood that visual effects should be a regular staple on his filmmaking menu of tricks. The movie included 470 digital effects shots, largely revolving around the creation of the massive 880-ship armada that brought U.S. invaders to the island.

Owens's way of working—pre-visualizing visual effects sections—allowed Eastwood and his team to keep moving forward, shooting live-action at their own pace and cutting the movie, even while vendor Digital Domain churned out shots under Owens's watchful eye. Furthermore, with the march of digital technology continuing unabated, Eastwood was able to shoot on the beaches of Iceland, where most of the battle sequences of the movie were filmed, without needing to stop and worry about the laborious use of green screen or blue screen. In other words, he didn't have to slow down much, if at all.

Indeed, Owens says that not slowing Eastwood down was the requirement of the visual effects methodology for *Flags*. "The goal was, let him do what he does, make him happy, change as little about the style as possible," Owens explains. "The tools and techniques were a lot more advanced by then [than earlier in the decade], and Clint allowed me to direct second unit for the staging of the landing craft and water vehicles [that would be part of eventual visual effects shots], so it was a lot more comfortable by that time."

Comfortable in production, but complicated in post for Owens and artists at Digital Domain, because shooting visual effects plates in this manner meant they had to extensively use a technique called rotoscoping to place actors into digital

(Above) Clint Eastwood observing Stephen Campanelli operating a Steadicam rig during a scene for *Changeling* with Angelina Jolie.

backgrounds. Without getting too technical about it, for visual effects, rotoscoping is essentially a laborious frame-by-frame method of separating a filmed foreground from its background, and then replacing the background with an entirely new background, often computer generated, to give the illusion of the scene taking place in an entirely different environment.

However, the tools and methods for such work continued to advance so dramatically that Owens was able to use rotoscoping even more extensively to create huge crowds to insert into empty rugby stadiums during *Invictus*, which, believe it or not, features six hundred digital shots. Owens insists that, to this day, *Invictus* and *Flags* may be the most extensively rotoscoped dramatic films ever.

In any case, the end result of the *Flags* effects work made Eastwood extremely confident about his growing relationship with visual effects.

"The best compliment we had on the visual effects in that film was from a guy who was a retired general," Eastwood chuckles. "He called me from New York and said he had seen the film, and that he thought it was pretty great the way we interspersed real footage with the story we shot. I took a little pause and said that while that was very complimentary, we, in fact, shot and made everything ourselves, and that there was no real war footage in the movie. He was surprised, and he was a combat guy who was there as a young captain on the first wave. That, coming from him, was a huge compliment."

(Opposite) *Flags of Our Fathers* combat scenes were shot on a beach at Sandvik, on the western coast of Iceland, near the capital, Reykjavik.

CUTTING EDGE

Changeling came along a couple of years later and used the art of digital set extensions liberally, along with the building of digital backgrounds and landscapes to illustrate 1920s-era Los Angeles. Then, as mentioned, *Invictus* digitally filled up stadiums to emulate the crowds that attended the real rugby matches documented in the film. The movie also took advantage of another technique Eastwood began using with Owens's help on *Flags of Our Fathers*—digital makeup.

In both films, to make soldiers for *Flags* and rugby players for *Invictus* look more battle-scarred, Eastwood directed Owens to strategically add realistic digital imperfections—cuts, bruises, scratches, dirt, and more to the faces and bodies of the actors. The technique was extremely effective in enhancing the sense of realism without bogging down Eastwood's production crew with having to agonize over the minute details of makeup on the faces of every single extra.

In *Invictus*, the digital intermediate color-timing process was also employed by Eastwood to smooth out some of actor Morgan Freeman's prosthetic makeup in terms of color and texture. Colorist Jill Bogdanowicz says that Freeman, playing the legendary Nelson Mandela, wore small prosthetics on his eyelids to make them look more hooded, like Mandela's eyes.

"On set, the prosthetic was the same color as Morgan's skin, but the film stock picked it up a bit differently," Bogdanowicz recalls. "You could see a bit of gray area on his eyes that was different than his skin. Clint asked me to [fix it using a digital color corrector] to make it the same color as Morgan's skin. I ended up doing that for every shot in the movie so that the prosthetic blended in better. The point is that Clint was aware at the start that I had the ability to do that."

(Above) Cécile de France and Thierry Neuvic act out the aftermath of the tsunami on location in Hawaii (*Hereafter*).

Although, later on, *J. Edgar* would rely heavily on traditional makeup techniques to age actors Leonardo DiCaprio, Armie Hammer, and Naomi Watts, digital tweaks were also used in that picture—primarily to smooth the prosthetics worn by Hammer and Watts. Since their makeup was far more extensive than Freeman's in *Invictus*, and required more than color adjustments, that work was done by a visual effects facility.

And in between all that, as mentioned earlier, came the tsunami sequence from *Hereafter*—Eastwood's biggest centerpiece visual effects sequence to date. Owens calls the birth of the sequence "a perfect unfolding" from the moment he and Eastwood first discussed it.

"Because of past experience, his confidence in me was maybe too high at that point," Owens says, smiling. "When I saw the sequence, I knew, just like *Invictus*, which had the digital crowd and stadiums, that here, all the water stuff had to be digital—that the majority of the sequence would be digital. But we had to worry about the design of the sequence and the close-ups."

Once again, Owens felt the need to pull out storyboards and animatics. However, he got swept up in the wake of Malpaso's lightning-quick production methods. He was still finishing shots for *Invictus* when Eastwood decided to go to London and shoot the water tank sequences of actress Cécile de France being consumed by the tsunami for *Hereafter*. The scene would be a combination of live-action

(Opposite) Eastwood reflects while on the set of *Invictus*. (Above) Morgan Freeman and Matt Damon, in character, before the big match.

shots from the tank, 3D water, and live-action pieces shot in Hawaii—tricky work. Owens hadn't had time yet to build an animatic for the tsunami, so "I went and showed Clint some storyboards, and explained that due to the complexity of the scene, it would unfortunately need to be shot in somewhat abstract places in order to achieve a natural final look. With these restrictions, starting with the water-tank shoot, Clint just let me have at it, and from then on, entrusted the design and execution of the sequence to me."

Owens eventually built an animatic, which was used as a blueprint for shooting the rest of the elements, and then Eastwood simply moved forward, as usual. "Occasionally, I would need to describe how something that was going to be added to the shot later needed to be framed for while they were shooting [elements]," Owens adds. "He would say OK and modify the angle. And that's all there was to it."

Owens says that Eastwood's team also learned the value of using animatics in the editing process. But Owens benefited, as well, from how he saw Eastwood and Cox utilize his pre-visualized material. "It's actually very progressive editing," he explains. "As you see it [cut with the rest of the film], you see where you can improve a sequence along the way. It can make a huge difference for six or eight or twelve frames. You see what they are doing to cut it, and you get new ideas."

To a degree, Owens concedes that visual effects will always be "square pegs in round holes" for Eastwood, but adds that such processes are now advanced enough that even the most extreme technical requirements can usually be handled without disturbing Eastwood's filmmaking zeitgeist. Rob Lorenz agrees, and suggests that Eastwood's success using visual effects and other modern digital filmmaking techniques within the context of the kinds of traditional dramas and working methods he prefers has actually enabled him creatively in recent years.

(Above) Clint Eastwood discusses choreography for an *Invictus* rugby scene with Matt Damon and other actors.

"Post is probably the most fun part for Clint creatively, now that he can do so many things," Lorenz suggests. "It's easier to experiment with things and to bring all the pieces together. In general, he loves new experiences, and he loves learning from and exploring new things. He'll try any new technique if he thinks it will help the final product without bogging him down."

"A real purist might not like using [digital technology], but I think the purists are gone now," Eastwood adds. "Using this technology can give you another toy. Sometimes the toys can get in the way, but only if you aren't decisive. If you are decisive, it can be a big help."

(Above L) Co-supervising sound editor Alan Murray records car interior sounds for *Mystic River*. He and Bub Asman manage all aspects of sound capture, editing, and manipulation for Eastwood's films. (Above R) Digital crowds in a South African rugby stadium (finished film frame).

(Above L) Wide shot showing the small percentage of the stadium that was filled with actors for *Invictus*. The final product featured packed stadiums thanks to visual effects. (Above R) Operator Stephen Campanelli follows Clint Eastwood out of the tunnel while filming. (Opposite) Shooting Morgan Freeman, as Nelson Mandela, greeting the crowd.

TRASH CAN SHOTS

Clint Eastwood was hell-bent on finding a way to visually illustrate the chaotic nature of combat in a powerful way as he set about designing the battle sequences seen in *Flags of Our Fathers*. To that end, it was his idea to incorporate the first digitally shot footage ever to appear in one of his films—an achievement handled by his high-definition (HD) video camera operator, Liz Radley, with assistant Alex Nicksay.

Radley was originally brought into Malpaso in 1999, to create video displays for on-screen playback on monitors and computers in *Space Cowboys*. Eastwood supported the idea of using what was then new technology for NASA's video displays, and so, for one of the first times ever in a motion picture, the production used high-definition imagery on the monitors seen in the film.

Next, on *Mystic River*, Radley set up Eastwood's first handheld wireless video monitoring system to use while directing (various generations of these handhelds can be seen throughout this book). Then, on *Flags of Our Fathers*, she also started shooting behind-the-scenes footage at Eastwood's request. On that same project, she configured a digital camera system for recording imagery in the midst of the choreographed battle scenes.

These experiences convinced her that, despite being labeled a "traditional filmmaker," her boss is as open-minded and modern a filmmaker as there is.

"I find it funny that Clint is seen as being old-school," she says. "In fact, he is incredibly interested, and is always soliciting opinions on 3D, HD cameras, and more. For him, it's more about when is the right time to try some of those things, but he is definitely open to them. He'll try something, and if it works, he'll go with it, and if it doesn't, he'll try something else."

On *Flags*, Eastwood asked Radley if there was a way to house small video cameras inside prop ammunition cases carried around the battlefield by extras, so they could wildly record the swirling madness. She provided the production with a series of Sony prosumer-level HDV cameras, wrapped in Bubble Wrap, foam, and waterproof housings, and then inserted into cutout spaces in the ammunition boxes.

Eastwood had Nicksay, extras, and stuntmen carry the cases around as they dashed, fell, and dropped during the battle sequences, with no regard for the cameras inside. He calls these "my trash can shots," and says they worked well because unique footage was captured without impacting his own process of shooting the wider action on location in Iceland.

Radley helped Eastwood execute the plan, but emphasizes, "it was all Clint's idea. It was a very specific request. He had assessed, based on his experience, that using small film cameras would be time-consuming because their run time with a film load is not as long as a video camera. So we did some tests and found the right cameras, and it worked nicely. Clint was fascinated by the footage."

Another thing Eastwood previously wanted to try in 2003, as Malpaso was rolling into *Mystic River*, was the use of a wireless video monitor that would allow him to watch the film camera's POV on set wherever he moved.

Since he is vehemently opposed to the video assist, or "video village," approach of having a crowd of people bunched around static monitors on set, as is so prevalent in the industry today, Eastwood had long been craving a mobile, private approach that would allow him to see the film camera's POV while he was standing, as always, as close to his actors as possible. He decided *Mystic River* was the time to give it a try, and asked Radley to devise such a system.

She built one with a wireless transmitter attached to the film camera, sending a live unrecorded signal directly to Eastwood's monitor. By the time of *Million Dollar Baby*, she had found a French company called Transvideo to supply a better, ultra-bright wireless monitor with a built-in microwave transmitter for Eastwood's use. Then, before *Letters from Iwo Jima*, Radley visited Transvideo's headquarters outside Paris to work with them on a customized design for handles on the monitor to accommodate Eastwood's large hands, so that he could easily grip it in his left hand and use the same thumb to quickly change channels between multiple cameras.

"Again, it's in keeping with how he likes to work," Radley suggests. "It's a real-time image for framing that Clint can view without any image delay, so that he can view it in tandem with looking at the actor himself and hearing the actor's voice in sync with the image. His only real requirements were that it be easy to use, work in real time, and be viewable in sunlight, and we met those."

Eastwood adds that the monitor has freed him from needing to run to the viewfinder after every lens change—once again speeding things up a bit. "[During a take], I can refer to it as needed," he says. "I usually watch the actors, but at some point, I can look down and make sure that everything is fitting into the frame the way I envisioned. I almost never have to look through the camera anymore."

(Bottom L) Eastwood organizes extras playing a motorcycle gang in the desert in *The Gauntlet*. During production of *J. Edgar*, (Below, Top R) Eastwood holds his monitor on set while (Below, Bottom R) Technicolor's senior colorist Jill Bogdanowicz, in her digital intermediate suite, does some fine-tuning.

(Opposite) A stylized *Bronco Billy* poster, designed by longtime Eastwood collaborator Bill Gold. (Top R and Center) Scenes from production of this film. (Bottom R) Eastwood uses a megaphone to orchestrate a chaotic *Bronco Billy* Wild West sequence—one of the few times on a movie set where Eastwood ever tried to amplify his voice.

(Page 226) Eastwood prepares for a scene in *Space Cowboys*. (Page 227) Eastwood examining a camera angle during shooting of *The Eiger Sanction*.

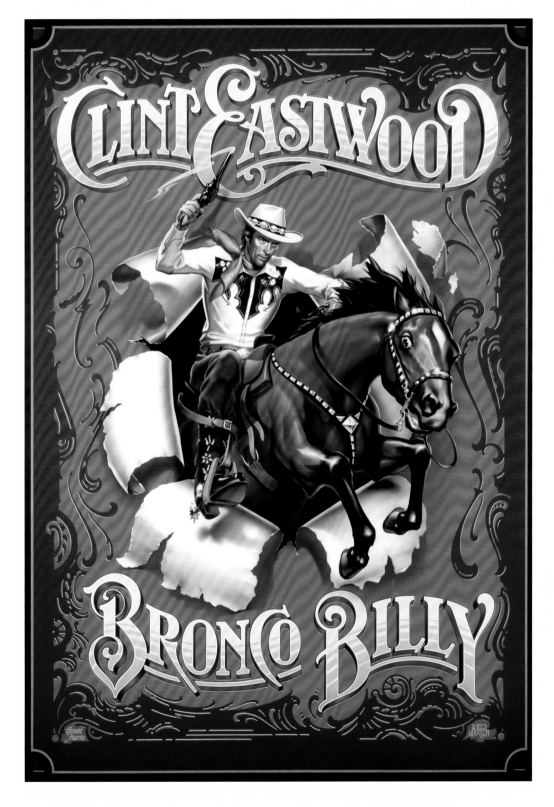

"JOHN HUSTON WAS MAKING GOOD MOVIES RIGHT UNTIL THE END, AND I HOPE I AM ALSO."

CLINT EASTWOOD, 2011

EPILOGUE
ANOTHER BREATH OF FRESH AIR

SO WHAT'S NEXT FOR CLINT EASTWOOD? IT'S A QUESTION HE GETS ASKED A LOT, FOR THE SIMPLE CHRONOLOGICAL REASON THAT HE IS NOW, AS OF THIS WRITING, IN HIS EARLY EIGHTIES. BUT IT'S HARDLY A NEW QUESTION—HE'S BEEN HEARING IT FOR YEARS.

Appearing on *Charlie Rose* in November of 1996, for instance, he was asked if or when he would be slowing down his filmmaking pace. In his mid-sixties at the time, Eastwood chuckled and declared, "I'm in the middle of [my career]. I'm not retiring. Maybe I'm at the sandwich station at the ninth hole, embarking on the back nine or something like that, but by the same token, I feel I have a lot more to do."

During the mid-1990s, Eastwood used the "back nine" golf analogy quite a bit, but he kept steadfastly making high-quality movies. Of course, that was fifteen years and fourteen movies ago, as of this writing. As 2011 wound down, following the release of *J. Edgar*, Eastwood was busy making plans for his next film, *A Star Is Born*. He also announced, to the surprise of many, that he would be acting again, and in a film directed by someone else—his partner and producer, Rob Lorenz—for the first time in almost twenty years. A few weeks before he made that announcement, though, Eastwood was asked for an update on the state of his career arc. With everything he is doing and planning to do—back nine or front nine, which is it today?

Smiling, as he characteristically hoisted his feet onto a coffee table in his Malpaso office, Eastwood admitted, "I was still playing the front nine back then [in the 1990s], and I'm still going on. *Unforgiven* was the start for me of getting another breath of fresh air and starting to work on different kinds of films. Then the same thing happened in the 2000s, beginning with *Mystic River*. I don't know that I was conscious of trying to make films of a different variety. I wasn't looking for that, necessarily—it all just sort of came to me, and the circumstances worked out the right way."

When reminded that most folks are hanging it up, or at least slowing down, long before the age of eighty-one, Eastwood insisted that not only didn't he have any plans to do so, but that he hadn't even thought about it. In fact, he seemed puzzled that more filmmakers, especially some of the legendary directors who came before him, had not pursued career arcs similar to his.

"Someday, I guess I'll probably say that's enough, but there is no reason to do that now because I'm still enjoying myself and feel like I'm doing as good as I can right now," he says. "I'm better maybe than I have been in a while, or at least, there are more things for me to do out there. So in that sense, it all depends upon the material and whether I think I can pull it off. I'm enjoying making movies right now. It's a nice time. I was always mystified why a great film director like Billy Wilder quit directing [in 1981, when Wilder was seventy-five years old]. He lived well into his nineties, and I knew him socially a little bit. He always seemed full of vinegar, and sharp, as far as I could tell."

(Opposite) Eastwood, in costume as the John Huston–inspired character John Wilson, studies a potential shot for *White Hunter, Black Heart*, a film based on a book about the making of Huston's *African Queen*. (Above) Clint Eastwood directing a group of extras portraying a motorcycle gang for *The Gauntlet*.

(Opposite) Clint Eastwood contemplates a wide shot inside the lobby of the Library of Congress building in Washington, D.C., during a location shoot for *J. Edgar*. (Above) Dressed in character for *High Plains Drifter* (1973), Clint Eastwood directs a scene.

"I also remember going to visit Frank Capra when I was making *High Plains Drifter* [in the early 1970s] because I was staying near where he lived. He was also lucid and interesting, and I wondered why he wasn't still making movies. [Capra stopped directing in his late sixties, about a decade earlier, and lived another twenty-seven years.] I don't know what age he was at the time, but he didn't seem 'old' to me.

"But John Huston, I remember he directed [his final film, in 1987] *The Dead*, while he was in a wheelchair with an oxygen mask on. He was about the age I am now [early eighties]. I don't know I'd want to do that—I guess he lived a little rougher lifestyle than I have. But he was making good movies right until the end, and I hope I am also."

Indeed, at the time of this writing, *J. Edgar* was debuting to critical buzz for Leonardo DiCaprio's performance and its stylized, noirish look and design. Plans were also being made for yet another movie of "a different variety"—a musical remake of *A Star Is Born*, starring Beyoncé. The exact timing of that movie was unclear at the time since Beyoncé had just announced her pregnancy [she gave birth early in 2012], but Eastwood's mind was well into it nonetheless.

"We have our leading lady, but need to cast the male star and then we will proceed," Eastwood explained. "It will be a drama about musicians, so there will be music in it, but it won't be a musical like Busby Berkeley with a high camera over top or anything. I'm playing the guy more as a veteran musician, like an Eric Clapton or a Carlos Santana or some other contemporary musician. I'm sure it will come out great."

The central point being that Eastwood is not only not contemplating retirement, he's continuing to make movies that are more dramatic, critically acclaimed, and profitable than ever before, and he is doing so at an unusually rapid and efficient clip. And he fully plans to keep doing exactly that.

The period of rejuvenation he refers to since *Mystic River* in 2003 shows no sign of fading. Every picture since then has generally been respected by critics, none have been formulaic or a revisitation of territory or genres he has already tackled, and all have done well at the box office. Indeed, *Gran Torino* was a dominant performer in 2009, and its worldwide receipts make it possibly the most profitable Eastwood picture ever—a monster success for a movie shot in just thirty-three days for $35 million (an amount recouped in its opening weekend).

Eastwood's colleagues see him enjoying the filmmaking process, the quality and success of his films, and the relationships that come out of the work far too much to slow down, combined with the fact, of course, that retirement isn't in his nature. His period of making, by his own admission, simpler and entertaining action pieces primarily to satisfy Warner Bros. box office needs—*Dirty Harry* sequels being the prototypical example—mixed in with thoughtful, psychological dramas is long over. Eastwood is only making thoughtful dramas at this stage, and increasingly unorthodox ones at that. He's earning nominations and winning awards with film themes and story lines the industry normally seeks to avoid in the mega–tent pole era—a small-time hood driven to the brink by his daughter's murder, an injured female boxer yearning to end her life, a foreign-language film about the losers of the world's greatest war, a tale about a dying bigot making peace with Asian neighbors, a psychological peek inside the head of one of the most disliked men in American history, and so on.

"He's making deeper, more thoughtful movies now," insists Barry Meyer, chairman/CEO of Warner Bros. "He's always done that, but interspersed them with what could be considered bigger, more commercial movies. Every so often, we felt he would give us a *Dirty Harry* in order to keep doing the movies he wanted to

(Above L) The crew filming exteriors during the *J. Edgar* Washington, D.C., location shoot. (Above R) J. Edgar Hoover and his mother from a key scene in the film.

make. But now, he's found, and shown us, that these [more thoughtful dramas] can be quite successful also. Some of them are among the most successful films he's made, like *Gran Torino*. At his age and this stage in his career, to shift the creative focus and get better is quite remarkable. No one else is doing it, that's for sure."

There is, of course, serendipity to Eastwood's latest period of rejuvenation since *Mystic River*. As his success as a filmmaker has grown along with the global and critical cementing of his status as an elite filmmaker, and as these successes pile up and the actors who work with him interact with their peers, Eastwood's ability to draw A-list actors into movies being made on accelerated timelines and slim budgets grows exponentially. In fact, this ability has proven to be uncanny in recent years. Stars the caliber of Sean Penn, Hilary Swank, Angelina Jolie, Matt Damon, Leonardo DiCaprio, and Beyoncé, among others, all happily appeared or were scheduled to appear in Eastwood films budgeted to pay far less than what such performers normally rake in these days.

"Clint's stature in the industry has gotten to a point where the great actors working today are actively seeking him out—they want to work for Clint Eastwood," Rob Lorenz elaborates. "That gives him an amazing talent pool to draw from. He's at a point where he is not burdened by financial considerations. He doesn't need money or more awards—he's not seeking acclaim. He's just making movies that he wants to make, and he's doing it with great people around him. I think that is why he has gotten more productive as he has gotten older, and it's a real pleasure for him."

Lorenz also suggests that Eastwood's age and half-century of experience on movie sets makes him naturally an authoritative figure whom actors and others want to please and are eager to learn from. Not so much in the sense of an elder statesman, per se. After all, Eastwood is often having to learn about new tools and techniques himself and is far more open than many filmmakers of his vintage to having those more expert than he on a particular technology or method take the lead on his behalf, as discussed elsewhere in this book. Rather, Lorenz means that Eastwood has seen and done just about everything that can be seen or done on a movie set, and so his wisdom is logically bound to be followed and respected and yearned for.

"It's just hard to argue with somebody with that much experience," Lorenz suggests. "Often, people bring us 'new' ideas, and Clint remarks that they knew that, or tried that, back in the '80s. In that sense, there are no new ideas for him, and you have to defer to his experience. But if you come up with something he thinks might be better, he'll be the first to give it a try."

As of this writing, Eastwood had not shot a movie with digital cameras yet, but he has Tom Stern's camera team constantly testing such cameras, and expects, eventually, that he will take that route. "After all, you have to keep up with the times," he suggests. Ironically, there may be no modern filmmaker better suited to keeping

(Opposite) The Eastwood team fills up a real apartment location in Boston while shooting a key *Mystic River* confrontation scene. Eastwood likes to shoot in real, cramped spaces for authenticity when feasible. (Top) Eastwood in a quiet moment. (Bottom L) Eastwood with Rob Lorenz during *J. Edgar*, and (Bottom R) with Tom Stern during the *Gran Torino* barbershop scene.

(Above, L-R) Producer Rob Lorenz, production manager/executive producer Tim Moore, Clint Eastwood, and cinematographer Tom Stern, during production of *Gran Torino*. The film's poster is at right.

up with the times than Clint Eastwood in his eighties. Those who work with him and know him best suggest the themes of his stories, while never overtly political or chosen with any agenda other than the notion they would make a good and interesting movie, somehow strike a consistent emotional chord with Eastwood's audiences in ways other filmmakers struggle to achieve.

Actor Ken Watanabe, speaking in his Santa Monica home while preparing in mid-2011 to return to his native Japan to aid in tsunami relief efforts, believes Eastwood is almost mystical in this ability. Despite Eastwood's uniquely American heritage, this ability makes him, in Watanabe's view, the most universally understandable filmmaker alive today, or maybe ever. And Watanabe is talking about a far deeper level than the simple fact that the initial drive to accept Eastwood as a critically substantive filmmaker started overseas, particularly in France.

"His movies are wide—all types of cultures and time periods," says Watanabe. "But for some reason, it seems to me that whenever one of his films comes out, it always fits the time in which it comes out. They are timely, even when he doesn't mean it that way. Like when *Gran Torino* came out—the auto industry in Detroit was having such problems. And then came *Hereafter*, which features a big tsunami, and the tsunami in Japan came right after that. Unfortunately, that movie was not released in Japan for that reason—it's too painful. But I'm just saying, I don't think it's all a coincidence. I know he can't know when things like that will happen, and moviemaking can take two or three years, so he can't plan it. But I'm saying that

with all the movie scripts he gets, he always follows his heart in choosing them, and somehow, they seem to match what is timely in the world. I can't really explain it, but I think he is just connected to the world somehow."

Many of Eastwood's oldest colleagues suggest his filmmaking success is possible because of his personal attention to small details and low-profile people and things. These traits, they imply, show up in his filmmaking. Leonard Hirshan, his agent of fifty years, calls him "an observer—a broad-minded observer. He's wide open, not close-minded at all. He has a demeanor that people trust and, even with changes in his life, that has been true from the very beginning, since I first met him on the set of *Rawhide*. He was observing directors, actors, but also the world around him, the people around him, and this has grown truer as he has gotten older."

Eastwood's longtime business manager, Howard Bernstein, describes him in similar terms—"a very smart man with an amazing memory for people and details," Bernstein insists. "That's why he is successful and why he's refreshing—he's someone who pays attention in our business, and that's important."

His cinematographer, Tom Stern, suggests that perhaps Eastwood's artistic psyche is not fully appreciated. After all, in Stern's view, the guy who made his bones as the ultimate movie tough guy is, in fact, far more focused on the frailties of human emotion in his capacity as a filmmaker. His boss, he suggests, is, and has always been, "on a quest for authenticity or truthfulness. He is trying to give us emotion—real emotion—in his movies. And so he keeps making them, and I expect he will as long as he is healthy."

As this book was being prepared, Beyoncé's pregnancy had cast doubt on whether Eastwood could get *A Star Is Born* together before the end of 2012. However, the potential for a delay did lead to asking Eastwood if he might, as he has done before, switch gears and pull another potential *Gran Torino* or *Letters from Iwo Jima* off the script pile and slip it into the tiniest of production windows.

(Above L) The chaos of combat from *Letters from Iwo Jima*, and (Above R) the joy of victory from *Flags of Our Fathers*. (Opposite) Clint Eastwood's character, Tom Highway, leads Marine recruits on a grueling training run during filming of *Heartbreak Ridge*.

"You never know," he said, smiling and unfolding his six-foot-two frame from the couch as early evening summer gloom took over his unlit office. "We have some good ideas lying around here somewhere."

The real surprise would come a few weeks later when news broke that Eastwood's next move would be to act in Lorenz's directorial debut—a baseball drama called *Trouble with the Curve*. It would mark the first time since Wolfgang Petersen directed him in *In the Line of Fire* in 1993 that Eastwood would perform for another director. Since *Gran Torino*, Eastwood had been insisting his acting days were probably over, unless he found "a really great script." Apparently, Lorenz found one, and the opportunity to act for his friend and partner, and alongside most

of his own crew, was something Eastwood didn't want to pass up. And, besides, Lorenz pledged the movie would be made in "the economical way"—the Malpaso way—just as Eastwood had taught him over the years.

But that decision wouldn't be announced for a few weeks yet. On this particular day, Eastwood apologized for needing to slip away for a meeting. The director said his farewells, slid into one of the golf carts parked in front of his bungalow, and drove away with a wave, Lorenz in the passenger seat. He swerved the cart down one of the crowded paths he has grown so familiar with over the decades, and off into the hustle and bustle of the Warner Bros. lot. There was more work to be done.

ACKNOWLEDGMENTS

WHEN I ARRIVED ON THE SET OF *HEREAFTER* IN EARLY 2010 WHILE RESEARCHING THIS BOOK, THE FIRST THING CLINT EASTWOOD TOLD ME WAS, "IF YOU ARE LOOKING FOR THE RIGHT WAY TO MAKE MOVIES, YOU ARE IN THE WRONG PLACE."

Far be it from me to disagree with Clint Eastwood, but in this case, I respect-fully have to. Clint was wrong that day—he certainly makes movies the right way. Not necessarily the most popular way, or the typical way, but if creative acclaim, financial success, entertainment value, economical methods, and harmonious teamwork add up to a high standard, then the Eastwood method is most certainly the right way to make movies. And that is why this book exists—to shine a spot-light from the inside out on the unique creative process of one of the world's most iconic filmmakers.

Therefore, the author would like to offer heartfelt thanks and appreciation to Mr. Eastwood. First, for giving the world his brilliant and influential forty-plus-year di-recting career. Second, for finding merit in my suggestion to highlight his method. And third, for allowing me unprecedented access to his sets and office for two movies, and to his employees, crew, colleagues, business associates, friends, and others, who helped me understand the artistic mind-set of the man virtually all of them call "the boss."

But not even Clint Eastwood does it alone. At Malpaso, Eastwood has an in-dispensable partner who is intimately involved in virtually every aspect of his business and creative success, just as he was intimately involved in making this book happen. That individual is his producer and colleague, Rob Lorenz. It was Rob who encouraged and listened to my proposition, waited patiently for me to hone my proposal, consumed it with an open mind, endorsed its value, and then brought it directly to Clint with that endorsement stamped on it. It was Rob who opened the door at Malpaso and Warner Bros., making it possible to poke around Clint's world, while offering help, encouragement, trust, and guidance throughout the process. Rob's active support was central to this project's suc-cess. I will always be grateful for your help, Rob, and I wish you much success in your directing career.

Many other Malpaso natives deserve special thanks. Among them is cinematog-rapher Tom Stern, ASC. It was Tom who first put the bug in my ear about doing this book while I was writing a magazine article about *Letters from Iwo Jima*. I shall

(Above) Clint Eastwood consults with producer Rob Lorenz, whom he says is a partner he is "very compatible" with. In 2012, Lorenz directed his first film, *Trouble with the Curve*, with Eastwood starring.

always be grateful for his suggestion, encouragement, insight, and time. This book would not have happened had he not casually said one day over lunch, "I think you should talk to Rob Lorenz." Thanks, Tom.

I'm also grateful to two other crucial players at Malpaso: Jessica Meier and Kristina Rivera. Jessica is technically Rob's assistant, and Kristina is Clint's, but in truth they are the hubs around which Malpaso operates, and both were essential in help-ing us navigate this project. Their generous assistance, time, and friendship were far above the call of duty, and I deeply appreciate it.

Virtually Eastwood's entire current crew and much of his former crew were also indispensable with their time, advice, insight, memories, and assets throughout the process, particularly editor Joel Cox, ACE; co–sound editors Alan Murray and Bub Asman; visual effects supervisor Michael Owens; gaffer Charlie Saldana; camera operator Stephen Campanelli; and video and computer graphics supervisor Liz Radley; among others. Liz, in particular, offered great insight into how Malpaso operates, and into the contributions to Eastwood's art provided by his late production designer, Henry Bumstead. Composer Lenny Niehaus and former crew members Jack Green, David Valdes, and Jack Taylor also gave far more than mere interviews, providing valuable time, intimate details, and assets to the cause.

There is another central figure whose role was invaluable in this book's evolution: Bob Hoffman, vice president of marketing and PR at Technicolor. Bob is a longtime friend, mentor, and supporter, and also a film expert and a major Clint-phile. He steadily encouraged me to push past any reservations I might have had in terms of tackling something this complex, with so many moving parts, gave me great insight into Clint Eastwood and filmmaking generally, and offered a reasoned and respected sounding board every step along the way. But that was only the start of his contribution. Bob also stepped up and brought Technicolor's generous financial and logistical assistance to bear on this project as a sponsor, helping us to incorporate spectacular imagery and other assets to enhance this book. Over time, Bob became a partner in pushing the project to fruition—the book is better for it, and so am I. Bob, I will always be grateful.

Deep thanks likewise to Bob's colleagues past and present at Technicolor, particularly Ahmad Ouri, currently president of Technicolor's Premier Retail Networks' business, but chief marketing officer at the time Technicolor joined this effort, and the man who officially green-lit Technicolor's sponsorship. Gracious thanks also to Benoit Joly, Technicolor's senior VP of operational marketing, who steadfastly maintained that support; Dana Ross, for all sorts of logistical help; and Clint Eastwood's colorist at Technicolor, Jill Bogdanowicz.

On the publishing side, great appreciation goes to Swan Studio's Lisa Fitzpatrick, who wore multiple hats while packaging and producing this book. Lisa believed in this project from the beginning, helped hone the idea, advocated for it across the industry, sold Abrams on it, put disparate pieces together, and oversaw its production over many months, doing whatever was required to move the project forward. Thanks, Lisa.

Kudos also to our top-notch designer, Mark Murphy, for performing valiantly under high-pressure conditions and handling a big menu with efficiency and artistry.

Thanks to Eric Himmel of Abrams not only for seeing the value in this project at a time when a horrible economic cloud was hovering over the publishing industry, but also for committing to it with gusto.

Thanks to Leith Adams, executive director of the Warner Bros. archive, for spending time with and educating me, advocating for this project inside Warner Bros., and helping us find assets; Diane Sponsler, Warner Bros.' longtime director of publicity photography, for tireless support and help with imagery; Janine Bassinger, curator of the Cinema Archives at Wesleyan University; Marvin Levy in Steven Spielberg's office; Charles "Chic" Scott; and countless publicists and assistants across the industry who aided the effort.

Gratitude also goes to current and former Warner Bros. executives, including chairman/CEO Barry Meyer, for giving of his own time and easing our ability to interface with the studio to find images, people, and information. Thanks also to Paul McGuire and Susan Fritz for helping me reach many friends of this project inside the studio.

Sincere appreciation also to Steven Spielberg and Morgan Freeman for taking time to contribute essays and insight to this book despite packed schedules, and to all the high-profile movie actors who took time to reminisce about working with Clint Eastwood. I particularly enjoyed sipping green tea with Ken Watanabe and absorbing his insight. Thanks also to his interpreter, Satch Watanabe. Thanks to Sean Penn, Forest Whitaker, Meryl Streep, Gene Hackman, Hilary Swank, Paul Haggis, Iris Yamashita, David Webb Peoples, and Dustin Lance Black. And deep gratitude to both Matt Damon and Leonardo DiCaprio for permitting me to watch them work for Clint Eastwood without letting my pesky presence interfere with their concentration.

Deep thanks to my attorney, Yonatan Hagos, and my business manager, Susan Richman.

Humble gratitude for believing in me, helping me, and putting up with me during this process goes to my dear mother, Lynn Einstein; my stepfather, Lionel Groberman; and many supportive friends and family members.

But most of all, my everlasting gratitude and love to my wife, Bari Berger Goldman, who put up daily with far more than any author's wife should have to during this process, and my two dear boys, Jake and Nathan. Both are on the vanguard of a new generation of Clint Eastwood fans, and Nathan, in fact, has vowed to one day have dinner with Clint Eastwood because "he's so cool." I can only agree.

—Michael Goldman
April 2012

ACKNOWLEDGMENTS

Like filmmaking, book packaging is a vastly collaborative enterprise. Although there are many people to mention, no greater appreciation could be extended than to my editor at Abrams, vice president and editor in chief Eric Himmel. Thank you for being a believer, once again.

Second, thank you to Abrams' contracts manager, Kristina Tully, whose steady hand guided me when this project's future was unsure. To producer Rob Lorenz: Thank you for showing faith and opening doors. It has been a privilege to participate in telling the story of Malpaso.

A round of thanks hardly befits the sense of appreciation I wish to extend to our book's subject, Clint Eastwood. I was speechless at the time you accepted our proposal and remain so other than to say thank you for granting me the unrestricted freedom to find a suitable home for this story.

Art director Jack Taylor proved to be an early and steady advocate. Thank you for your time, your art, and your stories. To Diane Sponsler, the vice president of photography at Warner Bros.: your attention, time, and counsel were invaluable. Thanks to the rest of the very talented Warner Bros. still photography staff, especially senior photo editor Jesse Mesa for assistance with the cover image and Greg Dyro, director, Warner Bros. Photo Lab, for watching over the quality. To Warner Bros. archivists Kim Payne, Jeff Briggs, and Steven Bingen: thank you for your endurance during my marathon image research trips. To my many licensing partners at Paramount and Universal, and to all you ladies at the Academy: many thanks, but most especially to Julie Heath, executive director of clip and still licensing at Warner Bros. At Abrams, I would also like to thank Scott Auerbach, Liam Flanagan, Ankur Ghosh, Michelle Ishay, Rob Sternitzky, and Kara Strubel. Thanks as well to Malpaso's Kristina Rivera and Jessica Meier, Warner Bros. museum curator Leith Adams, and my legal counsel, Jann Moorhead and Dana Newman, for lending your expertise early on.

To my partner in this enterprise, Michael Goldman: What to say? We did it; may it be the first of many in our Master Filmmaker at Work series. To the very talented designer Mark Murphy, who emerged as the clear choice to turn our dreams, words, and images into pages in a book—you raised the bar higher, and kept it there. To Technicolor vice president Bob Hoffman: Much appreciation for recognizing what we were aiming for, joining the project, and generously lending your considerable marketing expertise and resources.

Many colleagues showed support, interest, and encouragement in the run up to finding a publisher, including Elaine Piechowski, Iain Morris, Dan Farley, Paula Allen, Barbara Brogliatti, Risa Kessler, Patty Gift, Jan Miller, Janet Fletcher, Jim Muschett, Robb Pearlman, and the incredibly talented Ian Shimkoviak, but most especially Hope Innelli who advocated for the project early on. To my family: thank you for your endurance. Finally, for my part, I dedicate the work to my mother, Edith. Even when you didn't mean to, you've always known how to say the right thing.

—Lisa Fitzpatrick
April 2012

(Above) Clint Eastwood (R) with (L–R) Jean Pierre Barnard and Michael Grimm during filming of *The Eiger Sanction*. The Swiss Alp peak Jungfrau is in the background.

(Page 1) Clint Eastwood, dressed in character as William Munny, lines up a shot on the Alberta prairie during the making of *Unforgiven*. (Pages 2–3) Scene from *Letters from Iwo Jima*—radically de-saturated imagery from Eastwood. (Pages 4–5) Clint Eastwood watches the action unfold during the filming of *Million Dollar Baby*. (Page 6) Eastwood as Harry Callahan in *Sudden Impact*—the only Dirty Harry film he ever directed, and the first Eastwood film to be edited by Joel Cox as sole editor. (Page 7) Crew members take direction from Eastwood as he prepares to shoot the dining scene at the Monterey Municipal Wharf (*Play Misty for Me*). (Page 8) Eastwood pauses from acting in *The Gauntlet* to offer some direction to the actors during the railcar fight scene. He says directing himself "can be difficult, but over the years, I've learned to throw the switch." (Page 9) Eastwood (at camera) and his team use a single camera (as always) to shoot the gunning down of the Spider Conway character in *Pale Rider*. (Page 10) Clint Eastwood lines up a shot with actor William Holden during the filming of *Breezy*—the first time Eastwood directed a movie he did not act in. (Page 12) Cécile de France being filmed in a giant water tank for the drowning scene in *Hereafter*. (Page 13) An American soldier dug in on the black sand beach (*Flags of Our Fathers*). Iceland was chosen for its rich black sands that resemble Iwo Jima's, and the effect was further enhanced in postproduction. (Page 48) Scene underway (*Unforgiven*). (Page 49) Filming a boxing scene in one of several locations made up to resemble an arena (*Million Dollar Baby*). (Page 88) An evening shoot during production of *Letters from Iwo Jima*. (Page 89) The loneliness of war is captured in this scene from the same movie. (Page 98) Diane Venora, as Chan Parker, in stylized light that typifies *Bird*. (Page 99) Unit photography proof sheet showing Clint Eastwood at work figuring out a key scene during the making of *Firefox*. (Page 240) Clint Eastwood with actor John Russell (*Pale Rider*).

ILLUSTRATOR CREDITS

MALPASO ART DEPARTMENT
Jack Taylor pp. 70, 70, 95, 160, 166, 167, 170, 170
Joe Musso pp. 156, 216

UNIT PHOTOGRAPHY
Bob Akester—*Unforgiven*
Keith Bernstein—*J. Edgar, Invictus*
Murray Close—*White Hunter, Black Heart, The Rookie*
Sam Emerson—*Midnight in the Garden of Good and Evil*
Marcia Reed—*Bird, Heartbreak Ridge, Pale Rider, Sudden Impact, The Gauntlet*
Ken Regan—*Bridges of Madison County, A Perfect World*
Ken Regan, Mario Perez & Jay Maidment—*Hereafter*
Ken Regan & Merie Weismiller Wallace—*Space Cowboys*
Tony Rivetti, Jr.—*Gran Torino*
John Shannon—*Firefox, Bronco Billy*
Merie Weismiller Wallace—*Letters from Iwo Jima, Million Dollar Baby,*
Mystic River, Blood Work, True Crime
All of the above courtesy of Warner Bros.

Tony Rivetti, Jr.—*Changeling*
Unknown—*Play Misty for Me, The Eiger Sanction, High Plains Drifter, Breezy*
Courtesy of Universal Studios

Merie Weismiller Wallace—*Flags of Our Fathers*
Courtesy of Paramount Pictures

Henry Bumstead *Unforgiven* Drawing (page 93)
From the collection of the Margaret Herrick Library
(Academy of Motion Picture Arts and Sciences)

Produced by Lisa Fitzpatrick